Being-in-Dreaming

Being-in-Dreaming

Florinda Donner

HarperSanFrancisco
A Division of HarperCollins*Publishers*

FIRST EDITION

This edition is printed on acid-free paper that meets the American National Standards Institute Z39.48 Standard.

Library of Congress Cataloging-in-Publication Data

Donner, Florinda.
    Being-in-dreaming / Florinda Donner. — 1st ed.
        p.   cm.
    ISBN 0–06–250233–6 (alk. paper)
    1. Witchcraft—Mexico.   2. Donner, Florinda.   I. Title.
BF1584.M6D66   1991
133.4'3'0972—dc20   90–56444
                                                              CIP
                                                              r91

91 92 93 94 95 RRD 10 9 8 7 6 5 4 3 2 1

For all those who dream sorcerers' dreams.
And for the few who dreamt them with me.

Author's Note

My first contact with the sorcerers' world was not something I planned or sought out. It was rather a fortuitous event. I met a group of people in northern Mexico, in July of 1970, and they turned out to be the strict followers of a sorcerers' tradition belonging to the Indians of pre-Columbian Mexico.

That first meeting had a long-range, overpowering effect on me. It introduced me to another world that coexists with ours. I have spent twenty years of my life committed to that world. This is the account of how my involvement began and how it was spurred and directed by the sorcerers who were responsible for my being there.

The most prominent of them was a woman named Florinda Matus. She was my mentor and guide. She was also the one who gave me her name, Florinda, as a gift of love and power.

To call them sorcerers is not my choice. *Brujo* or *bruja,* which mean sorcerer or witch, are the Spanish terms they themselves use to denote a male or a female practitioner. I have always resented the negative connotation of those words. But the sorcerers themselves put me at ease, once and for all, by explaining that what is meant by sorcery is something quite abstract: the ability, which some people develop, to expand the limits of normal perception. The abstract quality of sorcery voids automatically, then, any positive or negative connotation of terms used to describe its practitioners.

Expanding the limits of normal perception is a concept that stems from the sorcerers' belief that our choices in life are limited, due to the fact that they are defined by the social order. Sorcerers believe that the social order sets up our lists of options, but we do the rest: by accepting only these choices, we set a limit to our nearly limitless possibilities.

This limitation, they say, fortunately applies only to our social side and not to the other side of us: a practically inaccessible side, which is not in the realm of ordinary awareness. Their main endeavor, therefore, is to uncover that side. They do this by breaking the frail, yet resilient, shield of human assumptions about what we are and what we are capable of being.

Sorcerers acknowledge that in our world of daily affairs there are people who probe into the unknown in pursuit of alternative views of reality. They contend that the ideal consequences of such probings should be the capacity to draw from our findings the necessary energy to change and to detach ourselves from our definition of reality. But they argue that unfortunately such probings are essentially mental endeavors. New thoughts, new ideas hardly ever change us.

One of the things I learned in the sorcerers' world was that without retreating from the world, and without injuring themselves in the process, sorcerers do accomplish the magnificent task of breaking the agreement that has defined reality.

Being-in-Dreaming

1

O N an impulse, after attending the baptism of a friend's child in the city of Nogales, Arizona, I decided to cross the border into Mexico. As I was leaving my friend's house, one of her guests, a woman named Delia Flores, asked me for a ride to Hermosillo.

She was a dark-complexioned woman, perhaps in her midforties, of medium height and stout build. She was powerfully big, with straight black hair arranged into a thick braid. Her dark, shiny eyes highlighted a shrewd, yet slightly girlish, round face.

Certain that she was a Mexican born in Arizona, I asked her if she needed a tourist card to enter Mexico.

"Why should I need a tourist card to enter my own country?" she retorted, widening her eyes with exaggerated surprise.

"Your mannerism and speech inflection made me think you were from Arizona," I said.

"My parents were Indians from Oaxaca," she explained. "But I am a *ladina*."

"What's a ladina?"

"Ladinos are sharp Indians who grow up in the city," she elucidated. There was an odd excitement in her voice I was at a loss to understand as she added, "They take up the ways of the white man, and they are so good at it that they can fake their way into anything."

"That's nothing to be proud of," I said judgingly. "It's certainly not too complimentary to you, Mrs. Flores."

The contrite expression on her face gave way to a wide grin. "Perhaps not to a real Indian or to a real white man," she said cheekily. "But I am perfectly satisfied with it myself." She leaned toward me and added, "Do call me Delia. I've the feeling we're going to be great friends."

Not knowing what to say, I concentrated on the road. We drove in silence to the check point. The guard asked for my tourist card, but didn't ask for Delia's. He didn't seem to notice her—no words or glances were exchanged between them. When I tried to talk to Delia, she forcefully stopped me with an imperious movement of her hand. Then the guard looked at me questioningly. Since I didn't say anything, he shrugged his shoulders and waved me on.

"How come the guard didn't ask for your papers?" I asked when we were some distance away.

"Oh, he knows me," she lied. And knowing that I knew she was lying, she burst into a shameless laughter. "I think I frightened him, and he didn't dare to talk to me," she lied again. And again she laughed.

I decided to change the subject, if only to save her from escalating her lies. I began to talk about topics of current interest in the news, but mostly we drove in silence. It was not an uncomfortable or strained silence; it was like the desert around us, wide and stark and oddly reassuring.

"Where shall I drop you?" I asked as we drove into Hermosillo.

"Downtown," she said. "I always stay in the same hotel when I'm in the city. I know the owners well, and I'm sure I can arrange for you to get the same rate I get."

I gratefully accepted her offer.

The hotel was old and run down. The room I was given opened to a dusty courtyard. A double, four-poster bed and a massive, old-fashioned dresser shrunk the room to claustrophobic dimensions. A small bathroom had been added, but a chamber pot was still under the bed; it matched the porcelain washing set on the dresser.

The first night was awful. I slept fitfully, and in my dreams I was conscious of whispers and shadows moving across the walls. Shapes of things and monstrous animals rose from behind the furniture. People materialized from the corners, pale, ghostlike.

The next day I drove around the city and its surroundings, and that night, although I was exhausted, I stayed awake. When I finally fell asleep, into a hideous nightmare, I saw a dark, amoeba-shaped creature stalking me at the foot of the bed. Iridescent tentacles hung from its cavernous crevices. As the creature leaned over me, it breathed, making short, raspy sounds that died out into a wheeze.

My screams were smothered by its iridescent ropes tightening around my neck. Then all went black as the creature—which somehow I knew to be female—crushed me by lying on top of me.

That timeless moment between sleep and wakefulness was finally broken by the insistent banging on my door and the concerned voices of the hotel guests out in the hall. I turned on the light and mumbled some apologies and explanations through the door.

With the nightmare still sticking to my skin like sweat, I went into the bathroom. I stifled a scream as I looked into the mirror. The red lines across my throat and the evenly spaced red dots running down my chest looked like an unfinished tattoo. Frantically, I packed my bags. It was three o'clock in the morning when I walked out into the deserted lobby to pay my bill.

"Where are you going at this hour?" Delia Flores asked, emerging from the door behind the desk. "I heard about your nightmare. You had the whole hotel worried."

I was so glad to see her I put my arms around her and began to sob.

"There, there," she murmured soothingly, stroking my hair. "If you want to, you can come and sleep in my room. I'll watch over you."

"Nothing in this world will make me stay in this hotel," I said. "I'm returning to Los Angeles this very instant."

"Do you often have nightmares?" she casually asked, leading me toward the creaky old couch in the corner.

"Off and on, I've suffered from nightmares all my life," I said. "I've gotten sort of used to them. But tonight it was different; it was the most real, the worst nightmare I've ever had."

She gave me an appraising, long look and then said, slowly dragging her words, "Would you like to get rid of your nightmares?" As she spoke, she gave a half glance over her shoulder toward the door, as if afraid that someone might be listening there. "I know someone who could truly help you."

"I would like that very much," I whispered, untying the scarf around my neck to show her the red marks. I told her the explicit details of my nightmare. "Have you ever seen anything like this?" I asked.

"Looks pretty serious," she pronounced, carefully examining the lines across my throat. "You really shouldn't leave before seeing the healer I have in mind. She lives about a hundred miles south of here. About a two-hour ride."

The possibility of seeing a healer was most welcome to me. I had been exposed to them since birth in Venezuela. Whenever I was sick, my parents called a doctor, and as soon as he left, our Venezuelan housekeeper would bundle me up and take me to a healer. As I grew older and no longer wanted to be treated by a witchdoctor —none of my friends were—she convinced me that it couldn't possibly do any harm to be twice protected. The habit was so ingrained in me that when I moved to Los Angeles I made sure to see a doctor as well as a healer whenever I was ill.

"Do you think she will see me today?" I asked. Seeing her uncomprehending expression, I reminded her that it was already Sunday.

"She'll see you any day," Delia assured me. "Why don't you just wait for me here, and I'll take you to her. It won't take me but a minute to get my belongings together."

"Why would you go out of your way to help me?" I asked, suddenly disconcerted by her offer. "After all, I'm a perfect stranger to you."

"Precisely!" she exclaimed, rising from the couch. She gazed down at me indulgently, as though she could sense the nagging doubts rising within me. "What better reason could there be?" she asked rhetorically. "To help a perfect stranger is an act of folly or one of great control. Mine is one of great control."

At a loss for words, all I could do was to stare into her eyes, which seemed to accept the world with wonder and curiosity. There was something strangely reassuring about her. It was not only that

I trusted her, but I felt as if I had known her all my life. I sensed a link between us, a closeness.

And yet, as I watched her disappear behind the door to get her belongings, I considered grabbing my bags and bolting for the car. I didn't want to end up in a predicament by being daring, as I had so many times before. But some inexplicable curiosity held me back, despite the familiar nagging feeling of alarm.

I had waited for nearly twenty minutes when a woman, wearing a red pantsuit and platform shoes, stepped out of the door behind the clerk's desk. She paused underneath the light. With a studied gesture, she threw her head back so that the curls of her blond wig shimmered in the light.

"You didn't recognize me, did you?" she laughed gleefully.

"It's really you, Delia," I exclaimed, staring at her, open-mouthed.

"What do you think?" Still cackling, she stepped out with me onto the sidewalk, toward my car parked in front of the hotel. She flung her basket and duffel bag in the back seat of my small convertible, then sat beside me and said, "The healer I'm taking you to see says that only the young and the very old can afford to look outrageous."

Before I had a chance to remind her that she was neither, she confided that she was much older than she appeared to be. Her face was radiant as she turned toward me and exclaimed, "I wear this outfit because I like to dazzle my friends!"

Whether she meant me or the healer, she didn't say. I certainly was dazzled. It wasn't only her clothes that were different; her whole demeanor had changed. There wasn't a trace of the aloof, circumspect woman who had traveled with me from Nogales to Hermosillo.

"This will be a most enchanting trip," she pronounced, "especially if we put the top down." Her voice was happy and dreamy. "I adore traveling at night with the top down."

I readily obliged her. It was almost four o'clock in the morning by the time we left Hermosillo behind. The sky, soft and black and speckled with stars, seemed higher than any other sky I had ever seen. I drove fast, yet it seemed we were not moving. The gnarled silhouettes of cactus and mesquite trees appeared and disappeared endlessly under the headlights; they seemed to be all the same shape, all the same size.

"I packed us some sweet rolls and a full thermos of *champurrado*," Delia said, reaching for her basket in the back seat. "It'll be morning before we get to the healer's house." She poured me half a cup of the thick hot chocolate made with cornmeal and fed me, bite by bite, a sort of Danish roll.

"We're driving through a magical land," she said as she sipped the delicious chocolate. "A magical land populated by warring people."

"What warring people are they?" I asked, trying not to sound patronizing.

"The Yaqui people of Sonora," she said and kept quiet, perhaps measuring my reaction. "I admire the Yaqui Indians because they have been in constant war," she continued. "The Spaniards first and then the Mexicans—as recently as 1934—have felt the savagery, cunning, and relentlessness of the Yaqui warriors."

"I don't admire war or warlike people," I said. Then by way of apologizing for my belligerent tone I explained that I came from a German family that had been torn apart by the war.

"Your case is different," she maintained. "You don't have the ideals of freedom."

"Wait a minute!" I protested. "It is precisely because I espouse the ideals of freedom that I find war so abhorrent."

"We are talking about two different kinds of war," she insisted.

"War is war," I interjected.

"Your kind of war," she went on, ignoring my interruption, "is between two brothers who are both rulers and are fighting for supremacy." She leaned toward me and in an urgent whisper added, "The kind of war I'm talking about is between a slave and the master who thinks that he owns people. Do you see the difference?"

"No. I don't," I insisted stubbornly and repeated that war is war, no matter what the reason.

"I can't agree with you," she said and, sighing loudly, leaned back in her seat. "Perhaps the reason for our philosophical disagreement is that we come from different social realities."

Astonished by her choice of words, I automatically slowed the car. I didn't mean to be rude, but to hear her spout academic concepts was so incongruous and unexpected that I couldn't help but laugh.

Delia didn't take offense; she watched me, smiling, thoroughly pleased with herself. "When you get to know my point of view, you may change your mind." She said this so seriously and yet so kindly I felt ashamed of myself for laughing at her. "You may even apologize for laughing at me," she added as if she had read my thoughts.

"I do apologize, Delia," I said and truly meant it. "I'm terribly sorry for my rudeness. I was so surprised by your statements that I didn't know what to do." I glanced at her briefly and added contritely, "So I laughed."

"I don't mean social apologies for your conduct," she said, shaking her head in disappointment. "I mean apologies for not understanding the plight of man."

"I don't know what you're talking about," I said uneasily. I could feel her eyes boring through me.

"As a woman, you should understand that plight very well," she said. "You have been a slave all your life."

"What are you talking about, Delia?" I asked, irritated by her impertinence, then immediately calmed down, certain that the poor Indian had no doubt an insufferable, overwhelming husband. "Believe me, Delia, I'm quite free. I do as I please."

"You might do as you please, but you're not free," she persisted. "You are a woman, and that automatically means that you're at the mercy of men."

"I'm not at the mercy of anybody," I yelled.

I couldn't tell whether it was my assertion or my tone of voice that made Delia burst into loud guffaws. She laughed at me as hard as I had laughed at her before.

"You seem to be enjoying your revenge," I said, peeved. "It's your turn to laugh now, isn't it?"

"It's not the same at all," she said, suddenly serious. "You laughed at me because you felt superior. A slave that talks like a master always delights the master for a moment."

I tried to interrupt her and tell her that it hadn't even crossed my mind to think of her as a slave or of me as a master, but she ignored my efforts. In the same solemn tone she said that the reason she had laughed at me was because I had been rendered stupid and blind to my own womanhood.

"What's with you, Delia?" I asked, puzzled. "You're deliberately insulting me."

"Certainly," she readily agreed and giggled, completely indifferent to my rising anger. She slapped my knee with a resounding whack. "What concerns me," she went on, "is that you don't even know that by the mere fact that you're a woman you're a slave."

Mustering up all the patience I was capable of, I told Delia that she was wrong. "No one is a slave nowadays."

"Women are slaves," Delia insisted. "Men enslave women. Men befog women. Their desire to brand women as their property befogs us," she declared. "That fog hangs around our necks like a yoke."

My blank look made her smile. She lay back on the seat, clasping her hands on her chest. "Sex befogs women," she added softly, yet emphatically. "Women are so thoroughly befogged that they can't consider the possibility that their low status in life is the direct end result of what is done to them sexually."

"That's the most ridiculous thing I've ever heard," I pronounced. Then, rather ponderously, I went into a long diatribe about the social, economic, and political reasons for women's low status. At great length I talked about the changes that have taken place in the last decades. How women have been quite successful in their fight against male supremacy. Peeved by her mocking expression, I couldn't refrain from remarking that she was no doubt prejudiced by her own experiences, by her own perspective in time.

Delia's whole body shook with suppressed mirth. She made an effort to contain herself and said, "Nothing has really changed. Women are slaves. We've been reared to be slaves. The slaves who are educated are now busy addressing the social and political abuses committed against women. None of the slaves, though, can focus on the root of their slavery—the sexual act—unless it involves rape or is related to some other form of physical abuse." A little smile parted her lips as she said that religious men and philosophers and men of science have for centuries maintained, and of course still do, that men and women must follow a biological, God-given imperative having to do directly with their sexual reproductive capabilities.

"We have been conditioned to believe that sex is good for us," she stressed. "This inherent belief and acceptance has incapacitated us to ask the right question."

"And what question is that?" I asked, trying hard not to laugh at her utterly erroneous convictions.

Delia didn't seem to have heard me; she was silent for so long I thought she had dozed off, and I was thus startled when she said, "The question that no one dares ask is, what does it do to us women to get laid?"

"Really, Delia," I chided in mock consternation.

"Women's befogging is so total, we will focus on every other issue of our inferiority except the one that is the cause of it all," she maintained.

"But, Delia, we can't do without sex," I laughed. "What would happen to the human race if we don't . . ."

She checked my question and my laughter with an imperative gesture of her hand. "Nowadays, women like yourself, in their zeal for equality, imitate men," she said. "Women imitate men to such an absurd degree that the sex they are interested in has nothing to do with reproduction. They equate freedom with sex, without ever considering what sex does to their physical and emotional well-being. We have been so thoroughly indoctrinated, we firmly believe that sex is good for us."

She nudged me with her elbow, and then, as if she were reciting a chant, she added in a sing-song tone, "Sex is good for us. It's pleasurable. It's necessary. It alleviates depression, repression, and frustration. It cures headaches, low and high blood pressure. It makes pimples disappear. It makes your tits and ass grow. It regulates your menstrual cycle. In short, it's fantastic! It's good for women. Everyone says so. Everyone recommends it." She paused for an instant, and then pronounced with dramatic finality, "A fuck a day keeps the doctor away."

I found her statements terribly funny but then sobered abruptly as I remembered how family and friends, including our family doctor, had suggested it—not so crudely to be sure—as a cure for all the adolescent ailments I had, growing up in a strictly repressive environment. He had said that once I was married, I would have regular menstrual cycles. I would gain weight. I would sleep better. I would be sweet tempered.

"I don't see anything wrong with wanting sex and love," I said defensively. "Whatever I've experienced of it, I have liked very much. And no one befogs me. I'm free! I choose whom I want and when I want it."

There was a spark of glee in Delia's dark eyes when she said, "Choosing your partner does in no way alter the fact that you're being fucked." Then with a smile, as if to mitigate the harshness of her tone, she added, "To equate freedom with sex is the ultimate irony. Men's befogging is so complete, so total, it has zapped us of the needed energy and imagination to focus on the real cause of our enslavement." She stressed, "To want a man sexually or to fall in love with one romantically are the only two choices given to the slaves. And all the things we have been told about these two choices are nothing but excuses that pull us into complicity and ignorance."

I was indignant with her. I couldn't help but think that she was some kind of repressed, man-hating shrew. "Why do you dislike men so much, Delia?" I asked in my most cynical tone.

"I don't dislike them," she assured me. "What I passionately object to is our reluctance to examine how thoroughly indoctrinated we are. The pressure put upon us is so fierce and self-righteous that we have become willing accomplices. Whoever dares to differ is dismissed and mocked as a man-hater or as a freak."

Blushing, I glanced at her surreptitiously. I decided that she could talk so disparagingly about sex and love because she was, after all, old. Physical desires were all behind her.

Chuckling softly, Delia put her hands behind her head. "My physical desires are not behind me because I'm old," she confided, "but because I've been given a chance to use my energy and imagination to become something different than the slave I was raised to be."

I felt thoroughly insulted rather than surprised that she had read my thoughts. I began to defend myself, but my words only triggered more laughter. As soon as she stopped, she turned toward me. Her face was as stern and serious as that of a teacher about to scold a pupil. "If you are not a slave, how come they reared you to be a *Hausfrau?*" she asked. "And how come all you think about is to *heiraten* and about your future *Herr Gemahl* who will *Dich mitnehmen?*"

I laughed so hard at her use of German I had to stop the car lest we have an accident. More interested in finding out where she had learned German so well, I forgot to defend myself from her unflattering remarks that all I wanted in life was to find a husband who would whisk me away. Regardless of how hard I pleaded, however, she disdainfully ignored my interest in her German.

"You and I will have plenty of time to talk about my German later," she assured me. She regarded me mockingly and added, "Or about your being a slave." Before I had a chance to retort, she suggested that we talk about something impersonal.

"Like what?" I asked, starting the car again.

Adjusting the seat in an almost reclining position, Delia closed her eyes. "Let me tell you something about the four most famous leaders of the Yaquis," she said softly. "I'm interested in leaders, in their successes or their failures."

Before I had a chance to grumble that I really wasn't that interested in war stories, Delia said that Calixto Muni was the first Yaqui leader who had attracted her attention. She wasn't a gifted storyteller; her account was straightforward, almost academic. Yet I was hanging on her every word.

Calixto Muni had been an Indian who had sailed for years under the pirates' flag in the Caribbean. On his return to his native Sonora, he led a military uprising against the Spaniards in the 1730s. Betrayed, he had been captured and executed by the Spaniards.

Then Delia gave me a long and sophisticated elucidation of how during the 1820s, after the Mexican independence was achieved and the Mexican government attempted to parcel out the Yaqui lands, a resistance movement turned into a widespread uprising. It was Juan Bandera, she said, who, guided by the spirit itself, organized military units among the Yaquis. Often armed only with bows and arrows, Bandera's warriors fought the Mexican troops for nearly ten years. In 1832, Juan Bandera was defeated and executed.

Delia said that the next leader of renown was José Maria Leyva, better known as Cajeme—the one who doesn't drink. He was a

11

Yaqui from Hermosillo. He was educated, and had acquired vast military skills fighting in the Mexican army. Thanks to those skills, he unified all the Yaqui towns. From his first uprising in the 1870s, Cajeme kept his army in an active state of revolt. He was defeated by the Mexican army in 1887 in Buatachive, a fortified mountain stronghold. Although Cajeme managed to escape and hide in Guaymas, he was eventually betrayed and executed.

The last of the great Yaqui heroes was Juan Maldonado, also known as Tetabiate—rolling stone. He reorganized the remnants of the Yaqui forces in the Bacatete Mountains, from which he waged ferocious and desperate guerrilla warfare against Mexican troops for more than ten years.

"By the turn of the century," Delia wrapped up her stories, "the dictator Porfirio Diaz had inaugurated a campaign of Yaqui extermination. Indians were shot down as they worked in the fields. Thousands were rounded up and shipped to Yucatan to work in the henequen plantations and to Oaxaca to work in the sugar cane fields."

I was impressed by her knowledge, but I still couldn't figure out why she had told me all this. "You sound like a scholar, a historian in the Yaqui way of life," I said admiringly. "Who are you really?"

For an instant she seemed to be taken aback by my question, which was purely rhetorical, then quickly recovered and said, "I've told you who I am. I just happen to know a great deal about the Yaquis. I live around them, you know." She was silent for a moment, then nodded as if she had reached some conclusion and added, "The reason I've told you about the Yaqui leaders is because it is up to us women to know the strength and the weakness of the leader."

"Why?" I asked, puzzled. "Who cares about leaders? They are all nincompoops as far as I'm concerned."

Delia scratched her head under the wig, then sneezed repeatedly and said with a hesitant smile, "Unfortunately, women must rally around them, lest they want to lead themselves."

"Whom are they going to lead?" I asked sarcastically.

She looked at me, astonished, then rubbed her upper arm, the gesture, like her face, girlish. "It's quite difficult to explain," she murmured. A peculiar softness had entered her voice, part tenderness, part indecision, part lack of interest. "I'd better not. I might lose you completely. All I can say, for the time being, is that I'm neither a scholar nor a historian. I'm a storyteller, and I haven't told you the most important part of my tale yet."

"And what might that be?" I asked, intrigued by her desire to change the subject.

"All I've given you so far is factual information," she said. "What I haven't mentioned is the world of magic from which those Yaqui leaders operated. To them, the actions of wind and shadows, of animals and plants were as important as the doings of men. That's the part that interests me the most."

"The actions of wind and shadows, of animals and plants?" I repeated mockingly.

Unperturbed by my tone, Delia nodded. She pushed herself up in the seat, pulled off the blond curly wig and let the wind blow through her straight black hair. "Those are the Bacatete Mountains," she said, pointing to the mountains to the left of us, barely outlined against the semidarkness of the dawn sky.

"Is that where we are going?" I asked.

"Not this time," she said, sliding down into her seat again. A cryptic smile played around her lips as she half turned toward me. "Perhaps one day you'll have a chance to visit those mountains," she mused, closing her eyes. "The Bacatetes are inhabited by creatures of another world, of another time."

"Creatures of another world, of another time?" I echoed her in mock seriousness. "Who or what are they?"

"Creatures," she said vaguely. "Creatures that don't belong to our time, to our world."

"Now, now, Delia. Are you trying to scare me?" I couldn't help laughing as I turned to glance at her. Even in the dark, her face shone. She looked extraordinarily young, the skin molded without wrinkles over curving cheeks, chin, and nose.

"No. I'm not trying to scare you," she said matter-of-factly, tucking a strand of hair behind her ear. "I'm simply telling you what is common knowledge around here."

"Interesting. And what kind of creatures are they?" I inquired, biting my lip to suppress my giggles. "And have you seen them?"

13

"Of course I've seen them," she said indulgently. "I wouldn't be talking about them if I hadn't." She smiled sweetly, without a trace of resentment. "They are beings that populated the earth at another time and now have retreated to isolated spots."

At first I couldn't help laughing out loud at her gullibility. And then, seeing how serious and how convinced she was that these creatures indeed existed, I decided that rather than make fun of her I should accept her credulousness. After all, she was taking me to a healer, and I didn't want to antagonize her with my rational probes.

"Are those creatures the ghosts of the Yaqui warriors who lost their lives in battle?" I asked.

She shook her head negatively, then, as if afraid someone might overhear, she leaned closer and whispered in my ear, "It's a well-known fact that those mountains are inhabited by enchanted creatures: birds that speak, bushes that sing, stones that dance. Creatures that can take any form at will."

She sat back and regarded me expectantly. "The Yaquis call these beings *surem*. They believe that the surem are ancient Yaquis who refused to be baptized by the first Jesuits who came to Christianize the Indians." She patted my arm affectionately. "Watch out, they say that the surem like blond women." She cackled with delight. "Maybe that's what your nightmare was all about. A surem trying to steal you."

"You don't really believe what you're saying, do you?" I asked derisively, unable to keep my annoyance in check.

"No. I've just made up that the surem like blonds," she said soothingly. "They don't like blonds at all."

Although I didn't turn to glance at her, I could feel her smile and the humorous twinkle in her eyes. It irked me to no end. I thought her to be either very candid, very coy, or, even worse, very mad.

"You don't believe that creatures from another world really exist, do you?" I snapped ill-humoredly. Then, afraid I had offended her, I glanced at her with a word of half-anxious apology ready. But before I could say anything, she answered in the same loud, ill-tempered tone of voice I had used.

"Of course I believe they exist. Why shouldn't they exist?"

"They just don't!" I snapped sharply and authoritatively, then quickly apologized. I told her about my pragmatic upbringing and how my father had guided me to realize that the monsters in my dreams and the playmates I had as a child—invisible to anyone but me, of course—were nothing but the product of an overactive imagination.

"From an early age I was reared to be objective and to qualify everything," I stressed. "In my world, there are only facts."

"That's the problem with people," Delia remarked. "They are so reasonable that just hearing about it lowers my vitality."

"In my world," I continued, ignoring her comment, "there are no facts anywhere about creatures from another world but only speculations and wishful thinking and," I emphasized, "fantasies of disturbed minds."

"You can't be that dense!" she cried out delightedly in between fits of laughter, as if my explanation had surpassed all her expectations.

"Can it be proven that those creatures exist?" I challenged.

"What would the proof consist of?" she inquired with an air of obvious false diffidence.

"If someone else can see them, that would be a proof," I said.

"You mean that if, for instance, you can see them, that'll be proof of their existence?" she inquired, bringing her head close to mine.

"We can certainly begin there."

Sighing, Delia leaned her head against the backrest of her seat and closed her eyes. She was silent for such a long time I was certain she had fallen asleep and was thus startled when she sat up abruptly and urged me to pull over to the side of the road. She had to relieve herself, she said.

To take advantage of our stop, I, too, went into the bushes. As I was about to pull up my jeans, I heard a loud male voice say, "How delicious!" and sigh just behind me. With my jeans still unzipped I dashed to where Delia was. "We'd better get out of here fast!" I cried out. "There is a man hiding in the bushes."

"Nonsense," she brushed my words aside. "The only thing behind the bushes is a donkey."

"Donkeys don't sigh like lecherous men," I pointed out, then repeated what I had heard the man say.

Delia collapsed into helpless laughter, then seeing how distressed I was, she held up her hand in a conciliatory gesture. "Did you actually see the man?"

"I didn't have to," I retorted. "It was enough to hear him."

She lingered for a moment longer, then headed toward the car. Right before we climbed up the embankment to the road, she stopped abruptly and, turning toward me, whispered, "Something quite mysterious has happened. I must make you aware of it." She led me by the hand back to the spot where I had squatted. And right there, behind the bushes, I saw a donkey.

"It wasn't there before," I insisted.

Delia regarded me with apparent pleasure then shrugged her shoulders and turned to the animal. "Little donkey," she cooed in a baby voice, "did you look at her butt?"

She's a ventriloquist, I thought. She's going to make the beast talk. However, all the donkey did was to bray loudly and repeatedly.

"Let's get out of here," I pleaded, tugging at her sleeve. "It must be the owner who's lurking in the bushes."

"But this little darling has no owner," she cooed in that same silly baby voice and scratched the animal's soft, long ears.

"It certainly has an owner," I snapped. "Can't you see how well fed and groomed it is?" In a voice that was getting hoarse with nervousness and impatience, I stressed again how dangerous it was for two women to be out alone on a deserted road in Sonora.

Delia regarded me silently, seemingly preoccupied. Then she nodded as if in agreement and motioned me to follow her. The donkey walked close behind me, nudging my buttocks repeatedly with its muzzle. Mumbling an imprecation, I turned around, but the donkey was gone.

"Delia!" I cried out in sudden fright. "What happened to the donkey?"

Startled by my cry, a flock of birds rose in raucous flight. The birds circled around us, then flew east toward that fragile crack in the sky that marked the end of the night and the start of the day.

"Where is the donkey?" I asked again in a barely audible whisper.

"Right here in front of you," she said softly, pointing to a gnarled, leafless tree.

"I can't see it."

"You need glasses."

"There is nothing wrong with my eyes," I said tartly. "I can even see the lovely flowers on the tree." Astonished at the beauty of the glowing, snow-white morning glory–shaped blossoms, I moved closer. "What kind of a tree is it?"

"Palo Santo."

For one bewildering second I thought that the donkey, which was emerging from behind the satiny, silver-gray trunk, had spoken. I turned to look at Delia.

"Palo Santo!" she laughed.

Then the thought crossed my mind that Delia was playing a joke on me. The donkey probably belonged to the healer, who, no doubt, lived nearby.

"What's so funny?" Delia asked, catching the all-knowing smirk on my face.

"I've got a most horrible cramp," I lied. Holding my hands against my stomach I squatted. "Please wait for me in the car."

The instant she turned to go, I took off my scarf and tied it around the donkey's neck. I enjoyed anticipating Delia's surprise upon discovering, once we were at the healer's place, that I had known about her joke all along. However, any hope of seeing the donkey or my scarf again were soon dashed. It took us almost two more hours to reach the healer's house.

2

IT was around eight o'clock in the morning when we arrived at the healer's house, in the outskirts of Ciudad Obregón. It was a massive old house, with whitewashed walls and a tile roof, gray with age. It had wrought-iron windows and an arched doorway.

The heavy door to the street was wide open. With the confidence of someone familiar with her surroundings, Delia Flores led me across the dark hall, down a long corridor, toward the back, to a sparsely furnished room with a narrow bed, a table, and several chairs. What was most unusual about the room was that it had a door in each of the four walls; they were all closed.

"Wait here," Delia ordered me, pointing with her chin toward the bed. "Take a little nap while I get the healer. It might take me some time," she added, closing the door behind her.

I waited for her footsteps to fade down the corridor before I inspected the most unlikely healing room I had ever seen. The whitewashed walls were bare; the light brown tiles of the floor shone like a mirror. There was no altar, no images or figurines of saints, the Virgin, or Jesus, which I had always assumed were customary in healing rooms. I poked my head through all four doors. Two opened into dark corridors; the other two led to a yard enclosed by a high fence.

As I was tiptoeing down a dark corridor, toward another room, I heard a low, menacing snarl behind me. Slowly, I turned around.

Barely two feet away there stood an enormous, ferocious-looking black dog. It didn't attack me but stood its ground growling, showing its fangs. Without directly meeting the animal's eyes, yet not letting it out of my sight, I walked backward to the healing room.

The dog followed me all the way to the door. I closed it softly, right on the beast's nose, and leaned against the wall until my heartbeat was back to normal. Then I lay down on the bed, and after a few moments—without the slightest intention of doing so—I fell into a deep sleep.

I was roused by a soft touch on my shoulder. I opened my eyes and looked up into an old woman's wrinkled pink face. "You're dreaming," she said. "And I'm part of your dream."

Automatically, I nodded in agreement. However, I wasn't convinced that I was dreaming. The woman was extraordinarily small. She wasn't a midget or a dwarf; rather, she was the size of a child, with skinny arms and narrow, fragile-looking shoulders.

"Are you the healer?" I asked.

"I'm Esperanza," she said. "I'm the one who brings dreams."

Her voice was smooth and unusually low. It had a curious, exotic quality, as though Spanish—which she spoke fluently—was a language to which the muscles of her upper lip were not accustomed. Gradually, the sound of her voice rose until it became a disembodied force filling the room. The sound made me think of running water in the depths of a cave.

"She's not a woman," I mumbled to myself. "She's the sound of darkness."

"I'll remove the cause of your nightmares now," she said, fixing me with an imperious gaze as her fingers closed lightly around my neck. "I'll get them out, one by one," she promised. Her hands moved across my chest like a soft wave. She smiled triumphantly, then motioned me to examine her opened palms. "See? They came out so easily."

She was gazing at me with an expression of such accomplishment and wonder, I couldn't bring myself to tell her that I didn't see anything in her hands.

Certain that the healing session was over, I thanked her and sat up. She shook her head in a gesture of reproach and gently pushed me back on the bed. "You're asleep," she reminded me. "I'm the one who brings dreams, remember?"

I would have loved to insist that I was wide awake, but all I managed to do was to grin foolishly as sleep pulled me into a comforting slumber.

Laughter and whispers crowded around me like shadows. I fought to wake myself. It took a great effort to open my eyes and sit up and look at the people gathered around the table. The peculiar dimness in the room made it difficult to see them clearly. Delia was among them. I was about to call out her name when an insistent scratching sound behind me made me turn around.

A man, precariously squatting on a high stool, was noisily shelling peanuts. At first sight he seemed to be a young man, but somehow I knew him to be old. He was slight of body, with a smooth, beardless face. His smile was a mixture of cunning and innocence.

"Want some?" he asked.

Before I could so much as nod, my mouth dropped open. All I could do was stare at him as he shifted his weight to one hand and effortlessly lifted his small, wiry body into a handstand. From that position he threw a peanut at me; it went straight into my gaping mouth.

I choked on it. A sharp tap between my shoulder blades immediately restored my breathing. Grateful, I turned, wondering who among the people, who were all standing by me now, had reacted so swiftly.

"I'm Mariano Aureliano," said the man who had tapped my back. He shook my hand. His gentle tone and the charming formality of his gesture mitigated the fierce expression in his eyes and the severity of his aquiline features. The upward slant of his dark brows made him look like a bird of prey. His white hair and his weathered, copperish face bespoke age, but his muscular body exuded the vitality of youth.

There were six women in the group, including Delia. All of them shook my hand in that same eloquent formality. They didn't tell me their names; they simply said that they were glad to meet me. Physically, they didn't resemble each other. Yet there was a striking alikeness about them, a contradictory blend of youth and age, a blend of strength and delicacy that was most baffling to me, accustomed as I was to the roughness and directness of my male-oriented, patriarchal, German family.

Just as with Mariano Aureliano and the acrobat on the stool, I could not tell the women's ages. They could have been as much in their forties as in their sixties.

I experienced a fleeting anxiety as the women kept staring at me. I had the distinct impression they could see inside me and were reflecting on what they saw. The amused, contemplative smiles on their faces did little to reassure me. Anxious to break that disturbing silence in any way I could, I turned away from them and faced the man on the stool. I asked him if he was an acrobat.

"I'm Mr. Flores," he said. He did a back flip from the stool and landed in a cross-legged position on the floor. "I'm not an acrobat," he pronounced. "I'm a wizard." There was a smile of unmistakable glee on his face as he reached into his pocket and pulled out my silk scarf, the one I had tied around the donkey's neck.

"I know who you are. You're her husband!" I exclaimed, pointing an accusing finger at Delia. "You two sure played a clever trick on me."

Mr. Flores didn't say a word. He simply gazed at me in polite silence. "I'm nobody's husband," he finally pronounced, then cartwheeled out of the room through one of the doors that led to the yard.

On an impulse, I jumped off the bed and went after him. Blinded momentarily by the brightness outside, I stood for a few seconds dazed by the glare, then crossed the yard and ran down the side of a dirt road into a recently ploughed field partitioned off by tall eucalyptus trees. It was hot. The sun bore down like flames. The furrows shimmered in the heat like effervescent giant snakes.

"Mr. Flores," I called out. There was no answer. Certain that he was hiding behind one of the trees, I crossed the field in a run.

"Watch those bare feet!" a voice, coming from above, warned me.

Startled, I looked up, straight into Mr. Flores' upside-down face. He was hanging from a branch, dangling from his legs.

"It's dangerous and utterly foolish to run about without shoes," he admonished sternly, swinging back and forth like a trapeze artist. "This place is infested with rattlesnakes. You'd better join me up here. It's safe and cool."

Knowing that the branches were far too high to reach, I nonetheless held up my arms with childish trust. Before I realized what he intended to do, Mr. Flores had grabbed my wrists and whisked me up into the tree with no more effort than if I had been a rag doll. Dazzled, I sat beside him staring at the rustling leaves; they glimmered in the sunlight like slivers of gold.

"Do you hear what the wind is telling you?" Mr. Flores asked after a long silence. He moved his head this way and that so I could fully appreciate the astounding manner in which he wiggled his ears.

"Zamurito!" I exclaimed in a whisper as memories flooded my mind. Zamurito, little buzzard, was the nickname of a childhood friend from Venezuela. Mr. Flores had the same delicate, birdlike features, jet-black hair, and mustard-colored eyes. And most astounding, he, like Zamurito, could wiggle his ears one at a time or both together.

I told Mr. Flores about my friend, whom I had known since kindergarten. In the second grade, we had shared a desk. During the long midday recess, instead of eating our lunch at the school grounds, we used to sneak outside and climb to the top of a nearby hill to eat in the shade of what we believed was the largest mango tree in the world. Its lowest branches touched the ground; its highest swept the clouds. In the fruit season, we used to gorge ourselves on mangoes.

The hilltop was our favorite place until the day we found the body of the school janitor hanging from a high branch. We didn't dare to move or to cry; neither of us wanted to lose face in front of the other. We didn't climb up the branches that day but tried to eat our lunch on the ground, practically under the dead man, wondering which of us would break down first. It was I who did.

"Have you ever thought of dying?" Zamurito had asked me in a whisper.

I had looked up at the hanged man. At that same instant the wind had rustled through the branches with an unfamiliar insistence. In the rustle I had distinctly heard the dead man whispering to me that death was soothing. It was so uncanny that I got up and ran away screaming, indifferent to what Zamurito might have thought of me.

"The wind made those branches and leaves speak to you," Mr. Flores said as I finished my story. His voice was soft and low. His golden eyes shone with a feverish light as he went on to explain that at the moment of his death, in one instantaneous flash, the old janitor's memories, feelings, and emotions were released and absorbed by the mango tree.

"The wind made those branches and leaves speak to you," Mr. Flores repeated. "For the wind is yours by right." Dreamily, he glanced through the leaves, his eyes searching beyond the field stretching away in the sun. "Being a woman enables you to command the wind," he went on. "Women don't know it, but they can have a dialogue with the wind any time."

I shook my head uncomprehendingly. "I really don't know what you're talking about," I said, my tone betraying my mounting unease. "This is like a dream. If it wouldn't be that it goes on and on, I'd swear it was one of my nightmares."

His prolonged silence annoyed me. I could feel my face flush with irritation. What am I doing here, sitting in a tree with a crazy old man? I pondered. And at the same time I was apprehensive that I may have offended him. I opted for apologizing for my bluntness.

"I realize that my words don't make much sense to you," he admitted. "That's because there is too much crust on you. It prevents you from hearing what the wind has to say."

"Too much crust?" I asked, puzzled and suspicious. "Do you mean that I'm dirty?"

"That, too," he said and made me blush. He smiled and repeated that I was enveloped by too thick a crust and that this crust couldn't be washed away with soap and water, regardless of how many baths I took. "You are filled with judgments," he explained. "They prevent you from understanding what I'm telling you and that the wind is yours to command."

He regarded me with narrowed, critical eyes. "Well?" he demanded impatiently. Before I knew what was happening he had taken hold of my hands and in one swift, fluid motion had swung me around and gently dropped me to the ground. I thought I saw his arms and legs stretch like rubber bands. It was a fleeting image, which I immediately explained to myself as a perceptual distortion caused by the heat. I didn't dwell upon it, for at that precise moment I was distracted by the sight of Delia Flores and her friends spreading a large canvas cloth under the next tree.

"When did you get here?" I asked Delia, baffled that I had failed to see or hear the group approach.

"We are going to have a picnic in your honor," she said.

"Because you joined us today," one of the women added.

"How did I join you?" I asked, ill at ease. I had failed to see who had spoken. I gazed from one to the other, expecting one of them to explain the statement.

Indifferent to my growing unease, the women busied themselves with the canvas cloth, making sure it was spread out smoothly. The longer I watched them, the more concerned I became. It was all so strange to me. I could easily explain why I had accepted Delia's invitation to see a healer, but I couldn't understand at all my subsequent actions. It was as if someone else had taken over my rational faculties and was making me stay there and react and say things I didn't mean to. And now they were going to have a celebration in my honor. It was disconcerting to say the least. No matter how hard I thought about it, I couldn't figure out what I was doing there.

"I certainly haven't merited any of this," I mumbled, my Germanic upbringing getting the better of me. "People don't just do things for others for the hell of it."

Only upon hearing Mariano Aureliano's exuberant laughter did I realize that all of them were staring at me.

"There's no reason to ponder so heavily what's happening to you today," he said, tapping me softly on the shoulder. "We're having a picnic because we like to do things on the spur of the moment. And since you have been healed by Esperanza today, my friends here like to say the picnic is in your honor." He spoke casually, almost indifferently, as if he were talking of some trifling matter. But his eyes said something else; they were hard and serious, as though it were vital I listen to him carefully.

"It's a joy for my friends to say that the picnic is in your honor," he continued. "Accept it, just as they say it, in simplicity and without premeditation." His eyes became soft as he gazed at the women, then he turned to me and added, "The picnic is not in your honor at all, I assure you. And yet," he mused, "it is in your honor. It's a contradiction that will take you quite some time to understand."

"I didn't ask anyone to do anything for me," I said sullenly. I had become inordinately ponderous, the way I always have been when threatened. "Delia brought me here, and I am thankful." I felt then compelled to add, "And I would like to pay for any services rendered to me."

I was certain I had offended them; I knew that any minute now I would be asked to leave. Other than hurting my ego, it wouldn't have bothered me much. I was frightened, and I had had enough of them.

To my surprise and annoyance, they didn't take me seriously. They laughed at me. The angrier I became, the greater their mirth. Their shiny, laughing eyes were fixed on me, as if I were an unknown organism.

Wrath made me forget my fear. I lashed out at them, accusing them of taking me for a fool. I charged that Delia and her husband —I didn't know why I insisted on pairing them together—had played a disgusting joke on me.

"You brought me here," I said, turning to Delia, "so you and your friends can use me as your clown."

The more I ranted, the more they laughed. I was about to weep with self-pity, anger, and frustration when Mariano Aureliano came to stand beside me. He began to talk to me as if I were a child. I wanted to tell him that I could take care of myself, that I didn't need his sympathy, and that I was going home, when something in his tone, in his eyes, appeased me so thoroughly that I was certain he had hypnotized me. And yet, I knew he hadn't.

What was so unknown and disturbing to me was the suddenness and completeness of my change. What would have ordinarily taken days had happened in an instant. All my life I had indulged in brooding over every indignity or affront—real or imagined—I had suffered. With systematic thoroughness, I would mull them over until every detail was explained to my satisfaction.

25

As I looked at Mariano Aureliano, I felt like laughing at my earlier outburst. I could hardly remember what it was that had infuriated me to the point of tears.

Delia pulled me by the arm and asked me to help the other women unpack the china plates, crystal goblets, and ornate silverware from the various baskets they had brought. The women didn't talk to me or to each other. Only little sighs of pleasure escaped their lips as Mariano Aureliano opened the serving dishes; there were tamales, enchiladas, a hot chili stew, and hand-made tortillas. Not flour tortillas—as was customary in northern Mexico and which I didn't much care for—but corn tortillas.

Delia handed me a plate with a little bit of everything on it. I ate so greedily I was finished before anyone else. "This is the most delicious food I've ever tasted," I gushed, hoping for seconds. No one offered them. To hide my disappointment, I commented on the beauty of the antique lace trim around the canvas cloth we were sitting on.

"I did that," the woman sitting on Mariano Aureliano's left said. She was old-looking, with disheveled gray hair that hid her face. In spite of the heat, she wore a long skirt, a blouse, and a sweater.

"It's authentic Belgian lace," she explained to me in a gentle, dreamy voice. Her long slender hands, glinting with exquisite jeweled rings, lingered lovingly on the broad trim. In great detail, she told me about her handiwork, showing me the kinds of stitches and threads she had used to sew on the trim. Occasionally, I caught a fleeting glimpse of her face through all that mass of hair, but I couldn't tell what she looked like.

"It's authentic Belgian lace," she repeated. "It's part of my trousseau." She picked up a crystal goblet, took a sip of water and added, "These, too, are part of my trousseau; they're Baccarat."

I didn't doubt that they were. The lovely plates—each one was different—were of the finest porcelain. I was wondering whether a discreet peek under mine would pass unnoticed, when the woman sitting to Mariano Aureliano's right encouraged me to do so.

"Don't be shy. Take a look," she urged me. "You're among friends." Grinning, she lifted her own plate. "Limoges," she pronounced, then lifted mine briefly and noted that it was a Rosenthal.

26

The woman had childlike, delicate features. She was small, with round, thickly lashed black eyes. Her hair was black, except for the crown of her head, which had turned white, and was combed back into a tight little chignon. There was a force, an edge to her that was quite chilling as she besieged me with direct, personal questions.

I didn't mind her inquisitor's tone. I was accustomed to being bombarded with questions by my father and brothers when I went on a date or embarked on any kind of activity on my own. I resented it, but it was the normal interaction at home. Thus, I never learned how to converse. Conversation for me was parrying verbal attacks and defending myself at any cost.

I was surprised when this woman's coercive interrogation didn't immediately make me feel like defending myself.

"Are you married?" the woman asked.

"No," I said softly but firmly, wishing that she would change the subject.

"Do you have a man?" she insisted.

"No. I don't," I retorted, beginning to feel the stirring of my old defensive self.

"Is there a type of man you're partial to?" she went on. "Are there any personality traits you prefer in a man?"

For an instant I wondered whether she was making fun of me, but she seemed to be genuinely interested, as did her companions. Their curious, anticipating faces put me at ease. Forgetting my belligerent nature and that these women might be old enough to be my grandmothers, I spoke to them as if they were friends my age and we were discussing men.

"He has to be tall and handsome," I began. "He has to have a sense of humor. He has to be sensitive without being wishy-washy. He has to be intelligent without being an intellectual." I lowered my voice and in a confidential tone added, "My father used to say that intellectual men are weak to the core and traitors, all of them. I think I agree with my father."

"That's all you want in a man?" the woman inquired.

"No," I hastened to say. "Above all, the man of my dreams has to be athletic."

"Like your father," one of the women interjected.

"Naturally," I said defensively. "My father was a great athlete. A fabulous skier and swimmer."

"Do you get along with him?" she asked.

"Marvelously," I enthused. "I adore him. Just the thought of him brings tears to my eyes."

"Why aren't you with him?"

"I'm too much like him," I explained. "There is something in me that I can't quite understand or control that pulls me away."

"What about your mother?"

"My mother." I sighed and paused for a moment to find the best words to describe her. "She's very strong. She's the sober part in me. The part that is silent and doesn't need reinforcement."

"Are you very close to your parents?"

"In spirit, I am," I said softly. "In practice, I am a loner. I don't have many attachments." Then, as if something inside me was pushing to come out, I revealed a personality flaw that not even in my most introspective moments would I admit to myself. "I use people rather than nourish or cherish them," I said, then immediately made amends. "But I'm quite capable of feeling affection."

With a mixture of relief and disappointment, I gazed from one to the other. None of them seemed to attach any importance to my confession. The women went on to ask if I would describe myself as a courageous being or as a coward.

"I'm a confirmed coward," I stated. "But unfortunately my cowardice never stops me."

"Stops you from what?" the woman who had been questioning me inquired. Her black eyes were serious and the wide span of her brows, like a line drawn with a piece of charcoal, was concentrated in a frown.

"From doing dangerous things," I said. Pleased to notice that they seemed to be hanging on my every word, I explained that another one of my serious flaws was my great facility to get into trouble.

"What trouble have you gotten into that you can tell us about?" she asked. Her face, which had been grave all this time, broke into a brilliant, almost malicious smile.

28

"How about the trouble I'm in now?" I said half in jest, yet fearing that they might take my comment the wrong way. To my surprise and relief they all laughed and yelled the way rural people are wont to do when something strikes them as daring or funny.

"How did you end up in the United States?" the woman asked when they had all calmed down.

I shrugged, not really knowing what to say. "I wanted to go to school," I finally mumbled. "I was in England first, but I didn't do much except have a good time. I really don't know what I want to study. I think I'm in search of something, although I don't know exactly what."

"That brings us back to my first question," the woman said, her thin, pert face and her dark eyes animated and peering like an animal's. "Are you in search of a man?"

"I suppose I am," I admitted, then added impatiently, "What woman isn't? And why do you ask me so insistently about it? Do you have someone in mind? Is this some kind of a test?"

"We do have someone in mind," Delia Flores interjected. "But he's not a man." She and the others laughed and shrieked with such abandon I could not help but giggle, too.

"This is definitely a test," the inquisitive woman assured me as soon as everyone was quiet. She was silent for a moment, her eyes watchful and considering. "From what you told me, I can conclude that you are thoroughly middle class," she went on. She flung her arms wide in a gesture of forced acceptance. "But then, what else can a German woman, born in the New World, be?" She saw the anger in my face and, with a barely suppressed grin on her lips, added, "Middle-class people have middle-class dreams."

Seeing that I was about to explode, Mariano Aureliano explained that she was asking all these questions because they were simply curious about me. Only seldom did they have visitors and hardly ever any young ones.

"That doesn't mean that I have to be insulted," I complained.

As though I hadn't said anything, Mariano Aureliano continued to make excuses for the women. His gentle tone and his reassuring pat on my back melted my anger, just as it had before. His smile was so touchingly angelic I didn't for a moment doubt his sincerity when be began to flatter me. He said that I was one of the most extraordinary, one of the most remarkable persons they had ever met. I was so moved that I encouraged him to ask anything he wanted to know about me.

"Do you feel important?" he inquired.

I nodded. "All of us are very important to ourselves," I stated. "Yes, I think I am important, not in a general sense, but specifically, just to myself." At great length I talked about a positive self-image, self-worth, and how vital it was to reinforce our importance in order to be psychically healthy individuals.

"And what do you think about women?" he asked. "Do you think they are more or less important than men?"

"It's quite obvious that men are more important," I said. "Women don't have a choice. They have to be less important in order for family life to roll on smooth wheels, so to speak."

"But is it right?" Mariano Aureliano insisted.

"Well, of course, it's right," I declared. "Men are inherently superior; that's why they run the world. I've been brought up by an authoritarian father, who, although he raised me as freely as my brothers, nevertheless let me know that certain things are not so important for a woman. That's why I don't know what I'm doing in school or what I want in life." I looked at Mariano Aureliano, then in a helpless, defeated tone added, "I suppose I'm looking for a man who is as sure of himself as my father."

"She's a simpleton!" one of the women interjected.

"No, no, she isn't," Mariano Aureliano assured everyone. "She's just confused and as opinionated as her father."

"Her German father," Mr. Flores corrected him emphatically, stressing the word *German*. He had descended from the tree like a leaf, softly and without a sound. He served himself an immoderate amount of food.

"How right you are," Mariano Aureliano agreed and grinned. "Being as opinionated as her German father, she's simply repeating what she has heard all her life."

My anger, which rose and fell like some mysterious fever, was not only due to what they were saying about me but also because they were talking about me as if I were not present.

"She's unredeemable," another woman said.

"She's fine for the purpose at hand," Mariano Aureliano defended me with conviction.

Mr. Flores backed Mariano Aureliano. And the only woman who had not spoken so far said in a deep, husky voice that she agreed with the men, that I was fine for the purposes at hand.

She was tall and slender. Her pale-complexioned face, gaunt and severe, was crowned by braided white hair and highlighted by large, luminous eyes. In spite of her worn, drab clothes, there was something innately elegant about her.

"What are you all doing to me?" I shouted, unable to contain myself any longer. "Don't you realize how horrible it is for me to hear you talk about me as if I were not here?"

Mariano Aureliano fixed his fierce eyes on me. "You are not here," he said in a tone that was devoid of all feeling. "At least not yet. And most important, you don't count. Not now or ever."

I almost fainted with wrath. No one had ever spoken to me so harshly and with such indifference to my feelings. "I puke and piss and shit on all of you, goddamned, cocksucking farts!" I yelled.

"My God! A German hick!" Mariano Aureliano exclaimed, and they all laughed.

I was about to jump up and stomp away when Mariano Aureliano tapped me repeatedly on my back.

"There, there," he murmured as if burping a baby.

And as before, instead of resenting being treated like a child, my anger vanished. I felt light and happy. Shaking my head uncomprehendingly, I looked at them and giggled. "I learned to speak Spanish in the streets of Caracas," I said, "with the riffraff. I can cuss horribly."

"Didn't you just love the sweet tamales?" Delia asked, closing her eyes in delicate appreciation.

Her question seemed to be a password; the interrogation ended.

"Of course she did!" Mr. Flores responded for me. "She only wishes she had been served more. She has an insatiable appetite." He came to sit beside me. "Mariano Aureliano outdid himself and cooked a delight."

"You mean *he* cooked the food?" I asked in disbelief. "He has all these women, and he *cooks?*" Mortified by how my words might be interpreted, I hastened to apologize. I explained that it surprised me to no end that a Mexican male would cook at home when there were women. Their laughter made me realize that I hadn't meant to say that either.

"Especially if the women are his women. Isn't that what you meant?" Mr. Flores asked, his words interspersed by everybody's laughter. "You're quite right, they are Mariano's women. Or to be more precise, Mariano belongs to them." He slapped his knee gleefully, then turned to the tallest of the women—the one who had only spoken once—and said, "Why don't you tell her about us."

"Obviously, Mr. Aureliano doesn't have that many wives," I began, still mortified by my gaffe.

"Why not?" the woman retorted, and everyone laughed again. It was a joyful, youthful laughter, yet it didn't put me at ease. "All of us here are bound together by our struggle, by our deep affection for one another, and by the realization that without one another nothing is possible," she said.

"You aren't part of a religious group, are you?" I asked in a voice that betrayed my growing apprehension. "You don't belong to some kind of a commune, do you?"

"We belong to power," the woman replied. "My companions and I are the inheritors of an ancient tradition. We are part of a myth."

I didn't understand what she was saying. I glanced uneasily at the others; their eyes were fixed on me. They were watching me with a mixture of expectation and amusement.

I shifted my attention back to the tall woman. She, too, was observing me with that same bemused expression. Her eyes were so shiny they sparkled. She leaned over her crystal goblet and daintily sipped her water.

"We are essentially dreamers," she explained softly. "We are all dreaming now, and, by the fact that you were brought to us, you are also dreaming with us." She said this so smoothly that I really didn't realize what she had said.

"You mean I am sleeping and having a dream with you?" I asked in mock incredulity. I bit my lip to suppress the laughter bubbling up within me.

"That's not exactly what you're doing, but it's close enough," she admitted. Unperturbed by my nervous giggles, she went on to explain that what was happening to me was more like an extraordinary dream where all of them were helping me by dreaming my dream.

"But that's idio——," I started to say, but she silenced me with a wave of her hand.

"We are all dreaming the same dream," she assured me. She seemed to be transported by a joy I was at a loss to understand.

"What about the delicious food I just ate?" I asked, looking for the chili sauce that had dribbled on my blouse. I showed her the spots. "That can't be a dream. I ate that food!" I insisted in a loud, agitated tone. "I did! I ate it myself."

She regarded me with a cool composure, as though she had been expecting just such an outburst. "But what about Mr. Flores lifting you up to the top of the eucalyptus tree?" she asked equably.

I was on the verge of telling her that he hadn't lifted me to the top of the tree but only to a branch when she whispered, "Have you thought about that?"

"No. I haven't," I said snappishly.

"Of course, you haven't," she agreed, nodding her head knowingly as if she were aware that I had that instant remembered that even the lowest branch of any of the trees around us was impossible to reach from the ground. She said then that the reason I hadn't thought about it was because in dreams we are not rational. "In dreams we can only act," she stressed.

"Wait a minute," I interrupted her. "I may be a little dizzy, I admit. After all, you and your friends are the strangest people I have ever met. But I am as awake as I can be." Seeing that she was laughing at me, I yelled, "This is not a dream!"

With an imperceptible nod of her head she motioned to Mr. Flores, who in one swift movement reached for my hand and propelled himself, with me in tow, to a branch of the nearest eucalyptus tree. We sat there for an instant, and before I could say anything, he pulled me back to the ground, to the same spot where I had been sitting.

"Do you see what I mean?" the tall woman asked.

"No, I don't," I screamed, knowing that I had had a hallucination. My fear turned to rage, and I let out a stream of the foulest imprecations. My rage spent, I was engulfed by a wave of self-pity, and I began to weep. "What have you people done to me?" I asked in between sobs. "Have you put something in the food? In the water?"

"We have done nothing of the sort," the tall woman said kindly. "You don't need anything . . ."

I could barely hear her. My tears were like some dark, gauzy veil; they blurred her face and also her words.

"Hold on," I heard her say, although I could no longer see her or her companions. "Hold on, don't wake up yet."

There was something so compelling about her tone, I knew that my very life depended on seeing her again. With some unknown and totally unexpected force, I broke through the veil of my tears.

I heard a soft clapping sound, and then I saw them. They were smiling, and their eyes shone so intensely their pupils seemed to be lit by some inner fire. I apologized first to the women and then to the two men for my silly outburst. But they wouldn't hear of it. They said that I had performed exceptionally well.

"We are the living parts of a myth," Mariano Aureliano said then puckered his lips and blew into the air. "I will blow you to the one person who now holds the myth in his hands. He will help you clarify all this."

"And who might he be?" I asked flippantly. I was going to ask whether he would be as opinionated as my father but was distracted by Mariano Aureliano. He was still blowing into the air. His white hair stood on end; his cheeks were red and distended.

As if in answer to his effort, a soft breeze began to rustle through the eucalyptus trees. He nodded, apparently aware of my unspoken thought and confusion. Gently, he turned me until I faced the Bacatete Mountains.

The breeze turned into a wind, a wind so harsh and cold it hurt to breathe. With a seemingly boneless, uncoiling movement, the tall woman rose, grabbed my hand, and pulled me with her across the ploughed furrows. We came to a sudden halt in the middle of the field. I could have sworn that, with her outstretched arms, she was luring the spiral of dust and dead leaves spinning in the distance.

"In dreams, everything is possible," she whispered.

Laughing, I opened my arms to beckon the wind. Dust and leaves danced around us with such force everything blurred before my eyes. The tall woman was suddenly far away. Her body seemed to be dissolving in a reddish light until it completely vanished from my field of vision. And then blackness filled my head.

3

IT was impossible for me to determine, at that time, whether the picnic had been a dream or had actually taken place. I was incapable of remembering, in a sequential order, all the events I had participated in from the moment I fell asleep on the bed in the healing room. My next clear recollection was that I found myself talking with Delia at the table, in that same room.

Familiar with such lapses of memory, which used to occur in my childhood, I didn't at first make much of this discrepancy. As a child, eager to play, I would often get out of my bed half asleep and sneak out of my house through the window grill. Many times, I did indeed wake up in the plaza, playing with other children who weren't put to bed as early as I was.

There was no doubt in my mind that the picnic had been real, although I couldn't immediately place it in a time sequence. I tried to think, to reconstruct the events, but it frightened me to bring forth the idea of my childhood memory lapses. Somehow, I was reluctant to ask Delia about her friends, and she didn't volunteer any information either. However, I did ask about the healing session, which I knew had been a dream.

"I had such an elaborate dream about a healer," I began cautiously. "Not only did she tell me her name, but she also assured me that she had made all my nightmares vanish."

"It wasn't a dream," Delia stated, her tone clearly revealing her displeasure. She stared at me with an intensity that made me want to fidget, to move away. "The healer did tell you her name," she went on. "And she certainly did cure you from your sleep maladies."

"But it was a dream," I insisted. "In my dream, the healer was the size of a child. She couldn't have been real."

Delia reached for the glass of water on the table, but she didn't drink. She turned it around, on and on, without spilling a drop, then looked at me with glittering eyes. "The healer gave you the impression of being little, that's all," she said, nodding to herself, as though the words had just occurred to her and she had found them satisfactory. She sipped her water with slow, slurping noises, and her eyes grew soft and reflective. "She had to be little in order to cure you."

"She had to be little? You mean I only saw her as being little?"

Delia nodded repeatedly then, leaning toward me, whispered, "You see, you were dreaming. Yet it wasn't a dream. The healer really came to you and cured you, but you were not in the place in which you are now."

"Come on, Delia," I objected. "What are you talking about? I know it was a dream. I am always totally aware that I am dreaming, even though the dreams are completely real to me. That's my malady, remember?"

"Maybe now that she has cured you, it's no longer your malady but your talent," Delia proposed, smiling. "But going back to your question, the healer had to be small, like a child, because you were quite young when your nightmares first began."

Her statement was so outlandish, I couldn't even laugh. "And now I am cured?" I asked facetiously.

"You are," she assured me. "In dreaming, cures are accomplished with great ease, almost effortlessly. What's difficult is to make people dream."

"Difficult?" I asked, my voice harsher than I had intended. "Everybody has dreams. We all have to sleep, don't we?"

Delia rolled her eyes derisively to the ceiling then gazed at me and said, "Those are not the dreams I am talking about. Those are ordinary dreams. Dreaming has purpose; ordinary dreams don't have any."

"They certainly do!" I emphatically disagreed with her, then went into a lengthy diatribe about the psychological importance of dreams. I cited works on psychology, philosophy, and art.

Delia wasn't in the least impressed with my knowledge. She agreed with me that ordinary dreams must indeed help maintain the mental health of individuals but insisted that she wasn't concerned with that. "Dreaming has a purpose; ordinary dreams don't," she reiterated.

"What purpose, Delia?" I said condescendingly.

She turned her head sideways, as if she wanted to hide her face from me. An instant later she looked back at me. Something cold and detached showed itself in her eyes, and the change of expression was altogether so ruthless that I was frightened. "Dreaming has always a practical purpose," she declared. "It serves the dreamer in simple or intricate ways. It has served you to get rid of your sleeping maladies. It served the witches at the picnic to know your essence. It served me to screen myself out of the awareness of the immigration guard patrol asking to see your tourist card."

"I'm trying to understand what you are saying, Delia," I mumbled. "Do you mean that you people can hypnotize others against their wills?" I asked forcefully.

"Call it that if you wish," she said. On her face was a look of calm indifference that bore little sympathy. "What you can't see yet is that you, yourself, can enter quite effortlessly into what you would call a hypnotic state. We call it dreaming: a dream that's not a dream, a dream where we can do nearly anything our hearts desire."

Delia almost made sense to me, but I had no words with which to express my thoughts, my feelings. I stared at her, baffled. Suddenly, I remembered an event from my adolescence. When I was finally allowed driving lessons in my father's jeep, I surprised my family by showing them that I already knew how to shift. I had been doing it for years in my dreams. With an assurance that was even baffling to me, I took the old road from Caracas to La Guayra, the port by the sea, on my first venture. I deliberated whether I should tell Delia about this episode but instead asked her about the healer's size.

"She is not a tall woman. Neither is she as small as you saw her. In her healing dream, she projected her smallness for your benefit, and in doing so, she was small. That's the nature of magic. You have to be what you want to give the impression of."

"Is she a magician?" I asked expectantly. The thought that they all worked in a circus, that they were part of some magic show, had crossed my mind at various times. It would explain so many things about them, I believed.

"No. She's not a magician," Delia said. "She's a sorceress."

Delia gazed at me so scornfully I was ashamed of my question. "Magicians are in a show," she explained, gazing at me pointedly. "Sorcerers are in the world without being part of the world." She was silent for a long time, then a sigh escaped her lips. "Would you like to see Esperanza now?" she asked.

"Yes," I said eagerly. "I would like that very much."

The possibility that the healer had been real and not a dream made my head spin. I didn't quite believe Delia, and yet I wanted to believe her in the worst way. My thoughts ran wild; suddenly I realized that I hadn't mentioned to Delia that the healer of my dream had told me her name was Esperanza.

I was so absorbed in my thoughts I failed to notice that Delia was speaking.

"I'm sorry, what did you say?"

"The only way you can make sense of all this is to call back dreaming," she maintained. Laughing softly, she waved her hand as if she were signaling someone to come.

Her words were of no importance to me. I was already pondering another train of thought. Esperanza was real. And I was certain she was going to clarify everything for me. Besides, she had not been at the picnic; she had not treated me as abominably as all the other women had. I harbored the vague hope that Esperanza had liked me, and this thought somehow restored my confidence. To disguise my feelings from Delia, I told her that I was anxious to see the healer. "I would like to thank her and, of course, pay her for all she did for me."

"It's already paid," Delia stated. The mocking glint in her eyes clearly revealed that she was privy to my thoughts.

"What do you mean it's already paid?" I asked in an involuntarily high-pitched voice. "Who paid for it?"

"It's hard to explain," Delia began with a distant kindness that put me momentarily at ease. "It all began at your friend's party in Nogales. I noticed you instantly."

"You did?" I asked expectantly, eager to hear some compliment on my tasteful and carefully chosen wardrobe.

There was an uncomfortable silence. I couldn't see Delia's eyes, veiled under her half-closed lids. There was something quiet yet oddly disturbing about her voice as she said that what she had noticed about me was that every time I had to talk to my friend's grandmother I seemed to be absentminded, as if I were asleep.

"Absentminded is putting it mildly," I said. "You have no idea what I went through, what I had to do to convince that old lady that I wasn't the devil incarnate."

Delia seemed not to have heard me. "I knew in a flash that you had great facility to dream," she went on. "So I followed you around through the house and saw you in action. You were not fully aware of what you were doing or saying. And yet you were doing fine, talking and laughing and lying your head off to be liked."

"Are you calling me a liar?" I asked in jest but betraying my hurt. I felt an impulse to get angry. I stared at the pitcher of water on the table until the threatening feeling had passed.

"I wouldn't dare call you a liar," Delia pronounced rather pompously. "I'd call you a dreamer." There was a heavy solemnity in her voice, but her eyes sparkled with mirth, with genial malice, as she said, "The sorcerers who reared me told me that it doesn't matter what one may say as long as one has the power to say it." Her voice conveyed such enthusiasm and approval that I was sure someone was behind one of the doors listening to us. "And the way to get that power is from dreaming. You don't know this because you do it naturally, but when you are in a pinch, your mind goes instantly into dreaming."

"Were you reared by sorcerers, Delia?" I asked in order to change the subject.

"Of course I was," she declared, as if it were the most natural thing in the world.

"Were your parents sorcerers?"

"Oh, no," she said and chuckled. "The sorcerers found me one day and reared me from then on."

"How old were you? Were you a child?"

Delia laughed, as if with my question I had reached the height of humor. "No, I wasn't a child," she said. "I was perhaps your age when they found me and began to rear me."

"What do you mean they began to rear you?"

Delia gazed at me but without focusing her eyes on me. For a moment I thought she hadn't heard me or, if she had, she wasn't going to answer me. I repeated my question. She shrugged and smiled. "They reared me as one rears a child," she finally said. "It doesn't matter how old you are; in their world, you are a child."

Suddenly afraid we might be overheard, I glanced over my shoulder and whispered, "Who are these sorcerers, Delia?"

"That's a very tough question," she mused. "At the moment, I can't even begin to answer it. All I can tell you about them is that they are the ones who said to me that one should never lie to be believed."

"Why should one lie then?" I asked.

"For the sheer pleasure of it," Delia promptly retorted. She then rose from the chair and walked toward the door that led to the yard. Before stepping outside, she turned and with a grin on her face asked, "Do you know the saying, 'If you are not lying to be believed, you can say anything you want, regardless of what anybody thinks of you'?"

"I've never heard such a saying." I suspected she had made it up; it had her stamp. "Besides, I don't understand what you're trying to say," I added primly.

"I'm sure you do," she said, looking sidelong at me through the strands of her black hair. Gesturing with her chin, she motioned me to follow her. "Let's go and see Esperanza now."

I jumped up and dashed after her, only to come to an abrupt halt by the door. Momentarily blinded by the brightness outside, I stood there, wondering what had happened. It seemed that no time had elapsed since I had run after Mr. Flores across the field. The sun, as it had been then, was still at the zenith.

I caught a glimpse of Delia's red skirt as she turned a corner. I rushed after her, across a stone archway that led to a most enchanting patio.

At first I saw nothing, so strong was the contrast between the dazzling sunlight and the intense shadows of the patio. Breathlessly, I simply stood there, perfectly still, inhaling the humid air; it was fragrant with the scent of orange blossoms, honeysuckle, and sweet peas. Climbing up strings that seemed to be suspended from the sky, the sweet peas hung like a brightly colored tapestry amidst the foliage of trees, shrubs, and ferns.

The healer I had seen before in my dream was sitting on a rocking chair in the middle of the patio. She was much older than Delia and the women at the picnic, though how I knew this I couldn't say. She was rocking to and fro with an air of dreamy abandon. I felt an anguishing pain that gripped my whole being, for I had the irrational certainty that her rocking movement was taking her farther and farther away from me. A wave of agony, an indescribable loneliness engulfed me as I kept staring at her. I wanted to cross the patio and hold her, but something about the patio's dark tiles, laid out in a most intricate pattern, held my feet in place.

"Esperanza," I finally managed to whisper in a voice so feeble it was barely audible even to myself.

She opened her eyes and smiled quite without surprise, as if she had been expecting me. She rose and walked toward me. She was not the size of a child but about my height, five feet and two inches. She was thin and fragile-looking, yet exuded a vitality that made me feel puny and shrunken.

"How happy I am to see you again." Her voice sounded sincere. She motioned me to grab one of the rush chairs and sit beside her.

As I looked about me, I discovered the other women, including Delia. They were sitting on rush chairs, half hidden by shrubs and trees; they, too, were watching me curiously. Some of them smiled, while the others kept on eating tamales from the plates on their laps.

In the shady, green light of the patio—in spite of the mundane task of eating—the women appeared insubstantial, imaginary. Yet, each one of them was unnaturally vivid without being distinct. They seemed to have absorbed the patio's greenish light, which had settled all around us like a transparent fog. The fleeting but awesome idea that I was in a house populated by ghosts crossed my mind.

"Would you like to eat something?" Esperanza asked me. "Delia has made the most delicious food you can imagine."

"No, thank you," I murmured in a voice that didn't sound like my own. Seeing her questioning expression, I added feebly, "I'm not hungry." I was so nervous and agitated that even if I had been starving I wouldn't have been able to swallow a bite.

Esperanza must have sensed my fear. She leaned toward me and patted my arm reassuringly. "What is it that you want to know?"

"I thought I had seen you in a dream," I blurted out, then, noticing the laughter in her eyes, added, "Am I dreaming now?"

"You are, but you are not asleep," she replied, enunciating her words slowly and precisely.

"How can I be dreaming and not be asleep?"

"Some women can do that with great ease," she maintained. "They can be dreaming and not be asleep. You are one of those women. Others have to work a lifetime to accomplish that."

I sensed a tinge of admiration in her voice, yet I wasn't in the least flattered. On the contrary, I was more worried than ever. "But how is it possible to dream without sleeping?" I insisted.

"If I explain to you how it is possible, you won't understand it," she pronounced. "Take my word for it, it's much better to postpone the explanations for the time being." Again she patted my arm and a gentle smile lit up her face. "For the moment it's enough for you to know that, for you, I am the one who brings dreams."

I didn't think it was enough, but I didn't dare to tell her so. Instead, I asked her, "Was I awake when you cured me of my nightmares? And was I dreaming when I sat outside in the field with Delia and all the others?"

Esperanza regarded me for a long moment then nodded sagely, as if she had decided to reveal some monumental truth. "You're too dumb to see the mystery of what we do." She said this so matter-of-factly, so nonjudgmentally, that it didn't occur to me to take offense or to attempt any kind of rebuttal.

"But you could make me see it, couldn't you?" I pleaded eagerly.

43

The other women giggled. It wasn't a mocking sound but a murmuring that echoed all around me like a muffled chorus. The sound didn't seem to come from the women but from the shadows of the patio. Rather than a giggle, it was a whisper, a delicate warning that not only made me lose my thrust but erased my troubling doubts, my desire to know. And I knew, without a shadow of doubt, that I had been awake and dreaming both times. It was a knowledge that I couldn't explain, however. It was something beyond words.

Yet, after a few moments, I felt compelled to dissect my realization, to put it all into some kind of logical framework.

Esperanza regarded me with apparent pleasure. Then she said, "I'm going to explain to you who we are and what we do."

She prefaced her elucidation with an admonition. She warned me that whatever she had to tell me wasn't easy to believe. Therefore, I had to suspend judgment and hear her out without interruptions, without questions. "Can you do that?"

"Naturally," I shot back.

She was silent for a moment, her eyes appraising me thoughtfully. She must have sensed my uncertainty and the question that was about to burst from my lips.

"It isn't that I don't want to answer your questions," she maintained. "It's rather that at this time it will be impossible for you to understand the answers."

I nodded—not in agreement—afraid that if so much as a peep came out of me she would stop talking altogether.

In a voice that was but a soft murmur, she told me something that was both incredible and fascinating. She said that she was the spiritual descendant of sorcerers who lived in the valley of Oaxaca millennia before the Spanish conquest.

Esperanza was silent for a long time. Her eyes, fixed on the bright, multicolored sweet peas, seemed to reach nostalgically into the past. "As it is for me, the part of those sorcerers' activities pertinent to you is called dreaming," she continued. "Those sorcerers were men and women who possessed extraordinary dreaming powers and performed acts that defied the imagination."

Hugging my knees, I listened to her. Esperanza was a brilliant raconteuse and a most gifted mimic. Her face changed with each

44

turn of her explanation. It was at times the face of a young woman, at other times an old woman's, or it was the face of a man or that of an innocent and impish child.

She said that millennia ago, men and women were the possessors of a knowledge that allowed them to slip in and out of our normal world. And thus they divided their lives into two areas: the day and the night. During the day they conducted their activities like everyone else: they engaged in normal, expected, everyday behavior. During the night, however, they became dreamers. They systematically dreamed dreams that broke the boundaries of what we consider to be reality.

Again she paused, as though giving me time to let her words sink in.

"Using the darkness as a cloak," she went on, "they accomplished an inconceivable thing; they were able to dream while they were awake."

Anticipating the question I was about to voice, Esperanza explained that to be dreaming while they were awake meant that they could immerse themselves in a dream that gave them the energy necessary to perform feats that stagger the mind, while they were perfectly conscious and awake.

Because of the aggressive mode of interaction at home, I never developed the ability to listen for very long. If I couldn't meddle with direct, belligerent questions, any verbal exchange, no matter how interesting, was meaningless to me. Unable to argue, I became restless. I was dying to interrupt Esperanza. I had questions, but to get answers, to have things explained to me, was not the thrust of my urge to interrupt. What I wanted to do was to give in to my compulsion to have a shouting match with her in order to feel normal again.

As if privy to my turmoil, Esperanza stared at me for an instant and then signaled me to speak. Or I thought she had given me such a command. I opened my mouth to say—as usual—anything that came to my mind even if it wasn't related to the subject. But I couldn't say a word. I struggled to speak and made gargling sounds to the delight of the women in the background.

Esperanza resumed talking, as if she hadn't noticed my futile efforts. It surprised me to no end that she had my undivided attention. She said that the origins of the sorcerers' knowledge could be understood only in terms of a legend. A superior being commiserating with the terrible plight of man—to be driven as an animal by food and reproduction—gave man the power to dream and taught him how to use his dreams.

"Legends, of course, tell the truth in a concealed fashion," she elucidated. "Their success in concealing the truth rests on man's conviction that they are simply stories. Legends of men changing into birds or angels are accounts of a concealed truth, which appears to be the fantasizing or, simply, the delusions of primitive or deranged minds.

"So it's been the task of sorcerers for thousands of years to make new legends and to discover the concealed truth of old ones.

"This is where dreamers come into the picture. Women are best at dreaming. They have the facility to abandon themselves, the facility to let go.

"The woman who taught me to dream could maintain two hundred dreams."

Esperanza regarded me intently, as if she were appraising my reaction, which was complete stupefaction, for I had no idea what she meant. She explained that to maintain a dream meant that one could dream something specific about oneself and could enter into that dream at will. Her teacher, she said, could enter at will into two hundred specific dreams about herself.

"Women are peerless dreamers," Esperanza assured me. "Women are extremely practical. In order to sustain a dream, one must be practical, because the dream must pertain to practical aspects of oneself. My teacher's favorite dream was to dream of herself as a hawk. Another was to dream of herself as an owl. So depending on the time of the day, she could dream about being either one, and since she was dreaming while she was awake, she was really and absolutely a hawk or an owl."

There was such sincerity and conviction in her tone and in her eyes, I was entirely under her spell. Not for a moment did I doubt her. Nothing she could have said would have seemed outlandish to me at that moment.

She further explained that in order to accomplish a dream of that nature, women need to have an iron discipline. She leaned toward me and in a confidential whisper, as though she didn't want the others to overhear her, said, "By an iron discipline I don't mean any kind of strenuous routine but rather that women have to break the routine of what is expected of them.

"And they have to do it in their youth," she stressed. "And most important, with their strength intact. Often, when women are old enough to be done with the business of being women, they decide it's time to concern themselves with nonworldly or other-worldly thoughts and activities. Little do they know or want to believe that hardly ever do such women succeed." She gently slapped my stomach, as if she were playing on a drum. "The secret of a woman's strength is her womb."

Esperanza nodded emphatically, as if she had actually heard the silly question that popped into my mind: "Her womb?"

"Women," she continued, "must begin by burning their matrix. They cannot be the fertile ground that has to be seeded by men, following the command of God himself."

Still watching me closely, she smiled and asked, "Are you religious by any chance?"

I shook my head. I couldn't speak. My throat was so constricted I could scarcely breathe. I was dumbstruck with fear and amazement, not so much by what she was saying, but by her change. If asked, I wouldn't have been able to tell when she changed, but all of a sudden her face was young and radiant; inner life seemed to have been fired up in her.

"That's good!" Esperanza exclaimed. "This way you don't have to struggle against beliefs," she pointed out. "They are very hard to overcome. I was reared a devout Catholic. I nearly died when I had to examine my attitude toward religion." She sighed. Her voice, turning wistful, became soft as she added, "But that was nothing compared to the battle I had to wage before I became a bona fide dreamer."

I waited expectantly, hardly breathing, while a quite pleasurable sensation spread like a mild electrical current through my entire body. I anticipated a tale of a gruesome battle between herself and terrifying creatures. I could barely disguise my disappointment when she revealed that she had to battle herself.

"In order to be a dreamer, I had to vanquish the self," Esperanza explained. "Nothing, but nothing, is as hard as that. We women are the most wretched prisoners of the self. The self is our cage. Our cage is made out of commands and expectations poured on us from the moment we are born. You know how it is. If the firstborn child is a boy, there is a celebration. If it's a girl, there is a shrug of the shoulders and the statement, 'It's all right. I still will love her and do anything for her.'"

Out of respect for the old woman, I didn't laugh out loud. Never in my life had I heard statements of that sort. I considered myself an independent woman. But obviously, in light of what Esperanza was saying, I was no better off than any other woman. And contrary to the manner in which I would have normally reacted to such an idea, I agreed with her. I had always been made aware that the precondition of my being a woman was to be dependent. I was taught that a woman was indeed fortunate if she could be desirable so men would do things for her. I was told that it was demeaning to my womanhood to endeavor to do anything myself if that thing could be given to me. It was drilled into me that a woman's place is in the home, with her husband and her children.

"Like you, I was reared by an authoritarian yet lenient father," Esperanza went on. "I thought, like yourself, that I was free. For me to understand the sorcerers' way—that freedom didn't mean to be myself—nearly killed me. To be myself was to assert my womanhood. And to do that took all my time, effort, and energy.

"The sorcerers, on the contrary, understand freedom as the capacity to do the impossible, the unexpected—to dream a dream that has no basis, no reality in everyday life." Her voice again became but a whisper as she added, "The knowledge of sorcerers is what is exciting and new. Imagination is what a woman needs to change the self and become a dreamer."

Esperanza said that if she had not succeeded in vanquishing the self, she would have only led a woman's normal life: the life her parents had designed for her. A life of defeat and humiliation. A

48

life devoid of all mystery. A life that had been programmed by custom and tradition.

Esperanza pinched my arm. I cried out in pain. "You'd better pay attention," she reprimanded me.

"I am," I mumbled defensively, rubbing my arm; I had been certain that no one would notice my waning interest.

"You won't be tricked or enticed into the sorcerer's world," she warned me. "You have to choose, knowing what awaits you."

The fluctuations of my mood were astonishing to me, because they were quite irrational. I should have been afraid. Yet I was calm, as if my being there were the most natural thing in the world.

"The secret of a woman's strength is her womb," Esperanza said and slapped my stomach once more. She said that women dream with their wombs, or rather, from their wombs. The fact that they have wombs makes them perfect dreamers.

Before I had even finished the thought "why is the womb so important?" Esperanza answered me.

"The womb is the center of our creative energy," she explained, "to the point that, if there would be no more males in the world, women could continue to reproduce. And the world would then be populated by the female of the human species only." She added that women reproducing unilaterally could only reproduce clones of themselves.

I was genuinely surprised at this specific piece of knowledge. I couldn't help interrupting Esperanza to tell her that I had read about parthenogenetic and asexual reproduction in a biology class.

She shrugged her shoulders and went on with her explanation. "Women, having then the ability and the organs for reproducing life, have also the ability to produce dreams with those same organs," she said. Seeing the doubt in my eyes, she warned me, "Don't trouble yourself wondering how it is done. The explanation is very simple, and because it's simple, it's the most difficult thing to understand. I still have trouble myself. So in a true woman's fashion, I act. I dream and leave the explanations to men."

Esperanza claimed that originally the sorcerers she had told me about used to pass their knowledge on to their biological descendants or to people of their private choice, but the results had been catastrophic. Instead of enhancing this knowledge, these new sorcerers, who had been selected by arbitrary favoritism, confabulated to enhance themselves. They were finally destroyed, and their destruction nearly obliterated their knowledge. The few sorcerers who were left then decided that their knowledge should never again be passed on to their descendants or to people of their choice but to those selected by an impersonal power, which they called the spirit.

"And now, all this brings us to you," Esperanza pronounced. "The sorcerers of ancient times decided that only the ones who were pinpointed would qualify. You were pointed out to us. And here you are! You are a natural dreamer. It's up to the forces that rule us where you go from here. It's not up to you. Nor to us, of course. You can only acquiesce or refuse."

From the urgency in her voice, and the compelling light in her eyes, it was obvious that she had given this explanation in complete seriousness. It was this earnestness that stopped me from laughing out loud. Also, I was too exhausted.

The mental concentration I had needed to follow her was too intense. I wanted to sleep. She insisted I stretch my legs, lie down, and relax. I did it so thoroughly that I dozed off.

When I opened my eyes, I had no idea how long I had slept. I sought the reassuring presence of Esperanza or the other women. There was no one with me on the patio. But I didn't feel alone; somehow their presence lingered amidst the green all around me, and I felt protected. A breeze rustled the leaves. I felt it on my eyelids, warm and soft. It blew around me, then passed over me the same way it was passing over the desert, quickly and soundlessly.

With my gaze fixed on the tiles, I walked around the patio trying to figure out its intricate design. To my delight, the lines led me from one rush chair to the other. I tried to recall who had sat in which chair, but hard as I tried, I couldn't remember.

I was distracted by a delicious scent of food, spiced with onions and garlic. Guided by that smell, I found my way to the kitchen, a large rectangular room. It was as deserted as the patio. And the bright tile designs adorning the walls reminded me of the patterns in the patio. I didn't pursue the similarities, for I had discovered the food left on the sturdy wooden table standing in the middle of the room. Assuming that it was for me, I sat down and ate it all. It was the same spicy stew I had eaten at the picnic; warmed over, it was even tastier.

As I gathered the dishes to take them to the sink, I discovered a note and a drawn map under my place mat. It was from Delia. She suggested I return to Los Angeles by way of Tucson, where she would meet me at a certain coffee shop specified on the map. Only there, she wrote, would she tell me more about herself and her friends.

4

EAGER to hear what Delia had to tell me about her friends, I returned to Los Angeles by way of Tucson. I arrived at the coffee shop in the late afternoon. An old man directed me to an empty space in the parking lot. Only when he opened my door did I realize who it was.

"Mariano Aureliano!" I exclaimed. "What a surprise. I'm so glad to see you. What are you doing here?"

"I was waiting for you," he said. "So my friend and I saved this space for you."

I caught a glimpse of a burly Indian driving an old red pickup truck. He had pulled out of the parking space as I drove into the lot.

"I'm afraid Delia couldn't make it," Mariano Aureliano said apologetically. "She had to leave for Oaxaca unexpectedly." He smiled broadly and added, "I'm here on her behalf. I hope I fit the bill."

"You've no idea how delighted I am to see you," I said truthfully. I was convinced that he, better than Delia, would help me make sense of all that had happened to me during the past few days. "Esperanza explained to me that I was in some sort of a trance when I met all of you," I added.

"Did she say that?" he asked almost absentmindedly.

His voice, his attitude, his whole demeanor was so different from what I remembered that I kept staring at him, hoping to discover what had changed. That fiercely chiseled face had lost all its fierceness. I was busy with my own turmoil, however, and didn't give it any more thought.

"Esperanza left me alone in the house," I went on. "She and all the women went away without even saying good-bye to me. But I wasn't disturbed," I hastened to point out. "Although I'm usually very put out when people are not courteous."

"Oh really!" he exclaimed as if I had said something extremely meaningful.

Afraid that he might take offense at what I was saying about his companions, I immediately started to explain that I hadn't really meant to say that Esperanza and the others had been un-friendly. "Quite the contrary, they were most gracious and kind," I assured him. I was about to reveal what Esperanza had told me, but his steady gaze stopped me. It wasn't an angry stare or a threatening one. It was a piercing look that cut through all my defenses. I had the certainty he was seeing right into the mess that my mind was.

I glanced away to hide my nervousness then told him in a light, almost joking tone that it hadn't really mattered to me that I had been left alone in the house. "I was intrigued that I knew every corner of that place," I confided, then paused for a moment, won-dering what impact my words were having on him. But he kept staring at me.

"I went to the bathroom, and I realized that I had been in that bathroom before," I continued. "There were no mirrors in it. I re-membered that detail before I actually entered the room. Then I remembered that there were no mirrors in the whole house. So I went through every room, and sure enough, I couldn't find any." Noticing that I was still getting no reaction from him, I went on to say that while listening to the radio on my way to Tucson I had realized that it was one day later than I expected. "I must have slept a whole day," I finished in a strained tone.

"You didn't quite sleep a whole day," Mariano Aureliano pointed out indifferently. "You walked through the house and talked to us a great deal before falling asleep like a log."

I started laughing. My laughter was very near to hysteria, but he didn't seem to notice this. He laughed too, and I relaxed.

"I don't sleep like a log, ever," I felt compelled to explain. "I'm an extremely light sleeper."

He was silent, and when he finally spoke his voice was serious, demanding. "Don't you remember being curious about how the women dressed and did their hair without glancing into mirrors?"

I could think of no reply, and he went on to say, "Don't you remember how odd you found it that there were no pictures on the walls and that there was no—"

"I have no recollection of having talked to anyone," I cut him off in midsentence. Then I glanced at him guardedly, thinking that perhaps, just in order to mystify me, he was saying I had interacted with everybody in that house, when in reality nothing of that sort had happened.

"Having no recollection of it doesn't mean it didn't take place," he said curtly.

My stomach fluttered involuntarily. It wasn't his tone of voice I took exception to but the fact that he had answered my unspoken thoughts.

Certain that if I kept on talking something would dispel my mounting apprehension, I went into a long and muddled recitation of how I felt. I recounted what had happened. There were gaps in the order of events as I tried to reconstruct all that had taken place between the healing session and my drive to Tucson, during which I knew that I had lost a whole day.

"You people are doing something to me, something strange and threatening," I finished, feeling momentarily righteous.

"Now you're being silly," Mariano Aureliano pronounced and smiled for the first time. "If something is strange and threatening, it is only because you're new at it. You're a tough woman. It'll make sense to you sooner or later."

I was annoyed at the sound of *woman*. I would have preferred if he had said *girl*. Accustomed as I was to being asked for my papers to prove that I was over sixteen, I suddenly felt old.

"Youth must be only in the eyes of the beholder," he said as if he were again reading my thoughts. "Whoever looks at you must see your youth, your vigor; but for you to feel you're a kid is wrong. You must be innocent without being immature."

For some inexplicable reason, his words were more than I could bear. I wanted to weep, not out of hurt but out of despondency. At a loss for what to do, I suggested we have something to eat. "I'm famished," I said, trying to sound cheerful.

"No, you're not," he said with authority. "You're just trying to change the subject."

Startled by his tone and his words, I looked at him, appalled. My surprise swiftly turned to anger. Not only was I hungry, but I was also exhausted and stiff from the long drive. I wanted to yell and vent on him all my wrath and frustration, but his eyes didn't let me move. There was something reptilian about those unblinking, burning eyes; for a moment I thought he might swallow me up, as a snake swallows a mesmerized, defenseless bird.

The mixture of fear and anger escalated to such heights I felt blood rushing to my face. And I knew by the slight curious lift of his brows that my face had turned purple. Since very early childhood, I had suffered from horrid attacks of temper. Other than trying to soothe me, no one had ever stopped me from indulging in these attacks, and I had indulged in them until I had refined them into king-sized temper tantrums. These tantrums were never caused by being denied what I wanted to have or wanted to do but by indignities—real or imagined—inflicted on my person.

Somehow the circumstances of that moment, however, made me feel ashamed of my habit. I made a conscious effort to control myself, which nearly consumed all my strength, but I calmed down.

"You were a whole day with us, a day which you can't remember now," Mariano Aureliano proceeded, seemingly unconcerned by my fluctuating mood. "During that time, you were very communicative and responsive. A thing which was extremely rewarding to us. When you are dreaming, you are a much better being, more appealing, more resourceful. You allowed us to know you in great depth."

His words threw me into a turmoil. Growing up asserting myself the way I did, I had become quite adept at detecting meaning hidden behind words. "To know me in great depth" bothered me to no end, especially "great depth." It could only mean one thing, I thought, and immediately discarded it as being preposterous.

I became so absorbed in my own calculations that I no longer paid any attention to what he was saying. He kept on explaining about the day I had lost, but I only caught bits and pieces. I must have been staring at him blankly, for all of a sudden he stopped talking.

"You're not listening," he reprimanded me sternly.

"What did you do to me when I was in a trance?" I shot back at him. More than a question, it was an accusation.

I was startled by my own words, for it was not a thought-out statement; the words had simply escaped me of their own accord. Mariano Aureliano was even more surprised. He almost choked on the burst of laughter that followed his wide-eyed expression of shock.

"We don't go around taking advantage of little girls," he assured me. Not only did he sound sincere, but he seemed to be offended by my accusation. "Esperanza told you who we are. We are very serious people," he stressed then in a mocking tone added, "And we mean business."

"What kind of business?" I demanded belligerently. "Esperanza didn't tell me what you want from me."

"She certainly did," he retorted with such assurance I wondered for an instant if he hadn't been concealed, listening to our conversation in the patio. I wouldn't have put it past him.

"Esperanza told you that you have been pointed out to us," he went on. "And now we are as driven by that as you are driven by fear."

"I'm not driven by anything or anybody," I shouted, quite forgetting that he hadn't told me what is was they wanted from me.

Without being in the least affected by my anger, he said that Esperanza had made it very clear to me that they were committed to rear me from now on.

"Rear me!" I yelled. "You're crazy. I've had all the rearing I need!"

Ignoring my outburst, he went on to explain that their commitment was total and whether or not I understood this was of no importance to them.

I stared at him, unable to hide my dread. Never before had I heard someone express himself with such compelling indifference and such concern at the same time. In an effort to conceal my alarm, I tried to imbue my voice with a spunkiness I was far from feeling when I asked, "What do you imply when you say you are going to rear me?"

"Just what you hear," he answered. "We're committed to guide you."

"But why?" I asked, frightened and curious at the same time. "Can't you see that I don't need any guidance, that I don't want any . . ."

My words were drowned by Mariano Aureliano's joyful laughter. "You certainly need guidance. Esperanza already showed you how meaningless your life is." Anticipating my next question, he motioned me to be silent. "As to why you and not someone else, she explained to you that we let the spirit tell us who we should guide. The spirit showed us that you were the one."

"Wait a minute, Mr. Aureliano," I protested. "I really don't want to be rude or ungrateful, but you must understand that I'm not seeking help. I don't want anybody to guide me, even though I probably need guidance. The mere thought is abhorrent to me. Do you see what I mean? Do I make myself clear?"

"You do, and I do see what you mean," he echoed, moving back a step away from my pointed finger. "But precisely because you don't need anything, you are a most adequate candidate."

"Candidate?" I yelled, fed up with his insistence. I looked around me, wondering if I had been overheard by the people going in and out of the coffee shop. "What is this?" I went on yelling. "You and your companions are all a bunch of nuts. You leave me alone, you hear? I don't need you or anyone."

To my surprise and morbid delight, Mariano Aureliano finally lost his temper and began to berate me like my father and brothers used to. In a tightly controlled voice that never rose to be heard beyond us, he insulted me. He called me stupid and spoiled. And then, as if insulting me had given him impetus, he said something unforgivable. He shouted that the only asset I ever had was to be born blond and blue-eyed in a land where blond hair and blue eyes were coveted and revered.

"You never had to struggle for anything," he asserted. "The colonial mentality of the *cholos* of your country made them regard you as if you really deserved special treatment. Privilege based merely on having blond hair and blue eyes is the dumbest privilege there is."

I was livid. I've never been one to take insults sitting down. My years of training at shouting matches at home and the extraordinarily descriptive vulgarities I learned—and never forgot—in the streets of Caracas in my childhood paid off that afternoon. I said things to Mariano Aureliano that embarrass me to this day.

I was so worked up I didn't notice that the burly Indian who was driving the pickup truck had joined us. I only realized he was there when I heard his loud laughter. He and Mariano Aureliano were practically on the ground, clasping their stomachs, shrieking with delight.

"What's so funny?" I yelled, turning to the burly Indian. I insulted him, too.

"What a foul-mouthed woman," he said in perfect English. "If I were your daddy I would wash your mouth with soap."

"Who asked you to butt in, you fat turd?" In blind fury, I kicked him in the shinbone.

He yelled out in pain and cursed me.

I was about to reach for his arm and bite him when Mariano Aureliano grabbed me from behind and tossed me in the air.

Time stopped. My descent was so slow, so imperceptible, it seemed to me that I was suspended in the air forever. I didn't land on the ground with my bones broken, as I expected, but in the arms of the burly Indian. He didn't even stagger but held me as if I weighed no more than a pillow, a ninety-five-pound pillow. Catching the wicked glint in his eyes, I was certain he was going to toss me again. He must have sensed my fear, for he smiled and gently put me down.

My wrath and strength spent, I leaned against my car and sobbed.

Mariano Aureliano put his arm around me and stroked my hair and shoulders, the way my father used to do when I was a child. In a soothing murmur, he assured me that he wasn't in the least upset at the barbarities I had yelled at him.

Guilt and self-pity only made me weep harder.

He shook his head in a sign of resignation, although his eyes shone with mirth. Then in an obvious effort to make me laugh, too, he confessed that he still couldn't believe I would know, let alone use, such foul language. "Well, I suppose language is there to be used," he mused, "and foul language should be used when the circumstances are called for."

I wasn't amused. And once the attack of self-pity had passed, I began, in my usual fashion, to mull over his assertion that all I had going for me was blond hair and blue eyes.

I must have cued Mariano Aureliano about my feelings, for he assured me that he had said that only to upset me and that there wasn't a shred of truth in it. I knew he was lying. For an instant I felt doubly insulted, and then I was appalled to realize that my defenses were shattered. I agreed with him. He had been right on target about everything he had said. With a single stroke, he had unmasked me, cut through my shield, so to speak. No one, not even my worst enemy, could have hit me with such an accurately devastating blow. And yet, whatever I might have thought about Mariano Aureliano, I knew he wasn't my enemy.

I felt quite dizzy with my realization. It was as if an unseen force were crushing something within me: the idea of myself. Something that had given me strength was now depleting me.

Mariano Aureliano took me by the arm and walked me toward the coffee shop. "Let's sign a truce," he said jovially. "I need you to do me a favor."

"You need only to ask," I responded, trying to match his tone.

"Before you got here, I went into this coffee shop to have a sandwich, and they practically refused to serve me. When I complained, the cook threw me out." Mariano Aureliano looked at me dejectedly and added, "That happens when one is an Indian."

"Report that cook to the manager," I cried out in righteous indignation, my own turmoil totally and most mysteriously forgotten.

"That wouldn't help me in the least," Mariano Aureliano confided. The only way I could help him, he assured me, was to go into

59

the coffee shop by myself, sit at the counter, order an elaborate meal, and drop a dead fly in my food.

"And blame the cook," I finished for him. The whole scheme sounded so preposterous it made me laugh. But when I caught sight of his genuine expectation, I promised to do what he asked of me.

"Wait here," Mariano Aureliano said, then together with the burly Indian—who had yet to be introduced to me—headed toward the old red pickup truck parked in the street. They returned within moments.

"By the way," Mariano Aureliano said, "this man here is John. He's a Yuma Indian from Arizona."

I wanted to ask him if he also was a sorcerer, but Mariano Aureliano beat me to the punch. "He is the youngest member of our group," he confided.

Giggling nervously, I extended my hand and said, "I'm glad to meet you."

"Likewise," John responded in a deep, resonant voice and clasped my hand warmly in his. "I hope you and I never come to blows again," he grinned.

Although he wasn't very tall, he exuded the vitality and strength of a giant. Even his big, white teeth seemed indestructible.

In a joking manner, John felt my biceps. "I'd bet you can knock a fellow out cold with one punch," he said.

Before I had a chance to apologize to him for my kicks and insults, Mariano Aureliano pressed a small box into my hand.

"The fly," he whispered. "John here suggests that you wear this," he added, retrieving a black, curly wig from a bag. "Don't worry, it's brand new," he assured me as he pulled the wig over my head. Then, holding me at arm's length, he regarded me critically. "Not bad," he mused, making sure my long, blond braid was tucked in properly. "I don't want anyone to recognize you."

"There's no need to disguise myself," I asserted. "Take my word for it, I don't know anyone in Tucson." I turned the side mirror of my car and looked at myself. "I can't go in looking like this," I protested. "I look like a poodle."

Mariano Aureliano gazed at me with an exasperating air of amusement as he arranged some stray curls. "Now, don't you forget that you have to sit at the counter and yell bloody murder when you discover the fly in your food."

"Why?"

He regarded me as if I were dim-witted. "You have to attract attention and humiliate the cook," he pointed out.

The coffee shop was packed with the early dinner crowd. However, it wasn't long before I was seated at the counter and was waited on by a harrassed-looking but friendly old waitress.

Half-hidden behind the order rack was the cook. Like his two helpers, he appeared to be Mexican or Mexican-American. He went about his job so cheerfully I was quite certain he was harmless, incapable of malice. But when I thought of the old Indian waiting for me in the parking lot, I felt no guilt whatsoever as I emptied the little matchbox—with such stealth and speed not even the men on either side of me noticed it—over the perfectly cooked hamburger steak I had ordered.

My shriek of revulsion was genuine upon seeing a large, dead cockroach on my food.

"What is it, dear?" the waitress asked concernedly.

"How does the cook expect me to eat this?" I complained. I didn't have to pretend anger. I was indignant, not at the cook but at Mariano Aureliano. "How can he do this to me?" I asked in a loud voice.

"It's all some dreadful accident," the waitress explained to the two curious and concerned customers on either side of me. She showed the plate to the cook.

"Fascinating!" the cook said, his voice loud and clear. Rubbing his chin thoughtfully, he studied the food. He wasn't in the least upset. I had the vague suspicion he was laughing at me. "This cockroach must have either fallen from the ceiling," he deliberated, gazing at my head in fascinated interest, "or perhaps from her wig."

Before I could retort indignantly and put the cook in his place, he offered me anything that was on the menu. "It'll be on the house," he promised.

I asked for a steak and a baked potato, which was almost immediately brought to me. As I was pouring some salad dressing over my lettuce, which I always ate last, I discovered a good-sized spider crawling from under a lettuce leaf. I was so taken aback by this obvious provocation I couldn't even shriek. I looked up. Waving from behind the order rack was the cook, a dazzling smile on his face.

Mariano Aureliano was waiting for me impatiently. "What happened?" he asked.

"You and your disgusting cockroach!" I spat out, then added resentfully, "Nothing happened. The cook didn't get upset. He enjoyed himself immensely, at my cost, of course. The only one who got upset was me."

At his urging, I gave Mariano Aureliano a detailed account of what took place. The more I talked, the more pleased he was. Disconcerted by his reaction, I glowered at him. "What's so funny?" I demanded.

He tried to keep a serious face, but his lips twitched. His soft chuckle exploded into a loud, delighted laughter. "You can't take yourself so seriously," he chided. "You're an excellent dreamer, but you're certainly no actress."

"I'm not acting now. And I certainly wasn't acting in there either," I said defensively in a high, shrill voice.

"I meant that I was counting on your ability to be convincing," he said. "You had to make the cook believe something that wasn't true. I really thought you could."

"How dare you criticize me!" I shouted. "I made a fool of myself on your behalf, and all you can say is that I don't know how to act!" I pulled off the wig and threw it at him. "I'm sure I've got lice now."

Ignoring my outburst, Mariano Aureliano went on to say that Florinda had already told him that I was incapable of pretending. "We had to know it for sure, in order to put you in your proper slot," he added equably. "Sorcerers are either dreamers or stalkers. Some are both."

"What are you talking about? What's this nonsense of dreamers and stalkers?"

"Dreamers deal with dreams," he explained softly. "They get their power, their wisdom, from dreams. Stalkers, on the other hand, deal with people, with the everyday world. They get their wisdom, their power, from interacting with their fellow men."

"You obviously don't know me at all," I said derisively. "I interact very well with people."

"No, you don't," he contradicted me. "You yourself said that you don't know how to converse. You're a good liar, but you lie only to get what you want. Your lies are too specific, too personal. And do you know why?" He paused for a moment, as if to give me time to respond. But before I could even think of what to say he added, "Because for you, things are either black or white with no shades of color in between. And I don't mean it in terms of morality, but in terms of convenience. Your convenience, that is. A true authoritarian." Mariano Aureliano and John exchanged glances, then both squared their shoulders, clicked their heels and did something unforgivable to me. They raised their arms in a fascist salute and said, "Mein Fuehrer!"

The more they laughed, the greater was my rage. I felt my blood ringing in my ears, rushing to my face. And this time, I did nothing to calm myself. I kicked my car and banged my arms against the roof.

The two men, instead of trying to soothe me—as my parents or my friends definitely would have done—stood there and laughed as if I were providing them with the funniest spectacle possible.

Their indifference, their complete lack of concern for me was so shocking that my wrath slowed down of its own accord. Never had I been so completely disregarded. I was lost. I realized then that I had no more maneuvers left. I had never known until that day that if the witnesses to my tantrums didn't show any concern, I didn't know what to do next.

"I think she's confused now," Mariano Aureliano said to John. "She doesn't know what to do." He put his arm around the burly Indian's shoulders and added softly, yet still loud enough for me to hear, "Now she is going to cry, and when she does, she's going to cry her head off until we console her. Nothing is as tiresome as a spoiled cunt."

That did it for me. Like an injured bull, I lowered my head and charged Mariano Aureliano.

He was so startled by my vicious, sudden attack, he almost lost his balance; it gave me enough time to sink my teeth in the fleshy part of his stomach. He let out a yell, a mixture of pain and laughter.

John grabbed me by the waist and pulled me away. I didn't let go of my bite until my partial bridge came off. I had knocked two of my upper front teeth out when I was thirteen in a fight between the Venezuelan and the German students at the German high school in Caracas.

Both men howled with laughter. John bent over the trunk of my Volkswagen, holding his stomach and banging my car. "She's got a hole in her teeth, like a football player," he cried out in between shrieks.

My embarrassment was beyond words. I was so vexed that my knees gave in on me and I slid to the paved ground, like a rag doll, and actually passed out.

When I came to my senses, I was sitting inside the pickup truck. Mariano Aureliano was pressing my back. Smiling, he stroked my head repeatedly and then embraced me.

I was surprised by my absence of emotion; I was neither embarrassed nor annoyed. I was relaxed, at ease. It was a tranquility, a serenity I had never known before. For the first time in my life, I realized that I had never been at peace with myself or with others.

"We like you immensely," Mariano Aureliano said. "But you have to cure yourself of your temper tantrums. If you don't, they will kill you. This time it was my fault. I must apologize to you. I did deliberately provoke you."

I was too calm to say anything. I got out of the truck to stretch my arms and legs. I had painful cramps in my calves.

After a few moments of silence, I apologized to the two men. I told them that my temper had gotten worse since I had started drinking colas compulsively.

"Stop drinking them," Mariano Aureliano suggested. Then he completely changed the subject and went on talking as if nothing had happened. He said that he was extremely pleased that I had joined them.

"You are?" I asked uncomprehendingly. "Did I join you?"

"You did!" he emphasized. "One day it will all make sense to you." He pointed to a flock of crows cawing above us. "The crows are a good omen. See how marvelous they look. They are like a painting in the sky. To see them now is a promise that we will see each other again."

I gazed at the birds until they flew out of sight. When I turned to look at Mariano Aureliano, he was no longer there. The pickup truck had rolled away without a sound.

5

ISREGARDING the scratchy bushes, I dashed after the dog, who was scurrying through the sagebrush with reckless speed. I soon lost sight of its golden fur shimmering amidst the fragrant wild shrubs and followed the sound of its barks, growing fainter and fainter in the distance.

Uneasily, I glanced at the thick fog advancing on me. It closed in around the spot where I stood and within moments there was no sight of the sky. The late afternoon sun, like a subdued ball of fire, was scarcely discernible. And the magnificent view of the Santa Monica Bay, now more imagined than seen from the Santa Susana Mountains, had disappeared with incredible speed.

I wasn't worried about the dog getting lost. I, however, had no idea where to find the secluded spot my friends had chosen for our picnic. Or where the hiking path was that I had taken to chase after the dog.

I took a few hesitant steps in the same general direction the dog had followed, when something made me stop. Emerging from above, through some crack in the fog, I saw a tiny point of light descending toward me. Another one followed, then another, like little flames tied to a string. The lights trembled and vibrated in the air, then just before they reached me, they vanished, as though the fog around me had swallowed them up.

Since they had disappeared only a few feet in front of me, I moved on, closer to the spot, eager to examine that extraordinary sight. As I peered intently into the fog, I saw dark, human shapes glide through the air, two or three feet off the ground, moving as though they were tiptoeing on clouds. One after the other, the human shapes squatted, forming a circle. I took a few more vacillating steps, then stopped as the fog thickened and absorbed them.

I remained still, not knowing what to do. I felt a most unusual fright. Not the fright I am familiar with, but one in my body, in my belly; the kind of fright animals must have. I don't know how long I stood there. When the fog cleared enough for me to see, I saw to my left, about fifty feet away, two men sitting cross-legged on the ground. They were whispering to each other. The sound of their voices seemed to be all around me, captured in small patches of fog that were like tufts of cotton. I didn't understand what they were saying, but I felt reassured as I caught a word here and there; they were speaking in Spanish.

"I'm lost!" I shouted in Spanish.

Both men slowly turned around, hesitant, disbelieving, as though they were seeing an apparition. I spun around, wondering if there was someone behind me that was causing their dramatic reaction. But there was no one.

Grinning, one of the men rose, stretched his limbs until his joints cracked, then covered the distance between us in quick strides. He was young, short, and powerfully built, with massive shoulders and a big head. His dark eyes radiated amusement and curiosity.

I told him that I had been hiking with friends and had gotten lost chasing after their dog. "I've no idea how to get back to them," I finished.

"You can't go any further this way," the man warned me. "We are standing on a cliff." He took me confidently by the arm and led me to the very edge of the precipice, no more than ten feet away from where I had been standing. "This friend of mine," he said, pointing to the other man, who had remained seated, staring at me, "had just finished telling me that there is an ancient Indian burial ground down below when you showed up and nearly scared us to death." He studied my face, my long blond braid, and asked, "Are you Swedish?"

Still bewildered by what the young man had said about the burial ground, I stared into the fog. Under normal circumstances, as a student of anthropology, I would have been thrilled to find out about an ancient Indian burial ground. At the moment, however, I couldn't care less if there was indeed one in that foggy emptiness below me. All I could think of was that if I hadn't been distracted by those lights I might have ended up buried myself.

"Are you Swedish?" the young man asked again.

"I am," I lied and immediately regretted it. I couldn't think of any way to correct it, though, without losing face.

"You speak Spanish perfectly," the man commented. "Swedish people have a marvelous ear for languages."

Although I felt terribly guilty, I couldn't help adding that more than a gift, it was a necessity for Scandinavians to learn various languages if they wanted to communicate with the rest of the world. "Besides," I confessed, "I grew up in South America."

For some strange reason this piece of information seemed to baffle the young man. He shook his head, as if in disbelief, and then remained silent for a long while, deep in thought. Then, as if he had arrived at some kind of a decision, he took me briskly by the hand and guided me to where the other man was sitting.

I had no intention of socializing. I wanted to get back to my friends as soon as possible. But the young man made me feel so at ease that instead of asking them to lead me back to the hiking path, I gave them a detailed account of the lights and human shapes I had just seen.

"How strange that the spirit would spare her," the seated man muttered as if to himself, his dark brows drawn together in a frown. But obviously he was talking to his companion, who mumbled something in return that I didn't catch. They exchanged conspiratorial glances, intensifying my feelings of unease.

"I beg your pardon?" I said, turning to the man who was sitting. "I didn't get what you were saying."

He stared at me aggressively and morosely.

"You were warned of the danger," he stated in a voice that was deep and resonant. "The emissaries of death came to your help."

"The who?" I felt compelled to ask, even though I had understood him perfectly well. I examined him closely. For an instant, I had the certainty I knew him, but as I kept staring at him, I realized I had never seen him before. Yet I couldn't completely discard the feeling of knowing him. He was not as young as the other man, but he wasn't old either. He was definitely an Indian. His skin was dark brown. His hair was blue-black, straight and thick as a brush. But it wasn't only his outward appearance that was almost familiar to me; he was morose, as only I could be morose.

Seemingly uncomfortable under my scrutiny, he rose abruptly. "I'll take you to your friends," he mumbled. "Follow me, and don't you dare fall down. You'll fall on top of me and kill us both," he added in a gruff tone.

Before I had the opportunity to say that I wasn't a clumsy oaf, he led the way down a very steep side of a mountain in the opposite direction of the cliff.

"Do you know where you are going?" I shouted after him, my voice sharp with nervousness. I couldn't orient myself—not that I am normally good at it—but I had not been aware of climbing up a hill as I chased the dog.

The man turned around. An amused little grin quickly lit his face, though his eyes did not smile. He looked at me with a black, stony look. "I'm going to take you to your friends," was all he said.

I didn't like him, yet I believed him. He wasn't too tall—about five feet ten—and he was small boned, yet his body projected the massiveness and compactness of a stocky person. He moved in the fog with extraordinary confidence, stepping with ease and grace down what I thought was a vertical drop.

The younger man climbed down behind me, helping me every time I got stuck. He had the solicitous manner of an old-fashioned gentleman. His hands were strong and beautiful and incredibly soft to the touch. His strength was tremendous. He easily lifted me up and over his head several times. Perhaps not an extraordinary feat considering my puny weight, but quite impressive taking into account that he was standing on shale ledges and was no more than two or three inches taller than I.

"You have to thank the emissaries of death," the man who had led the way insisted as soon as we had reached level ground.

"I do?" I asked mockingly. The thought of saying thank you to the "emissaries of death" seemed ridiculous to me. "Do I have to go down on my knees?" I asked in between a fit of giggles.

The man didn't think I was being funny. He rested his hands on his hips and looked me full in the eye, his narrow, gaunt face unsmiling. There was something menacing about his stance, about his slanted dark eyes under the bristly eyebrows running together over the bridge of his chiseled nose. Abruptly, he turned his back to me and moved away to sit on a nearby rock. "We can't leave this spot until you thank the emissaries of death," he pronounced.

Suddenly, the realization that I was alone in a godforsaken place hit me. I was fogged in with two strange men, one of them perhaps dangerous. I knew he wouldn't budge from the spot until I fullfilled his ludicrous request. To my amazement, instead of feeling frightened, I felt like laughing.

The all-knowing smile on the younger man's face clearly revealed that he knew how I felt and was quite delighted by it.

"You don't have to go as far as kneeling," he told me, and then, no longer able to hold back his mirth, he began to laugh. It was a bright, raspy sound; it rolled like pebbles all around me. His teeth were snow-white and perfectly even, like a child's. His face had a look at once mischievous and gentle. "It's enough to say thank you," he prompted me. "Say it. What do you have to lose?"

"I feel stupid," I confided, deliberately trying to win him over. "I won't do it."

"Why?" he asked in a nonjudgmental tone. "It'll only take a second, and," he stressed, smiling, "it won't hurt a bit."

In spite of myself, I had to giggle. "I'm sorry, but I can't do it," I repeated. "I'm like that. The moment someone insists that I do something I don't want to do, I get all tense and angry."

Eyes on the ground, his chin resting on his knuckles, the young man nodded his head thoughtfully. "It's a fact that something prevented you from getting hurt, perhaps even killed," he said after a long pause. "Something inexplicable."

I agreed with him. I even admitted that it was all very baffling to me. And I tried to make a point about phenomena happening coincidentally at the right time, in the right place.

"That's all very appropriate," he said. Then he grinned and daringly nudged me on the chin. "But it doesn't explain your particular case," he said. "You have been the recipient of a gift. Call the giver coincidence, circumstances, chain of events, or whatever, the fact remains that you were spared pain, injury."

"Perhaps you're right," I conceded. "I should be more grateful."

"Not more grateful. More pliable, more fluid," he said and laughed. Seeing that I was getting angry, he opened his arms wide as if to encompass the sagebrush around us. "My friend believes that what you saw has to do with the Indian burial ground, which happens to be right here."

"I don't see a burial ground," I said defensively.

"It's hard to recognize it," he explained, squinting at me as if he had trouble with his eyes. "And it isn't the fog that prevents one from seeing it. Even on a sunny day, one sees nothing but a patch of sagebrush." He went down on his knees and, grinning, looked up at me. "However, for the knowing eye, it's an unusually shaped patch of sagebrush." He lay flat on the ground, on his stomach, his head tilted to the left, and motioned me to do the same.

"This is the only way to see it clearly," he explained as I lay down beside him on the ground. "I wouldn't have known this but for my friend here, who knows all kinds of interesting and exciting things."

At first I saw nothing, then one by one I discovered the rocks in the thick underbrush. Dark and shiny, as though they had been washed by the mist, they sat hunched in a circle, more like creatures than stones.

I stifled a scream as I realized that the circle of rocks was exactly like the circle of human figures I had seen earlier in the fog.

"Now I am truly frightened," I mumbled, shifting uncomfortably. "I told you that I saw human figures sitting in a circle." I looked at him to see if his face betrayed any disapproval or mockery before I added, "It's too preposterous, but I could almost swear those rocks were the people I saw."

"I know," he whispered, so softly I had to move closer to him. "It's all very mysterious," he went on. "My friend, who, you must have noticed, is an Indian, says that certain Indian burial grounds, such as this one, have a row or a circle of boulders. The boulders are the emissaries of death." He looked at me closely and then, as if he wanted to make sure he had my full attention, confided, "They are the emissaries, mind you, and not the representation of the emissaries."

I kept staring at the man, not only because I didn't know what to make of his statements, but because his face kept changing as he talked and smiled. It wasn't that his features changed, but his face was at moments that of a six-year-old child, a seventeen-year-old boy, and that of an old man, too.

"These are strange beliefs," he continued, seemingly oblivious to my scrutiny. "I didn't put too much stock in them until the moment you came out of the blue, as my friend was telling me about the emissaries of death, and then you told us that you had just seen them.

"If I were given to distrust," he went on, his tone suddenly menacing, "I would believe that you and he are in cahoots."

"I don't know him!" I defended myself, indignant at the mere suggestion, then whispered softly, so only he could hear, "To be quite frank, your friend gives me the creeps."

"If I were given to distrust," the young man repeated, ignoring my interruption, "I would believe that you two are actually trying to scare me. But I'm not distrustful. So the only thing I can do is suspend judgment and wonder about you."

"Well, don't wonder about me," I said irritably. "And I don't know what the hell you're talking about anyway." I glared at him angrily. I had no sympathy for his dilemma. He too was giving me the creeps.

"He's talking about thanking the emissaries of death," the older man said. He had walked to where I was lying and was peering down at me in a most peculiar manner.

Eager to get away from that place and those two crazy people, I stood up and shouted my thanks. My voice echoed, as if the underbrush had turned into rocks. I listened until the sound died away.

Then, as if possessed, and quite against my better judgment, I cried out my thanks again and again.

"I'm sure the emissaries are more than satisfied," the younger man said, nudging my calf. Laughing, he rolled on his back. There was a wonderful strength in his eyes, in the delighted power of his laugh. I didn't doubt for an instant, despite the levity, that indeed I had thanked the emissaries of death. And most oddly, I felt myself protected by them.

"Who are you two?" I directed my question at the younger man.

In one agile, smooth motion he sprang to his feet. "I'm José Luis Cortéz; my friends call me Joe," he said, holding out his hand to clasp mine. "And this here is my friend Gumersindo Evans-Pritchard."

Afraid I would laugh out loud at the name, I bit my lip and bent to scratch an imaginary bite on my knee. "A flea, I think," I said, gazing from one man to the other. Both stared back at me, defying me to make fun of the name. There was such a serious expression on their faces that my laughter vanished.

Gumersindo Evans-Pritchard reached for my hand—hanging limply at my side—and shook it vigorously. "I'm delighted to make your acquaintance," he said in perfect English with an upper-class British accent. "For a moment I thought you were one of those stuck-up cunts."

Simultaneously, my eyes widened and my mouth opened. Although something in me registered that his words were meant as a compliment rather than an insult, my shock was nevertheless so intense that I just stood there as if paralyzed. I wasn't prudish— under the proper circumstances I could outswear anyone—but to me there was something so appallingly offensive about the sound of the word *cunt*, it rendered me speechless.

Joe came to my rescue. He apologized for his friend, explaining that Gumersindo was an extreme social iconoclast. Before I had a chance to say that Gumersindo had definitely shattered my sense of propriety, Joe added that Gumersindo's compulsion to be an iconoclast had to do with the fact that his last name was Evans-Pritchard. "It shouldn't surprise anyone," Joe noted. "His father is an

Englishman who abandoned his mother, an Indian woman from Jalisco, before Gumersindo was born."

"Evans-Pritchard?" I repeated guardedly, then turned to Gumersindo and asked him if it was all right for Joe to reveal to a stranger his family's skeletons in the closet.

"There aren't skeletons in the closet," Joe answered for his friend. "And do you know why?" He fixed me with his shiny, dark eyes that were neither brown nor black but the color of ripe cherries.

Helplessly, I shook my head to say no, my attention held by his compelling gaze. One eye seemed to be laughing at me; the other one was dead serious, ominous and menacing.

"Because what you call skeletons in the closet are Gumersindo's source of strength," Joe went on. "Do you know that his father is now a famous English anthropologist? Gumersindo hates his guts."

Gumersindo nodded his head almost imperceptibly, as if he were proud of his hatred.

I could hardly believe my good fortune. They were referring to none other than E. E. Evans-Pritchard, one of the most important social anthropologists of the twentieth century. And it was precisely during this term at UCLA that I was researching a paper on the history of social anthropology and the most eminent proponents in the field.

What a scoop! I had to restrain myself from shouting out loud and jumping up and down with excitement. To be able to come with some awful secret like that. A great anthropologist seducing and abandoning an Indian woman. I was not in the least concerned that Evans-Pritchard hadn't done any fieldwork in Mexico—he was mainly known for his research in Africa—for I was certain I would discover that during one of his visits to the United States he had gone into Mexico. I had the very proof standing before me.

Smiling sweetly, I gazed at Gumersindo and made the silent promise that, of course, I wouldn't reveal anything without his permission. Well, perhaps I would just say something to one of my professors, I thought. After all, one didn't come across this kind of information every day.

My mind was spinning with possibilities. Perhaps a small lecture with only a few selected students at the home of one of my professors. In my mind, I had already selected the professor. I didn't particularly like him, but I appreciated the rather childish manner in which he tried to impress his students. Periodically, we met at his home. Every time I had been there, I had discovered on his desk a note, left there as if by mistake, written to him by a famous anthropologist, Claude Lévi-Strauss.

"You didn't tell us your name," Joe said politely, gently pulling me by my sleeve.

"Carmen Gebauer," I said without hesitation, giving the name of one of my childhood friends. To ease my discomfort and guilt at having lied again with such facility, I asked Joe if he was from Argentina. Seeing his puzzled frown, I hastened to add that his inflection was definitely Argentinian. "Even though you don't look like an Argentinian," I noted.

"I'm Mexican," he said. "And judging by your accent, you grew up either in Cuba or in Venezuela."

I didn't want to continue on that line of conversation and swiftly changed the subject. "Do you know how to get back to the hiking path?" I asked, suddenly concerned that my friends might be worried by now.

"No, I don't," Joe confessed with childish candor. "But Gumersindo Evans-Pritchard does."

Gumersindo led the way across the chaparral, up a narrow trail on the other side of the mountain. It wasn't long before we heard my friends' voices and the barking of their dog.

I felt intense relief, and at the same time I was disappointed and puzzled that neither man tried to find out how to get in touch with me.

"I'm sure we'll meet again," Joe said perfunctorily by way of farewell.

Gumersindo Evans-Pritchard surprised me by gallantly kissing my hand. He did this so naturally and gracefully that it didn't occur to me to laugh at him.

"It's in his genes," Joe explained. "Even though he's only half English, his refinement is beyond reproach. He's totally gallant!"

Without another word or backward glance, both of them disappeared in the mist. I doubted very much that I would ever see them again. Overcome with guilt for having lied about my name, I was on the verge of running after them when my friends' dog almost knocked me to the ground as it jumped on me and tried to lick my face.

6

DUMBFOUNDED, I stared at the guest speaker. In his three-piece suit, short, curly hair, and clean-shaven face, Joe Cortéz looked like someone from another time amidst the long-haired, bearded and beaded, casually dressed students in one of the large lecture auditoriums at the University of California in Los Angeles.

Hastily, I slipped into the empty seat in the back row of the packed auditorium, a seat saved for me by the same friend I had gone hiking with in the Santa Susana Mountains.

"Who is he?" I asked her.

Shaking her head in disbelief, she regarded me impatiently, then scribbled *Carlos Castaneda* on a piece of paper.

"Who in the dickens is Carlos Castaneda?" I asked and giggled involuntarily.

"I gave you his book," she hissed, then added that he was a well-known anthropologist who had done extensive fieldwork in Mexico.

I was about to confide to my friend that the guest speaker was the same man I had met in the mountains the day I had gotten lost. However, for some very good reason, I didn't say anything. That man was responsible for almost destroying our friendship, which I treasured immensely. My friend had been adamant in her opinion that the story about Evans-Pritchard's son was hogwash. I had insisted that the two men had nothing to gain by telling me a tall tale. I just knew that they had candidly spoken the truth. My friend, mad at me for believing them, had called me a gullible fool.

Since neither of us had been willing to yield, our argument had become quite heated. Her husband, hoping to bring us out of our frenzy, had suggested that perhaps I had been told the truth. Irked by his lack of solidarity with her, my friend had yelled at him to shut up.

We had driven home in a morose state, our friendship strained. It took a couple of weeks to wash away the bad feeling. In the meantime, I had tried my information on Evans-Pritchard's son on several people more versed in anthropological matters and in anthropologists than I or my friend. Needless to say, I was made to feel like an idiot. Out of stubbornness, I held on to my blind belief that I alone knew the truth. I had been reared to be practical; if one lies, it has to be to gain something that can't be gained otherwise. And I was at a loss to figure out what those men could have had to gain.

I paid little attention to Carlos Castaneda's lecture. I was too absorbed with wondering about his reason for lying to me about his name. Given as I was to deducing other people's motives from a simple statement or an observation, I had a field day trying to search for a clue to his. But then I remembered that I, too, had given him a false name. And I couldn't determine why I had done so.

After long mental deliberation, I decided that I had lied because automatically I hadn't trusted him. He was too self-confident, too cocky to inspire my trust. My mother had reared me to distrust Latin men, especially if they were not somewhat subservient. She used to say that Latin machos were like bantam cocks, interested only in fighting, eating, and having sex, in that order. And I suppose I had believed her without even thinking about it.

I finally looked at Carlos Castaneda. I couldn't make heads or tails of what he was talking about. But I became fascinated by his movements. He seemed to speak with his whole body, and his words, rather than emerging from his mouth, seemed to flow from his hands, which he moved with the gracefulness and agility of a magician.

Boldly, I walked up to him after the lecture. He was surrounded by students. He was so solicitous and engaging with the women that I automatically despised him.

"You've lied to me about your name, Joe Cortéz," I said in Spanish, pointing an accusing finger at him.

Holding his hand over his stomach, as if he had received a blow, he gazed at me with that same hesitant, disbelieving expression he had had when he first saw me in the mountains.

"It is also a lie that your friend Gumersindo is the son of Evans-Pritchard," I added before he recovered from his surprise at seeing me. "Isn't it?"

He made a pleading gesture for me not to say any more. He didn't seem to be in the least embarrassed. But there was such plain and simple wonder in his eyes that my righteous wrath was stopped short. Gently, he held me by the wrist, as if afraid I would leave.

After he finished talking with the students, he silently led me to a secluded bench, shaded by a gigantic pine tree, in the north campus.

"All this is so strange that I am truthfully speechless," he said in English as we sat down. He gazed at me as if he still couldn't believe I was sitting beside him. "I never thought I would find you again," he mused. "After we left, my friend—his name, by the way, is Nestor—and I discussed you at great length. We concluded that you were a semiapparition." He abruptly changed to Spanish and said that they even went back to the place where they had left me in the hope of finding me.

"Why did you want to find me?" I asked in English, confident that he would respond in English that he went there because he liked me.

In Spanish, there is no way to say that one just likes someone else. The response has to be more florid and at the same time more precise. In Spanish, one can either happen to evoke a good feeling— *me caes bien*—or arouse total passion—*me gustas*.

My candid question plunged him into a long silence. He seemed to be fighting whether he ought to speak or not. At last, he said that finding me in the fog that afternoon had caused him a profound upheaval. His face was enraptured as he revealed all this, and his voice betrayed the deepest awe as he added that finding me in the lecture room had been nearly the end of him.

"Why?" I asked, my vanity pricked. And I instantly regretted it because I was convinced he was going to tell me he was head over heels in love with me, and that would have been too disturbing. I wouldn't have known how to respond.

"It's a very long story," he said, still in a pensive mood. He puckered his lips, as if he were talking to himself, rehearsing what he was going to say next.

I knew the signs of a man who is preparing to make his pitch. "I haven't read your work," I said in order to head him off in a different direction. "What is it about?"

"I've written a couple of books about sorcery," he replied.

"What kind of sorcery? Voodoo, spiritualism, or what?"

"Do you know anything about sorcery?" he asked with a note of expectation in his voice.

"Of course I do. I grew up with it. I've spent a great deal of time in the coastal region of Venezuela; it's an area that is famous for its sorcerers. Most summers of my childhood were spent with a family of witches."

"Witches?"

"Yes," I said, pleased with his reaction. "I had a nanny who was a witch. She was a black woman from Puerto Cabello. She took care of me until I was an adolescent. Both my parents worked, and when I was a child, they were quite happy to leave me in her care. She could handle me much better than either of my parents. She would let me do as I pleased. My parents, of course, let her take me everywhere. During the school holidays she would take me with her to visit her family. It was not her biological family but her witch family. Although I wasn't allowed to participate in any of their rituals and trance sessions, I did manage to see a great deal."

He regarded me curiously, as if he didn't believe me. Then he asked with a bemused smile, "What made her a witch?"

"All sorts of things. She killed chickens and offered them to the gods in exchange for favors. She and her fellow witches—men and women—would dance until they would go into a trance. She recited secret incantations that had the power to heal her friends and injure her enemies. Her specialty was love potions. She prepared them with medicinal plants and all sorts of bodily refuse, such as menstrual blood, nail clippings, and hair, preferably pubic hair. She made amulets for good luck in gambling or in matters of love."

80

"And your parents allowed all this?" he asked in disbelief.

"At home, no one knew about it, except myself and my nanny's clients, of course," I explained. "She made house calls, as any doctor would. All she ever did at home was to burn candles behind the toilet bowl whenever I had nightmares. Since it seemed to help me and there was no danger of anything catching fire amidst the tiles, my mother openly allowed her to do this."

He suddenly stood up and began to laugh.

"What's so funny?" I asked, wondering whether he thought I had made it all up. "It's the truth, I assure you."

"You assert something to yourself, and, as far as you are concerned, once you make the assertion it turns into the truth," he said with a serious face.

"But I told you the truth," I insisted, certain that he was referring to my nanny.

"I can see through people," he said calmly. "For instance, I see you're convinced that I am going to make a pass at you. You've convinced yourself about it and now it is the truth. That's what I am talking about."

I tried to say something, but indignation took my breath away. I would have liked to run away. But that would have been too humiliating.

He frowned slightly, and I had the unpleasant impression that he knew what I was feeling. My face got red. I trembled with suppressed anger. Nonetheless, within moments I felt extraordinarily calm. It wasn't due to any conscious effort on my part; yet I had the distinct sensation that something in me had shifted. I had the vague recollection that I had gone through a similar experience before, but my memory faded away as fast as it came.

"What are you doing to me?" I muttered.

"I just happen to see through people," he said in a contrite tone. "Not all the time and certainly not with everybody, but only with the people I am intimately associated with. I don't know why I can see through you."

His sincerity was apparent. He seemed much more baffled than I was. He sat down again and moved closer to me on the bench. We remained in total silence for a while. It was a most pleasant experience to be able to drop all effort at making conversation and not feel that I was being stupid. I looked up at the sky; it was cloudless and transparent like blue glass. A soft breeze blew through the pine branches, and the needles fell on us like a gentle rain. Then the breeze turned into a wind, and the dry, yellow, fallen leaves of the nearby sycamore blew toward us; they swirled around us with a soft, rhythmic sound. In one abrupt swoop, the wind carried the leaves high up into the air.

"That was a fine display of the spirit," he murmured. "And it was for you. The wind, the leaves spinning in the air in front of us. The sorcerer I work with would say that that was an omen. Something pointed you out to me, at the precise moment I was thinking that I'd better leave. I cannot leave now."

Thinking only about his last statement, I felt inexplicably happy. It wasn't a triumphant happiness, the kind of glee one feels when getting one's way. It was rather a feeling of profound well-being that didn't last long. My ponderous self took over suddenly and demanded that I be rid of those thoughts and feelings. I had no business being there. I had cut a class, missed lunch with my real friends, missed my daily laps at the pool in the women's gym.

"Perhaps it'll be better if I leave," I said. I intended it as a statement of relief, but when I said it, it sounded as if I were feeling sorry for myself—which somehow I was.

But instead of leaving, I asked him, as casually as I could, whether he had always been able to see through people.

"No, not always." His kind tone clearly betrayed that he was conscious of my inner turmoil. "The old sorcerer I work with has recently taught me how."

"Do you think that he could teach me, too?"

"Yes, I think he would." He seemed amazed at his own statement. "If he feels about you the way I do, he'll certainly try to."

"Did you know about sorcery before?" I asked timidly, slowly coming out of my agitation.

"In Latin America everybody thinks that they know, and I believed I did. In that sense, you remind me of myself. Like you, I was convinced that I knew what sorcery was. But then, when I really encountered it, it wasn't like I thought it was."

"How was it?"

"Simple. So simple that it's scary," he confided. "We think that sorcery is scary because of its malignancy. The sorcery I encountered is not malignant at all, and because of that, it's the scariest thing there is."

I interrupted him and commented that he must be referring to white as opposed to black sorcery.

"Don't talk nonsense, damn it!" he impatiently snapped at me.

The shock of hearing him speak to me in that manner was so great that I gasped for breath. I was instantly thrown back into turmoil. He turned his face to avoid my gaze. He had dared to yell at me. I became so angry I thought I was going to have a fit. My ears were buzzing. I saw dark spots in front of my eyes. I would have hit him, if he hadn't jumped out of my reach so swiftly.

"You're very undisciplined," he said and sat down again. "And quite violent. Your nanny must have indulged your every whim and treated you as if you were made of precious glass." Seeing my scowling frown, he went on to say that he hadn't really yelled at me out of impatience or anger. "It doesn't matter to me personally whether you listen or not," he explained. "But it matters to someone else on whose behalf I shouted at you. Someone who is watching us."

I was perplexed at first, then uneasy. I looked all around me, wondering whether his sorcerer teacher might be watching us.

He ignored me and went on to say, "My father never mentioned to me that we have a constant witness. And he never mentioned it because he didn't know it. Just like you, yourself, don't know it."

"What kind of nonsense are you talking about?" My raspy, angry voice reflected my feelings at the moment. He had yelled at me, he had insulted me. I resented that he was talking his head off as if nothing had happened. If he believed that I was going to overlook his actions, he was in for a surprise. "You won't get away with it," I thought, smiling at him maliciously. "Not with me, buddy."

"I'm talking about a force, an entity, a presence which is neither a force nor an entity nor a presence," he explained with an angelic smile. He seemed totally oblivious to my belligerent mood. "Sounds like gibberish, but it isn't. I am referring to something that only sorcerers know about. They call it the spirit. Our personal watcher, our perennial witness."

I don't know exactly how or what precise word triggered it, but suddenly he had my full attention. He went on talking about this force, which he said wasn't God or anything to do with religion or morality, but an impersonal force, a power that was there for us to use if we only learned to reduce ourselves to nothing. He even held my hand, and I didn't mind it. In fact, I liked the feel of his strong, soft touch. I became morbidly fascinated with the strange power he had over me. I was aghast that I longed to sit with him on that bench indefinitely with my hand in his.

He went on talking. And I went on listening to every word he said. But at the same time I perversely wondered when he was going to grab my leg. For I knew that he wasn't going to have enough with my hand, and I couldn't do anything to stop him. Or was it that I didn't want to do anything to stop him?

He explained that he had been as careless and undisciplined as one could be but that he never knew the difference because he was imprisoned by the mood of the time.

"What's the mood of the time?" I asked in a rough, unfriendly voice, lest he think I was enjoying being with him.

"Sorcerers call it the modality of the time," he said. "In our day, it's the concern of the middle class. I am a middle-class man, just like you're a middle-class woman—"

"Classifications of that nature don't hold any validity," I interrupted him rudely, yanking my hand out of his. "They are simply generalizations." I scowled at him suspiciously. There was something startlingly familiar about his words, but I couldn't think where I had heard them before or what significance I was attaching to them. Yet I was sure they had a very vital significance for me if I could only recall what I already knew about them.

"Don't give me this social scientist gaff," he said jovially. "I'm as aware of it as you are."

Giving in to a wave of total frustration, I took his hand and bit it. "I'm truly sorry about that," I instantly mumbled, before he recovered from his surprise. "I don't know why I did it. I haven't bitten anyone since I was a child." I sidled to the far edge of the bench, in readiness for his retaliation. It didn't come.

"You're absolutely primitive" was all he said, rubbing his hand in a dazed sort of way.

I let out a deep sigh of relief. His power over me was shattered. And I remembered that I had an old score to settle with him. He had turned me into the laughingstock of my anthropology student friends. "Let's go back to our original problem," I said, trying to arouse my anger. "Why did you tell me all that nonsense about Evans-Pritchard's son? You must have realized that I was going to make a fool of myself." I watched him carefully, certain that confronting him like this after the bite would finally break his self-control or at least rattle him. I expected him to yell, to lose his confidence and impudence. But he remained unperturbed. He took a deep breath and adopted a serious expression.

"I know that it looks like a simple case of people telling tall tales for their amusement," he began in a light, casual tone. "But it's more complex than that." He chuckled softly, then reminded me that he hadn't known at that time that I was a student of anthropology and that I would make a fool of myself. He paused for a moment, as if searching for the proper words, then he shrugged helplessly and added, "I really can't explain to you now why I introduced my friend to you as Evans-Pritchard's son, unless I tell you much more about myself and my aims. And that's not practical."

"Why not?"

"Because the more you know about me, the more entangled you'll become." He regarded me thoughtfully, and I could see in his eyes that he was sincere. "And I don't mean a mental entanglement. I mean you'll become personally entangled with me."

This was such a blatant display of gall that I regained all my confidence. I fell back on my well-tried sarcastic laughter and said in a cutting tone, "You are perfectly disgusting. I know your kind. You are the typical example of the conceited Latin macho I have battled with all my life." Seeing the expression of surprise on his face, I pressed on in my most haughty tone, "How dare you to think that I'll be entangled with you?"

He didn't become red in the face as I expected. He slapped his knee and laughed uproariously, as if that was the funniest thing he had ever heard. And to my utter dismay, he began to tickle me in the ribs as if I were a child.

Afraid to laugh—I was ticklish—I screeched with indignation. "How dare you to touch me!" I stood up to leave. I was shaking. And then I shocked myself even further by sitting down again.

Seeing that he was about to tickle me again, I curled my hands into fists and held them before me. "I'll smash your nose if you touch me again," I warned him.

Thoroughly unconcerned by my threat, he reclined his head against the back of the bench and closed his eyes. He laughed gaily, a deep chortling laugh that made him shiver all over. "You're a typical German girl who grew up surrounded by brown people," he said, turning sideways toward me.

"How do you know I am German? I never told you that," I said in a faltering voice I intended to be softly menacing.

"I knew that you were German when I first met you," he said. "You confirmed it the moment you lied that you were Swedish. Only Germans born in the New World after the Second World War lie like that. That is, of course, if they live in the United States."

Although I wasn't going to admit this to him, he was right. I had often felt people's hostility as soon as they learned that my parents were Germans; in their eyes it automatically made us Nazis. It didn't make any difference when I told them that my parents were idealists. Of course, I had to admit to myself that, like good Germans, they believed that their kind were inherently better, but basically they were gentle souls who had been apolitical all their lives.

"All I did was to agree with you," I pointed out acidly. "You saw blond hair, blue eyes, high cheekbones, and all you could think of was a Swede. You are not very imaginative, are you?" I pushed my advantage. "You had no business lying yourself, unless you're a fucking liar by nature," I went on, my voice rising against my will. Tapping his chest with my index finger I added derisively, "Joe Cortéz, eh?"

"Is your name really Cristina Gebauer?" he shot back, imitating my odious, loud voice.

"Carmen Gebauer!" I shouted, offended that he hadn't remembered the name correctly. Then, suddenly ashamed of my outburst, I went into a chaotic defense of myself. After a few moments, realizing that I didn't know what I was saying, I abruptly stopped and confessed that I was indeed German and that Carmen Gebauer was the name of a childhood friend.

"I like that," he said softly, a barely suppressed grin on his lips. Whether he was referring to my lying or to my confession I couldn't tell. His eyes were brimming with kindness and with amusement. In a tender, wistful voice he proceeded to tell me the story of his childhood girlfriend, Fabiola Kunze.

Confused by his reaction, I turned away and gazed at the nearby sycamore and the pine trees beyond. Then, eager to hide my interest in his story, I began to play with my fingernails; I pushed back the cuticles and peeled off the nail polish, methodically and thoughtfully.

The story of Fabiola Kunze resembled my own life so closely that after a few moments I forgot all about my pretense at indifference and listened to him attentively. I suspected that he was fabricating the story, and yet I had to give him credit for coming up with details that only a daughter of a German family in the New World would know.

Fabiola allegedly was mortally afraid of dark Latin boys, but she was equally afraid of the Germans. The Latins scared her because of their irresponsibility; the Germans, because they were so predictable.

I had to restrain myself from laughing out loud when he described scenes of Fabiola's home on a Sunday afternoon when two dozen Germans would sit around a beautifully set table—with the best china, silver, and crystal—and she would have to listen to two dozen monologues that passed for conversation.

As he went on giving specific details of those Sunday afternoons, I began to feel more and more uncomfortable: there was Fabiola's father prohibiting political debates in his house but compulsively aiming at starting one, seeking devious ways to tell dirty jokes about Catholic priests. Or her mother's mortal dread: her fine china was in the hands of these clumsy oafs.

His words were cues to which I unconsciously responded. I began to see scenes of my Sunday afternoons like pictures flashed on the wall for my observation.

I was a veritable bundle of nerves. I wanted to stomp and carry on as only I knew how. I wanted to hate this man, but I couldn't. I wanted vindication, apologies, but I couldn't get any from him. I wanted to dominate him. I wanted him to fall in love with me so I could reject him.

Ashamed of my immature feelings, I made a great effort to pull myself together. Pretending to be bored, I leaned toward him and asked, "Why did you lie about your name?"

"I didn't lie," he pronounced. "That's my name. I have several names. Sorcerers have different names for different occasions."

"How convenient!" I exclaimed sarcastically.

"Very convenient," he echoed and gave a slight wink, which infuriated me beyond measure.

And then he did something completely outlandish and unexpected. He put his arms around me. There was no sexual overtone in his embrace. It was the spontaneous, sweet, and simple gesture of a child who wants to comfort a friend. His touch soothed me instantly and so completely that I began to sob uncontrollably.

"I'm such a shit," I confessed. "I want to beat you, and look at me. I am in your arms." I was about to add that I was enjoying it when a surge of energy rushed through me. As if I had awakened from a dream, I pushed him away. "Let go of me," I hissed and stomped away.

I heard him choking with laughter. I wasn't in the least concerned about his chuckles; my outburst had dissipated instantly. I stood rooted to the spot, trembling all over, unable to walk away. And then, as if I had a giant rubber band attached to me, I returned to the bench.

"Don't feel bad," he said kindly. He seemed to know exactly what it was that was pulling me back to the bench. He patted my back as one does a baby's after a meal.

"It isn't what you or I do," he continued. "It's something outside the two of us which is acting upon us. It's been acting upon me for a long time. Now I am accustomed to it. But I can't understand why it acts upon you. Don't ask me what it is," he said, anticipating my question. "I can't yet explain it to you."

I wasn't going to ask him anything anyway. My mind had stopped functioning. I felt exactly as if I were asleep, dreaming that I was talking.

Moments later, my numbness passed. I felt more animated yet not quite like my usual self. "What's happening to me?" I asked.

"You are being focused and pushed by something that doesn't stem from you," he said. "Something is pushing you, using me as a tool. Something is superimposing another criterion on your middle-class convictions."

"Don't start on that middle-class idiocy," I said feebly. It was more like I was pleading with him. I smiled helplessly, thinking that I had lost my usual gall.

"These, by the way, are not my own opinions or ideas," he said. "I'm like you, strictly a product of middle-class ideology. Imagine my horror when I came face to face with a different and a more prevailing ideology. It ripped me apart."

"What ideology is that?" I asked meekly, my voice so low it was barely audible.

"A man brought that ideology to me," he explained. "Or rather, the spirit spoke and acted on me through him. That man is a sorcerer. I've written about him. His name is Juan Matus. He's the one who made me face my middle-class mentality.

"Juan Matus once asked me a grand question: 'What do you think a university is?' I, of course, answered him like a social scientist: 'A center of higher learning.' He corrected me and declared that a university should be called a 'Middle-Class Institute' because it is the institution we attend to further perfect our middle-class values. We attend the institute to become professionists, he said. The ideology of our social class tells us that we must prepare ourselves for occupying managerial positions. Juan Matus said that men go to the middle-class institute to become engineers, lawyers, doctors, etc., and women go there to get a suitable husband, provider, and father of their children. Suitable is naturally defined by middle-class values."

I wanted to contradict him. I wanted to shout at him that I knew people who weren't necessarily interested in a career or looking for a spouse, that I knew people who were interested in ideas, in learning for its own sake. But I didn't know such people. I felt a terrible pressure in my chest and had an attack of dry coughing. It wasn't the cough or the physical discomfort that made me wriggle in my seat and prevented me from arguing with him. It was the certainty that he was speaking about me: I was going to a university precisely to find a suitable man.

Again I stood up, ready to leave. I had even extended my hand to shake his in farewell when I felt a powerful tug on my back. It was so strong I had to sit down, lest I fall. I knew he hadn't touched me; I had been looking at him all the time.

Thoughts of people I didn't quite remember, of dreams I hadn't quite forgotten, came crowding into my mind, forming an intricate pattern from which I couldn't extricate myself. Unknown faces, half-heard sentences, dark images of places, and blurred images of people threw me momentarily into some kind of limbo. I was close to remembering something about all this kaleidoscope of visualizations and sounds. But the knowledge flittered away, and a feeling of calm and ease overtook me, a tranquility so deep that it screened out all my desire to assert myself.

I stretched my legs in front of me as if I didn't have a care in the world—and at the moment I didn't—and began to talk. I couldn't remember ever talking about myself so frankly before, and I couldn't fathom why I was suddenly so unguarded with him. I told him about Venezuela, my parents, my childhood, my restlessness, my meaningless life. I told him of things I wouldn't even admit to myself.

"I've been studying anthropology since last year. And I really don't know why," I said. I was beginning to feel slightly uncomfortable by my own revelations. I shifted restlessly on the bench, but I couldn't stop myself from adding, "Two subjects that interest me more are Spanish and German literature. To be in the anthropology department defies all I know about myself."

"That detail intrigues me to no end," he said. "I can't get into it now, but it seems as if I had been placed here for you to find me, or vice versa."

"What does all this mean?" I asked, then blushed, realizing that I was interpreting and centering everything on my womanhood.

He seemed to be thoroughly aware of my state of mind. He reached for my hand and pressed it against his heart. "*Me gustas, nibelunga!*" he exclaimed dramatically, and for good measure he translated the words into English, "I'm passionately attracted to you, Nibelung." He looked at me with the eyes of a Latin lover and then burst into raucous laughter. "You're convinced I have to say this to you sooner or later, so it might as well be now."

Instead of getting angry at being teased, I laughed; his humor gave me great pleasure. The only Nibelungen I knew were from my father's German mythology books. Siegfried and the Nibelungen. As far as I could remember, they were underground, magical, dwarfish beings.

"Are you calling me a dwarf?" I asked in jest.

"God forbid!" he protested. "I'm calling you a German mythical being."

Shortly afterwards, as if it were the only thing we could have done, we drove to the Santa Susana Mountains, to the place we had met. Neither of us said a single word as we sat on the cliff overlooking the Indian burial ground. Moved by a pure impulse of companionship, we sat there in silence, oblivious to the afternoon turning into night.

7

JOE Cortéz parked his van at the bottom of a hill. He came around to open my door and with a gallant flair helped me alight from the car. I felt relieved that we had finally stopped, although I couldn't imagine why. We were in the middle of nowhere. We had been driving since early morning. The day's heat, the flat desert, the merciless sun, and the dust of the road were but a vague memory as I breathed in the cold, heavy night air.

Agitated by the wind, the air swirled about us like something palpable, something alive. There was no moon. And the stars, incredible in number and brilliance, only seemed to intensify our isolation. Under that uneasy splendor, the hills and the desert stretched all around us, nearly invisible, full of shadows and murmuring sounds. I tried to orient myself by looking at the sky, but I didn't know how to identify the constellations.

"We're facing east," Joe Cortéz whispered, as if I had spoken out loud; then patiently he tried to teach me the major constellations in the summer sky. I could only remember the star Vega, because the name reminded me of a seventeenth-century Spanish writer, Lope de Vega.

While we sat in silence on the top of his van looking at the sky, my mind wandered through the events of our journey.

Less than twenty-four hours ago, while we were eating in a Japanese restaurant in downtown Los Angeles, he had asked me, out of the blue, if I would accompany him to Sonora for a few days.

"I would love to go," I said impulsively. "The school term is over. I'm free. When do you plan to leave?"

"Tonight!" he said. "In fact, right after we finish our meal."

I laughed, certain that his invitation had been a joke. "I can't leave on such short notice," I pointed out. "What about tomorrow?"

"Tonight," he insisted softly, then held out his hand to clasp mine in a formal handshake. Only when I saw the delight and mischief in his eyes did I realize that he wasn't saying good-bye but sealing an agreement.

"When decisions are made, they have to be acted upon immediately," he pronounced, leaving the words hanging in midair in front of me. Both of us stared at them as though we could indeed see their size and shape.

I nodded, hardly aware of having made the decision. The chance had been there, outside of me, ready, inevitable. I didn't have to do anything to bring it about.

Suddenly, with shattering vividness, I then remembered my other trip to Sonora a year before. My body stiffened with fear and shock as images—disconnected in their sequence—stirred deep within me. The events of that odd trip had faded from my conscious mind so totally and absolutely that, only until a moment before, it was as if they had never taken place. But now the events were as clear in my mind as they were the day they happened.

Shivering not with cold but with an undefinable dread, I turned to face Joe Cortéz and tell him about that trip. He was staring at me with an odd intensity; his eyes were like tunnels, deep and dark; they absorbed my dismay. But they also made the images of that trip recede. Once the images had lost their impulse, all that was left in my mind was a trite, empty thought. I believed at that instant, in my usual assertive manner, that I couldn't tell anything to Joe Cortéz, because a true adventure always dictates its own course and the most memorable, exciting events in my life had always been those whose course I had not interfered with.

"What do you want me to call you? Joe Cortéz or Carlos Castaneda?" I asked with nauseating feminine joviality.

His copper-colored face crinkled up in a smile. "I'm your childhood companion. Give me a name. I call you *nibelunga*."

I couldn't come up with a suitable name. I asked him, "Is there any order to your names?"

"Well," he mused, "Joe Cortéz is a cook, a gardener, a handyman; a solicitous and thoughtful man. Carlos Castaneda is a man from the academic world, but I don't think you have met him yet." He looked at me fixedly and smiled; there was something childlike and intensely trusting about that smile.

I decided to call him Joe Cortéz.

We spent the night—in separate rooms—in a motel in Yuma, Arizona. After leaving Los Angeles, all through the long drive I had worried myself sick about the sleeping arrangements. I had at moments feared he would pounce on me before we got to the motel. After all, he was a strong young man, too self-confident and aggressive. I wouldn't have been so worried if he had been American or European. But because he was Latin, I simply knew what his assumptions were. Accepting his invitation to spend a few days with him meant that I was willing to share his bed.

His thoughtfulness and considerate behavior toward me throughout the long drive was a detail that fit perfectly with what I thought and expected of him: he was preparing the ground.

It was late when we got to the motel. He went to the manager's office to see about our rooms. I stayed in the car, imagining scenario upon lurid scenario.

I had been so absorbed with my fantasies, I failed to notice his return from the office. Hearing him dangle a set of keys before me, I jumped in my seat and dropped the brown paper sack I had been holding, unconsciously clutched against my breast. It contained all my toiletries, which we had bought on the way.

"I got you a room at the back of the motel," he said. "It's away from the highway." He pointed to the door a few steps away from us and added, "I'll sleep in this one, close to the street. I'm used to sleeping through any kind of noise." He chuckled to himself. "These were the only two rooms they had left."

Disappointed, I took the key from his hand. All my scenarios fell apart. I wasn't going to have the opportunity to refuse him. Not that I really wanted to do so. Yet my very soul clamored for a victory, no matter how small.

"I don't see why we have to rent two rooms," I said with studied casualness. My hand was shaking as I retrieved the toiletries on the floor and stuffed them into the paper sack. What I had said sounded incredible to me, yet I couldn't stop myself. "The traffic won't let you rest, and you need your sleep as much as I do." I didn't for a moment believe that anyone could sleep through the noise coming from the highway.

Without looking at him, I got out of the car, and then I heard myself propose, "We could sleep in the same room—in two beds, that is."

I stood there for a moment, numbed and appalled. Never before had I done such a thing, nor had I had such a schizoid reaction. I was saying things that I didn't mean. Or did I mean them but didn't know what I felt?

His mirth put an end to my confusion. He laughed so hard people turned on the light in one of the rooms and yelled at us to shut up.

"Stay in the same room and have you take advantage of me in the middle of the night," he said in between waves of hilarity. "Right after my shower. No way!"

I blushed so intensely my ears were burning. I wanted to die of shame. This was not one of my scenarios. I went back inside the car and slammed the door. "Take me to the Greyhound bus," I hissed at him with suppressed wrath. "Why in the hell did I come with you? I should have my head examined!"

Still laughing, he opened the door and gently pulled me out. "Let's sleep not only in the same room but in the same bed." He looked at me sheepishly. "Please, let me make love to you!" he pleaded as if he really meant it.

Aghast, I tore myself loose from his hold and yelled, "Not in your fucking life!"

"There," he said. "This is such a fierce refusal that I dare not insist." He reached for my hand and kissed it. "You have refused me and put me in my place. No more problems. You're vindicated."

I turned away from him, ready to weep. My chagrin was not due to his unwillingness to spend the night with me—had he expected to do so, I truly wouldn't have known what to do—but to the fact that he knew me even better than I knew myself. I had refused to give credence to what I thought was a way of flattering himself. He was able to see through me. Suddenly, it frightened me.

He moved closer and hugged me. It was a sweet, simple embrace. As had happened before, my turmoil vanished completely, as though it had never existed. I hugged him back and said yet the most incredible thing, "This is the most exciting adventure of my life." I immediately wanted to retract my statement. The words that had escaped were not mine. I didn't even know what I meant. This was not the most exciting adventure of my life. I had taken many exciting trips. I had been around the world.

My irritation reached its peak when he kissed me goodnight, swiftly and softly, as one kisses a child, and I liked it against my will. I had no will. He pushed me down the corridor toward my room.

Cursing myself, I sat down on my bed and wept in frustration, in anger and self-pity. Since as far back in life as I could remember, I had always had my way. I was accustomed to it. To be confused and not know what I wanted was a brand-new sensation for me and a most unwelcome one.

I slept restlessly with my clothes on until he banged on the door, early in the morning, to wake me up.

We drove all day, meandering along out-of-the-way roads. As he had told me, Joe Cortéz was indeed a solicitous man. Throughout the long drive, he was the kindest, the most considerate and entertaining companion one could wish for. He pampered me with food and songs and stories. He had an astonishingly deep yet clear baritone voice. And he knew all my favorite songs. Corny love songs from every South American country, all their national anthems, old ballads, and even nursery rhymes.

His stories made me laugh until my abdominal muscles hurt. As a storyteller, he kept me enraptured with every turn of his tale.

He was a born mimic. His uncanny imitation of every conceivable South American accent—including the distinctive Portuguese of Brazil—was more than mimicry, it was magic.

"We'd better climb down from the car's roof." Joe Cortéz's voice broke into my reveries. "It gets cold at night in the desert."

"It's a tough environment," I said, wishing we would get back into the van and drive off. Ill at ease, I watched him retrieve some bags from the car. He had bought all kinds of presents for the people we were going to visit. "Why did you park here in the middle of nowhere?"

"You ask the dumbest questions, nibelunga," he replied. "I parked here because it is here where our car journey ends."

"Have we arrived at our mysterious destination that you can't talk about?" I asked in a sarcastic tone.

The only thing that had marred the enchanting drive had been his refusal to tell me where exactly we were going.

In a matter of milliseconds, I became so angry with him that I was ready to punch him in the nose. The thought that my sudden irritability was simply the result of a long, exhausting day, brought me a needed sense of relief.

"I'm getting nasty now, but I don't mean to," I said in a jovial tone that sounded phony even to me. My voice was so strained it revealed just how much it cost me to hold back my temper. It worried me that I could get mad at him so easily and so quickly.

"You really don't know how to converse," he said with a big smile. "You only know how to coerce."

"Oh! I see, Joe Cortéz has left. Are you going to start insulting me again, Carlos Castaneda?"

He chortled gaily at my remark, which by then wasn't meant to be funny. "This place is not in the middle of nowhere," he said. "The city of Arizpe is nearby."

"And the U.S. border is to the north," I recited. "And Chihuahua to the east. And Los Angeles is somewhere northwest of here."

He shook his head disparagingly and took the lead. Silently, we walked through the chaparral, which I could feel more than see, along a winding narrow trail. The path grew wider as we approached a vast clearing fenced in by short mesquite trees. The silhouettes of two houses could be discerned in the darkness. The bigger of the two had lights inside. The small dark house stood some distance away.

We walked up to the large house. Pale moths fluttered in the light slanting through the windowpanes.

"I have to warn you that the people you're going to meet are a bit strange," he said in a whisper. "Don't say anything. Let me do the talking."

"I always say whatever I please," I asserted. "And I don't like to be told how to behave. I'm not a child. Besides, my social manners are impeccable. I can assure you that I won't embarrass you."

"Get off your high horse, goddamn it!" he hissed in a tightly controlled voice.

"Don't treat me like I am your wife, Carlos Castañeda," I yelled at the top of my voice, pronouncing his last name the way I felt it ought to be pronounced: with a tilde on the *n*, which I knew he much disliked.

But he didn't get angry. It made him laugh as he so often did when I expected him to explode with wrath. He never does, I thought, and sighed despondently. He had the most extraordinary equanimity. Nothing ever seemed to ruffle him or cause him to lose his temper. Even when he shouted, it somehow always sounded phony.

Just as he was about to knock, the door opened. A thin man formed a black shadow in the rectangle of light. With an impatient gesture of his arm, he bade us in. We entered a plant-filled vestibule. Swiftly, as though afraid to show his face, the man moved ahead of us and, without a word of greeting, opened an inner door with rattly glass panes.

We followed him along a dark corridor and across an inside patio, where a young man sitting on a rush chair was playing a guitar and singing in a soft, grief-stricken voice. He paused the instant he noticed us. He didn't return my greeting and resumed his playing as we turned a corner and went down another equally dark corridor.

"Why is everyone so impolite?" I whispered into Joe Cortéz's ear. "Are you sure this is the right house?"

He chuckled softly. "I've told you, they are eccentric," he murmured.

"Are you sure you know these people?" I insisted.

"What kind of a question is that?" he snapped in a quiet yet menacing tone. "Of course I know them."

We had reached a lighted doorway. His pupils gleamed.

"Are we going to stay here overnight?" I asked uneasily.

"I've no idea," he whispered in my ear and then kissed my cheek. "And please, don't ask any more questions. I'm trying my best to accomplish a nearly impossible maneuver."

"What maneuver is that?" I whispered back. A sudden realization made me feel anxious and uncomfortable but also excited. The word *maneuver* had been the clue.

Seemingly aware of my innermost feelings, he shifted the bags he was carrying into one arm and gently took my hand and kissed it—his touch sent pleasurable shivers throughout my body—and led me across the threshold. We entered a large, dimly lit, sparsely furnished living room. It was not what I expected a provincial Mexican living room to look like. The walls and the low ceiling were immaculately white; there wasn't a picture or a wall decoration to mar that whiteness.

Against the wall opposite the door stood a large couch. On it sat three elderly, elegantly dressed women. I couldn't quite see their faces, but in the dim light they looked peculiarly alike—without actually resembling one another—and vaguely familiar. I was so baffled by this I barely noticed the two people sitting on the spacious armchairs nearby.

In my eagerness to reach the three women, I took an involuntary giant leap. I had failed to notice that the room had a split-level brick floor. As I steadied myself, I noticed the beautiful oriental rug and the woman sitting in one of the armchairs.

"Delia Flores!" I exclaimed. "My God! I can't believe this!" I touched her, for I needed to make sure she was not a figment of my imagination. "What is going on?" I asked instead of greeting her. At that same instant I realized that the women on the couch were the same women I had met the previous year at the healer's house.

I stood gaping, frozen, my mind dazed with shock. A quick, faint smile twitched the corners of their mouths as they turned toward the white-haired old man sitting in the other armchair.

"Mariano Aureliano." My voice was but a soft, shaky whisper. All the energy was gone from me. I turned to face Joe Cortéz and in that same feeble voice accused him of tricking me. I wanted to scream at him, insult him, do him bodily harm. But I had no strength left in me, not even to lift my arm. I barely realized that, like me, he stood rooted to the floor, his face ashen with shock and bewilderment.

Mariano Aureliano rose from his chair and moved toward me, arms extended to embrace me. "How happy I am to see you again." His voice was soft and his eyes shone brightly with excitement and joy. He lifted me off the ground in a bear's hug. My body was limp. I had no strength—or desire—to reciprocate his warm embrace. I could not say a word. He put me down and went over to greet Joe Cortéz with that same effusive warmth.

Delia Flores and her friends came over to where I stood. One by one they embraced me and whispered something in my ear. I felt comforted by their affectionate touches and by their soft voices, but I didn't understand a thing they said. My mind wasn't there with me. I could feel and hear but I couldn't make sense of what I felt and heard.

Mariano Aureliano gazed at me and said in a clear voice that pierced the fog of my mind, "You haven't been tricked. I told you from the beginning that I would blow you to him."

"So you're . . ." I shook my head, unable to finish my sentence as it finally dawned on me that Mariano Aureliano was the man Joe Cortéz had told me so much about: Juan Matus, the sorcerer who had changed the course of his life.

I opened my mouth to say something but shut it again. I had the sensation of being cut loose from my own body. My mind couldn't accommodate any further astonishment. And then I saw Mr. Flores emerge from the shadows. Upon realizing that he was the man who had let us in, I simply passed out.

When I regained consciousness, I was lying on the couch. I felt extraordinarily well rested and free of anxiety. Wondering how long I had been out, I sat up and lifted my arm to look at my wristwatch.

"You have been out for exactly two minutes and twenty seconds," Mr. Flores announced, studying his watchless wrist. He was sitting on a leather ottoman near the couch. In a sitting position he appeared much taller than he did standing up, for his legs were short and his torso long.

"How terribly dramatic to swoon away," he said, coming to sit beside me on the couch. "I'm truly sorry we have frightened you." His yellow-amber eyes, shiny with laughter, belied the genuinely concerned tone of his voice. "And I do apologize for not greeting you at the door." His face reflected a bemusement bordering on fascination as he pulled my braid. "With your hair hidden under the hat and with that heavy leather jacket I thought you were a boy."

I stood up and had to hold on to the couch. I was still a bit dizzy. Uncertainly, I looked around me. The women were no longer in the room, and neither was Joe Cortéz. Mariano Aureliano was sitting in one of the armchairs, staring fixedly ahead of him. Perhaps he was asleep with his eyes open.

"When I first saw the two of you holding hands," Mr. Flores went on, "I was afraid that Charlie Spider had turned queer." He said the whole sentence in English. He pronounced his words beautifully and precisely and with genuine relish.

"Charlie Spider?" I laughed at the name and at his formal English pronunciation. "Who is he?"

"Don't you know?" he asked, his eyes wide with genuine puzzlement.

"No, I don't. Should I know?"

He scratched his head, perplexed by my denial, then asked, "With whom have you been holding hands?"

"Carlos held my hand as we stepped into this room."

"There you are," Mr. Flores said, gazing at me with rapt approval, as if I had resolved a particularly difficult riddle. Then seeing my still-mystified expression he added, "Carlos Castaneda is not only Joe Cortéz, but he's also Charlie Spider."

"Charlie Spider," I mumbled softly. "That's a very catchy name." Of all the three names, it was the one I liked best, no doubt because I was exceedingly fond of spiders. They didn't frighten me in the least, not even big, tropical spiders. The corners of my apartment were always spotted with spider webs. Whenever I cleaned, I could not bring myself to destroy those gauzy webs.

"Why does he call himself Charlie Spider?" I asked curiously.

"Different names for different situations." Mr. Flores recited the answer as if it were a slogan. "The one who should explain all this to you is Mariano Aureliano."

"Is Mr. Aureliano's name also Juan Matus?"

Mr. Flores nodded emphatically. "It most certainly is," he said, with a broad, gleeful smile. "He also has different names for different situations."

"How about yourself, Mr. Flores? Do you also have different names?"

"Flores is my only name. Genaro Flores." His tone was flirtatious. He leaned toward me and in an insinuating whisper proposed, "You can call me Genarito."

I shook my head involuntarily. There was something about him that scared me more than Mariano Aureliano did. On a rational level, I couldn't decide what it was that made me feel this way. Outwardly, Mr. Flores seemed much more approachable than the other man. He was childlike, playful, and easygoing. And yet, I didn't feel at ease with him.

"The reason I only have one name," Mr. Flores broke into my reveries, "is that I am not a nagual."

"And what is a nagual?"

"Ah, that's a terribly difficult thing to explain." He smiled disarmingly. "Only Mariano Aureliano or Isidoro Baltazar can explain that."

"Who is Isidoro Baltazar?"

"Isidoro Baltazar is the new nagual."

"Don't tell me any more, please," I said fretfully. Holding my hand to my forehead I sat down again on the couch. "You're confusing me, Mr. Flores, and I'm still kind of weak." I looked at him pleadingly and asked, "Where is Carlos?"

"Charlie Spider is spinning some spiderish dream." Mr. Flores said the whole sentence in his extravagantly pronounced English then chuckled contentedly as though he were savoring a particularly clever joke. He glanced gleefully at Mariano Aureliano—still staring fixedly at the wall—then back at me and back at his friend. He must have sensed my growing apprehension, for he shrugged helplessly, held up his hands in a resigned gesture, and said, "Carlos, also known as Isidoro Baltazar, went to visit . . ."

"He left?" My shriek made Mariano Aureliano turn to look at me. I was more distraught at being left alone with the two old men than I was about learning that Carlos Castaneda was known by yet another name and that he was the new nagual, whatever that meant.

Mariano Aureliano rose from his chair, bowed deeply, and, holding out his hand to help me up, said, "What could possibly be more delightful and rewarding for two old men than to guard you until you awoke from your dreams?"

His engaging smile and his old-fashioned courtesy were irresistible. I relaxed instantly. "I can't think of anything more delightful," I cheerfully agreed and let him lead me to a brightly lit dining room across the corridor, to an oval-shaped mahogany table at the far end of the room. Gallantly, he held out a chair for me, waited until I was comfortably seated, then said that it was not too late for supper and that he would go himself to the kitchen and bring me something delicious to eat. My offer to help him was graciously rejected.

Mr. Flores, instead of walking to the table, cartwheeled across the room, calculating the distance with such precision he landed a few inches away from the table. Grinning, he sat beside me. His face showed no trace of exertion; he wasn't even out of breath.

"In spite of your denial that you aren't an acrobat, I believe that you and your friends are part of some magic show," I said.

Mr. Flores sprang from his chair, his face crinkling with mischief. "You're absolutely right. We are part of some magic show!" he exclaimed, reaching for one of the two earthenware jugs standing on the long sideboard. He poured me a cup of hot chocolate. "I make a meal of it by eating a piece of cheese with it." He cut me a slice of Manchego cheese.

Together they were superb.

I wanted seconds, but he didn't offer me any. I thought that a cup—and it had only been half full—was not enough. I had always been partial to chocolate and could eat inordinate amounts of it without ill effects. I was certain that if I concentrated on my desire to have more of it, he would be obliged to pour me another cup without my having to ask. I was able to do this as a child when I wanted something badly enough.

Greedily, I watched him remove two extra cups and two saucers from the tall china closet. I noticed that between the crystal, the china, and the silverware on the shelves stood an odd assortment of prehispanic clay figurines and plastic prehistoric monsters.

"This is the witches' house," Mr. Flores said in a conspiratorial tone, as if to explain the incongruity of the decor in the china closet.

"Mariano Aureliano's wives?" I asked daringly.

He didn't answer but gestured for me to turn around. Mariano Aureliano was standing right behind me.

"The same ones," Mariano Aureliano said cheerfully, placing a porcelain tureen on the table. "The same witches who made this delicious oxtail soup." With a silver ladle he served me a plateful and urged me to add to it a wedge of lime and a slice of avocado.

I did so, then devoured it all in a few gulps. I ate several platefuls, until I felt physically satisfied, almost stuffed. We sat around the table for a long time. The oxail soup had the most soothing effect on me. I was at ease. Something that was usually very nasty in me had been turned off. My whole being, body and spirit, was thankful that I didn't have to use up energy to defend myself.

Nodding his head, as though silently confirming each of my thoughts, Mariano Aureliano watched me with keen, amused eyes.

I was about to address him as Juan Matus, when he anticipated my intent and said, "I'm Juan Matus for Isidoro Baltazar. For you, I'm the nagual Mariano Aureliano." Smiling, he leaned closer and whispered in a confidential tone, "The man who drove you here is the new nagual, the nagual Isidoro Baltazar. That's the name you should use when you talk to him or about him.

"You're not quite asleep but not quite awake either," Mariano Aureliano went on explaining, "so you'll be able to understand and remember everything we say to you." Seeing that I was about to interrupt him, he added sternly, "And tonight, you're not going to ask stupid questions."

It wasn't so much his tone, but a force, an edge to him that was chilling. It paralyzed my tongue; my head, however, of its own accord, made a nodding gesture of affirmation.

"You have to test her," Mr. Flores reminded his friend. A definite wicked gleam appeared in his eyes as he added, "Or better yet, let me test her myself."

Mariano Aureliano paused, a long, deliberate moment charged with ominous possibilities, and regarded me critically, as if my features would give him a clue to some important secret.

Mesmerized by his keen, piercing eyes, I didn't so much as blink.

He nodded thoughtfully, and Mr. Flores asked me in a deep, grave tone, "Are you in love with Isidoro Baltazar?"

And I'll be damned if I didn't say yes in a mechanical, unanimated voice.

Mr. Flores moved closer, until our heads almost touched, and in a whisper that shook with suppressed laughter asked, "Are you really madly, madly in love with him?"

I said yes again, and both men burst into loud, elated guffaws. The sound of their laughter, bouncing around the room like ping-pong balls, finally broke my trancelike state. I hooked onto the sound and pulled myself out of the spell.

"What in the name of hell is this," I shouted at the top of my voice.

Startled, both men jumped out of their chairs. They looked at me, then at each other, and burst out laughing again with ecstatic abandon. The more eloquent my insults, the greater their mirth. There was something so infectious about their laughter, I couldn't help but giggle, too.

As soon as we had all calmed down, Mariano Aureliano and Mr. Flores bombarded me with questions. They were particularly interested in how and when I first met Isidoro Baltazar. Every absurd little detail overjoyed them. By the time I had gone over the events for the fourth and fifth time, I had either improved and enlarged my story with each telling, or I had remembered details I wouldn't have dreamed I could remember.

"Isidoro Baltazar saw through you and through the whole thing," Mariano Aureliano judged when I finally finished with my various accounts. "But he doesn't see well enough yet. He couldn't even conceive that I had sent you to him." He regarded me wickedly and corrected himself. "It wasn't really I who sent you to him. It was the spirit. The spirit chose me to do its bidding, though, and I blew you to him when you were most powerful, in the midst of your dreaming-awake." He spoke lightly, almost listlessly; only his eyes conveyed the urgency of his knowledge. "Perhaps your dreaming-awake power was the reason Isidoro Baltazar didn't realize who you were, even though he was seeing. Even though the spirit let him know the very first time he set eyes on you. A display of lights in the fog is the ultimate give-away. How stupid of Isidoro Baltazar not to see the obvious."

He chuckled softly, and I nodded in agreement, without knowing what I was agreeing to.

"That'll show you that to be a sorcerer is no big deal," he continued. "Isidoro Baltazar is a sorcerer. To be a man of knowledge is something else. For that, sorcerers have to wait sometimes a lifetime."

"What's the difference?" I asked.

"A man of knowledge is a leader," he explained, his voice low, subtly mysterious. "Sorcerers need leaders to lead us into and through the unknown. A leader is revealed through his actions. Leaders have no price tag on their heads, meaning that there is no way to buy them or bribe them or cajole them or mystify them."

He settled more comfortably in his chair and went on to say that all the people in his group had made it a point to study leaders throughout the ages in order to see if any of them fulfilled the requirements.

"Have you found any?"

"Some," he admitted. "Those we have found could have been naguals." He pressed his finger against my lips and added, "Naguals are, then, natural leaders, men of tremendous energy, who become sorcerers by adding one more track to their repertoire: the unknown. If those sorcerers succeed in becoming men of knowledge, then there is practically no limit to what they can do."

"Can women—" He didn't let me finish.

"Women, as you will learn someday, can do infinitely more complex things than that," he affirmed.

"Did Isidoro Baltazar remind you of someone you met before?" Mr. Flores interrupted.

"Well," I began expansively, "I felt thoroughly at ease with him. I felt as if I had known him all my life. He reminded me of someone perhaps in my childhood, a forgotten childhood friend perhaps."

"So you really don't remember meeting him before?" Mr. Flores interjected.

"You mean at Esperanza's house?" I asked, wondering whether I had seen him at the healer's place and didn't recall it.

He shook his head disappointedly. Then, apparently no longer interested in my response, he went on to ask if I had seen someone waving at us on our way to the house.

"No," I said. "I didn't seen anyone waving at us."

"Think hard," he insisted.

I told the two men that after Yuma, instead of going east to Nogales on Highway 8—the most logical route—Isidoro Baltazar headed south into Mexico, then east through "El Gran Desierto," then north again into the United States through Sonoyta, to Ajo, Arizona, and back into Mexico to Caborca, where we had a most delicious lunch of beef tongue in a green chili sauce.

"After getting into the car with a full stomach, I hardly paid any attention to the road," I admitted. "I know we passed through Santa Ana, and then we headed north again to Cananea, and then south again. A veritable mess, if you ask me."

"Can't you remember seeing anyone on the road?" Mr. Flores insisted. "Anyone waving at you?"

I shut my eyes tightly in an effort to visualize anyone waving at us. But my memory of the trip was one of stories and songs and of physical exhaustion. And then as I was about to open my eyes, the image of a man flashed before me. I told them that I vaguely recalled there had been a young man in the outskirts of one of those towns who I thought was trying to catch a ride.

"He might have waved at us," I said. "But I'm not sure."

Both men chuckled like children trying hard not to give away a secret.

"Isidoro Baltazar wasn't too sure of finding us," Mariano Aureliano remarked gleefully. "That's why he followed this outlandish route. He followed the sorcerers' path, the coyote trail."

"Why wouldn't he be sure of finding you?" I interrupted.

"He didn't know whether he would find us until he saw the young man waving at him," Mariano Aureliano explained. "That young man is a sentry from the other world. His waving was a sign that it was all right to continue. Isidoro Baltazar should have known right then who you really were, but he is very much like you, extremely cautious, and when he's not cautious, he's extremely reckless." He paused for a moment to let the words sink in then added meaningfully, "Moving between those two points is the surest way to miss the boat. Cautiousness blinds as surely as recklessness."

"I can't understand the logic of all this," I murmured wearily.

Mariano Aureliano elucidated, "Whenever Isidoro Baltazar brings a guest, he has to heed the sentry's signal before he can continue on his journey."

"Once he brought a girl he was in love with." Mr. Flores chuckled, closing his eyes as if transported by his own memory of the girl. "A tall, dark-haired girl. Strong girl. Big feet. Nice face. He drove all over Baja California, and the sentry never let him through."

"Do you mean he brings his girlfriends?" I asked with morbid curiosity. "How many has he brought?"

"Quite a few," Mr. Flores said candidly. "He did that, of course, entirely on his own. Your case is different," he pointed out. "You're not his girlfriend; you were just coming back. Isidoro Baltazar nearly croaked when he found out he was so stupid to miss all the indications of the spirit. He was merely your chauffeur. We were waiting for you."

"What would have happened if the sentry hadn't been there?"

"What always occurs when Isidoro Baltazar comes accompanied," Mariano Aureliano replied. "He wouldn't have found us, because it's not up to him to choose whom to bring into the sorcerers' world." His voice was enticingly soft as he added, "Only those the spirit has pointed out may knock on our door, after they have been ushered into it by one of us."

108

I was about to interrupt, then remembering his admonition that I wasn't to ask stupid questions, I quickly pressed my hand against my mouth.

Grinning appreciatively, Mariano Aureliano went on to say that in my case Delia had brought me into their world. "She's one of the two columns, so to speak, that make the door of our door. The other one is Clara. You'll meet her soon."

There was genuine admiration in his eyes and in his voice as he went on to say, "Delia crossed the border just to bring you home. The border is an actual fact, but sorcerers use it symbolically. You were on the other side and had to be brought here, to this side. Over on the other side is the daily world, here on this side is the world of sorcerers.

"Delia ushered you in smoothly, a real professional job. It was an impeccable maneuver that you will appreciate more and more as time passes."

Mariano Aureliano half-rose from his chair and reached for the porcelain compote on the sideboard. He placed it in front of me. "Help yourself. They're delicious."

Enraptured, I gazed at the pulpy dry apricots on the hand-painted dish then tried one. They were more than wonderful. I put three in my mouth.

Mr. Flores winked at me. "Go ahead," he urged me. "Put all of them in your mouth before we take the plate away."

I blushed and tried to apologize with a mouth full of apricots.

"Don't apologize!" Mariano Aureliano exclaimed. "Be yourself, but be yourself in control. If you want to finish the apricots, then finish them, and that should be all there is to it. What you should never do is finish them, and then feel sorry you did."

"Well, I'll finish them," I said. And that made them laugh.

"Do you know that you met Isidoro Baltazar last year?" Mr. Flores said. He was balancing so precariously on his tilted chair, I feared he would fall backwards and crash into the china closet. A wicked glint of delight dawned in his eyes as he began to hum a well-known *ranchera* song. Instead of the words that went with it, he made up a little ditty that told the story of Isidoro Baltazar, a famous cook in Tucson. A cook who never lost his cool, not even when he was accused of putting dead cockroaches in the food.

"Oh!" I exclaimed. "The cook! The cook in the coffee shop was Isidoro Baltazar! But that can't be true," I mumbled. "I don't think he would . . ." I stopped myself in midsentence.

I kept staring at Mariano Aureliano, hoping to discover something in his face, in that aquiline nose, in those piercing eyes. I shook involuntarily, as if I were suddenly chilled. There was something savage in his cold eyes.

"Yes?" he prompted me. "You don't think he would . . . ," he urged me with a movement of his head to finish my sentence.

I was going to say, inanely, that I didn't think Isidoro Baltazar could lie to me so despicably. I couldn't quite bring myself to say it, though.

Mariano Aureliano's eyes became even harder, but I was too upset, too sorry for myself to feel frightened.

"So, I was tricked after all," I finally blurted out, glowering at him. "Isidoro Baltazar knew all along who I was. It's all a game."

"It's all a game," Mariano Aureliano readily agreed. "A marvelous game, though. The only game worth playing." He paused as if to give me time to complain some more. But before I had a chance to do so, he reminded me of the wig he had pulled over my hair. "If you didn't recognize Isidoro Baltazar—who wasn't disguised— what makes you think that he recognized you in your poodle outfit?"

Mariano Aureliano kept watching me. His eyes had lost their hardness; now they were sad, weary. "You weren't tricked. You weren't even enticed. Not that I wouldn't do so if I deemed it necessary," he noted in a light, soft tone. "I told you what was what from the beginning. You have witnessed stupendous events, still you haven't noticed them. As most people do, you associate sorcery with bizarre behavior, rituals, drugs, incantations." He leaned closer and lowered his voice to a mere whisper, then added that true sorcery was a most subtle and exquisite manipulation of perception.

"True sorcery," Mr. Flores interjected, "does not allow for human interference."

110

"But Mr. Aureliano claims that he blew me to Isidoro Baltazar," I pointed out with immature impertinence. "Isn't that interfering?"

"I'm a nagual," Mariano Aureliano said simply. "I'm the nagual Mariano Aureliano, and the fact that I am the nagual enables me to manipulate perception."

I had paid close attention to his words, but I didn't have the vaguest idea what he meant by manipulating perception. Out of sheer nervousness, I reached for the last dry apricot on the plate.

"You're going to get sick," Mr. Flores said. "You're so tiny, and yet you're such a super pain in the . . . eye."

Mariano Aureliano came to stand behind me, then pressed my back in such a way it made me cough up the last apricot I had had in my mouth.

8

AT this point, the sequence of events, as I remember it, becomes blurry. I don't know what happened next. Perhaps I fell asleep and wasn't aware of it, or perhaps the pressure Mariano Aureliano exerted on my back was so great that I passed out.

When I came to my senses again, I was lying on a mat on the floor. I opened my eyes and instantly became conscious of the intense brightness around me. There seemed to be sunlight in the room. I blinked repeatedly, wondering whether there was something wrong with my eyes. I couldn't focus them.

"Mr. Aureliano," I called out. "There seems to be something wrong with my eyes." I tried to sit up but couldn't.

It wasn't Mr. Aureliano or Mr. Flores who was standing by my side; a woman was there. She was leaning over me, blotting out the brightness, so to speak. Her black hair hung loosely down her sides and shoulders; she had a round face and an imposing bust. Again I tried to sit up. She didn't touch me, yet I knew that somehow she was holding me down.

"Don't call him Mr. Aureliano," she said. "Or Mariano either. That's very disrespectful of you. Call him nagual, and when you talk about him, call him the nagual Mariano Aureliano. He likes his full name." Her voice was melodious. I liked her.

I felt feisty. I wanted to ask her why all the nonsense about being disrespectful. I had heard Delia and all the other women call him the most ridiculous pet names and fuss over him as if he were their favorite doll. He certainly had enjoyed every minute of it. But I couldn't remember when and where I had witnessed that.

"Do you understand?" the woman asked.

I wanted to say yes, but I didn't have a voice. I tried, to no avail, to open my mouth and say something. When she insisted on knowing if I had understood, all I could do was nod.

She offered me her hand to help me up. Before she touched me I was up, as if my desire to rise had superseded the actual contact with her hand and had pulled me into a sitting position before she did.

Astonished by this occurrence, I wanted to ask her about it, but I could barely keep myself upright. And as for talking, words simply refused to come out of my mouth.

She stroked my hair repeatedly. Obviously, she was thoroughly aware of my plight. She smiled kindly and said, "You're dreaming."

I didn't hear her say that, but I knew that her words had moved directly from her mind into mine. She nodded and told me that, indeed, I could hear her thoughts and that she could hear mine. She assured me that she was like a figment of my imagination, yet she could act with me or upon me.

"Pay attention!" she commanded me. "I'm not moving my lips, and yet I am talking to you. Do the same."

Her mouth didn't move at all. Wondering whether I could feel a movement in her lips when she silently enunciated her words, I wanted to press my fingers against her mouth. She was actually very good-looking but menacing. She reached for my hand and pressed it against her smiling lips. I didn't feel a thing.

"How can I talk without my lips?" I thought.

"You have a hole between your legs," she said directly into my mind. "Focus your attention on it. The pussy talks."

That remark hit a funny chord in me. I laughed so hard I lost my breath and blacked out again.

The woman shook me awake. I was still on the same mat on the floor, but I was propped up with a thick cushion behind my back. I blinked and shuddered, then drew a long breath and looked at her. She was sitting on the floor beside me.

"I'm not given to fainting," I said and surprised myself by being able to utter the words. The sound of my own voice was so reassuring that I laughed out loud and repeated the same sentence several times.

"I know, I know," she appeased me. "Don't worry, you're not quite awake anyway. I am Clara. We have already met at Esperanza's."

I should have protested or asked her what she meant. Instead, without doubting for an instant, I accepted that I was still asleep and that we had met at Esperanza's.

Memories, foggy thoughts, visions of people, of places, began to emerge slowly. A clear thought popped into my mind: I had dreamt once that I met her. It was a dream. Thus, I never had thought about it in terms of real events. The moment I hooked onto that realization, I remembered Clara.

"Of course, we've met," I said triumphantly. "But we met in a dream, so you are not real. I must be dreaming now, therefore I can remember you."

I sighed, content that it could all be explained so easily, and relaxed against the thick pillow. Another clear memory of a dream popped into my mind. I couldn't recall exactly when I had dreamt this dream, but I remembered it as clearly as if the event had actually taken place; in it, Delia had introduced me to Clara. She had described Clara as the most gregarious of the women dreamers. "She actually has friends who adore her," Delia had confided in me.

The Clara of that dream was quite tall, strong, and rotund. She had observed me insistently as one observes a member of an unknown species, with careful eyes and nervous smiles. And yet, in spite of her demanding scrutiny, I had liked her immensely. Her eyes were speculating and smiling and green. What I remembered best about her intense watchfulness was that she had looked at me with the unblinking stare of a cat.

"I know this is just a dream, Clara," I repeated, as if I needed to reassure myself.

"No. This is not just a dream, it's an special dream," Clara contradicted me forcefully. "You're wrong to entertain such thoughts. Thoughts have power; be watchful of them."

"You're not real, Clara," I insisted, in a strained, high-pitched voice. "You're a dream. That's why I can't remember you when I am awake."

My stubborn persistence made Clara chuckle. "You have never tried to remember me," she finally explained. "There was no point to it, no reason for it. We women are excruciatingly practical. Our great flaw or our great asset."

I was about to ask her what the practical aspect of remembering her now was, when she anticipated my question.

"Since I am in front of you, you need to remember me. And you do." She bent lower and, fixing me with her catlike stare, added, "And you won't forget me anymore. The sorcerers who reared me told me that women need two of anything in order to solidify it. Two sights of something, two readings, two frights, etc. You and I have now met twice. Now I am solid and real."

To prove how real she was, she pushed up the sleeves of her blouse and flexed her biceps. "Touch them," she urged me.

Giggling, I did. She indeed had hard, powerfully defined muscles. They felt as real as anything. She also made me touch the muscles of her thigh and calf.

"If this is a special dream," I said cautiously, what do I do in this dream?"

"Anything your heart desires," she said. "You're doing fine so far. I cannot guide you, though, for I am not your dreaming teacher. I am simply a fat witch who actually takes care of the other witches. It was my partner, Delia, who delivered you into the sorcerers' world, just like a midwife. But she was not the one who first found you. Florinda did."

"Who is Florinda?" I giggled uncontrollably. "And when did she find me?"

"Florinda is another witch," Clara said matter-of-factly, then began to giggle too. "You met her. She's the one who took you into her dream in Esperanza's house. Do you remember the picnic?"

"Ah," I sighed appreciatively. "You mean the tall woman with the husky voice?" A radiance filled me. I had always admired tall women.

"The tall woman with the husky voice," Clara confirmed. "She found you a couple of years ago at a party you attended with your boyfriend. A plush dinner in Houston, Texas, at the house of an oilman."

"What would a witch be doing at a party in an oilman's house?" I asked. Then the full impact of her claim hit me. I was dumbstruck. Although I didn't remember seeing Florinda, I certainly did recall the party. I had gone with a friend who flew in his private jet from Los Angeles just to attend that party and flew back the next day. I was his translator. There had been several Mexican businessmen at that party who didn't speak English.

"Jesus!" I exclaimed under my breath. "What a weird turn of events!" In great detail I described the party to Clara. It was the first time I had been to Texas. Like some star-struck movie fan, I ogled the men, not because they were handsome but because they looked so outlandish to me in their Stetson hats, pastel-colored suits, and cowboy boots. The oilman had hired entertainers. They had staged a variety show, worthy of Las Vegas, in a nightclub grotto built especially for the occasion. It throbbed with loud music and strobe lights. And the food had been superb.

"But why would Florinda attend such a party?" I asked.

"The world of sorcerers is the strangest thing there is," Clara said by way of an answer. She jumped up, like an acrobat, from a sitting position to a standing one, without using her arms. She paced about the room, back and forth in front of my mat. She looked formidable in her full, dark skirt, her cowboy denim jacket—colorfully embroidered in the back—and her sturdy cowboy boots. An Australian hat, pulled low over her brow as if to protect her from the noonday sun, added the last touch to her eccentric, outlandish appearance.

"How do you like my outfit?" she asked, pausing in front of me. Her face was radiant.

"It's great," I gushed. She certainly had the flair, the confidence to carry off any kind of outfit. "It's really cool."

She kneeled beside me on the mat and in a confidential whisper said, "Delia is green with envy. We are always in competition to see who comes up with the nuttiest getup. It has to be crazy without being stupid." She was silent for a moment, and her eyes watched me, considering. "You're welcome to compete," she offered. "Do you want to join us in our game?"

I nodded emphatically, and she spelled out the rules for me.

"Originality, practicality, low price, and no self-importance," she rattled off. Then she rose again and twirled a few more times around the room. Laughing, she collapsed beside me and said, "Florinda thinks I should encourage you to participate. She says that in that party, she found out that you had a touch for thoroughly practical outfits."

She could barely finish the sentence; she was overcome by a great burst of giggles.

"Did Florinda talk to me there?" I asked and gazed at her slyly, wondering whether she would tell me what I had omitted from my account, information that I wasn't going to volunteer.

Clara shook her head then gave me a distracted smile, meant to deflect further questions about the party.

"How did Delia happen to be at the baptism in Nogales, Arizona?" I asked, shifting the conversation to the events of the other party.

"Florinda sent her there," Clara admitted, tucking all her loose hair into her Australian hat. "She crashed the party by telling everyone that she had come with you."

"Wait a minute!" I interrupted her. "This is no dream. What are you trying to do to me?"

"I'm trying to instruct you," Clara insisted, without altering her air of indifference. Her tone was even, almost casual. She didn't seem to be interested in the effect her words were having on me. Yet she watched me carefully as she added, "This is a dream, and we are certainly talking in your dream, because I am also dreaming your dream."

That her outlandish statements should have been enough to appease me was proof that I was dreaming. My mind became calm, sleepy, and capable of accepting the situation. I heard myself speak, a voice detached from my volition. "There is no way Florinda could have known about my driving to Nogales," I said. "My girlfriend's invitation was accepted on the spur of the moment."

"I knew that this would be incomprehensible to you," Clara sighed. Then, looking into my eyes and weighing her words carefully, she declared, "Florinda is your mother more than any mother you ever had."

I found her statement preposterous, but I couldn't say a word.

"Florinda feels you," Clara continued. She had a devilish glint in her eyes as she added, "There is a homing device she uses. She knows wherever you are."

"What homing device?" I asked, my mind suddenly completely in control. The thought that someone might know at all times what I was up to filled me with dread.

"Her feelings for you are a homing device," Clara said with beautiful simplicity and in a tone so soft and harmonious that it made my apprehension vanish.

"What feelings for me, Clara?"

"Who knows, child?" she said wistfully. She drew her legs up, wrapped her arms around them, and rested her chin on her knees. "I've never had a daughter like this."

My mood changed abruptly from amusement back to apprehension. In the rational, thought-out manner that was my style, I began to worry about the subtle implications of Clara's statement. And it was precisely my rational deliberations that again turned on my doubts. This couldn't possibly be a dream. I was awake; my concentration was too keen for me to be otherwise.

Sliding down the cushion propped against my back, I half closed my eyes. I kept watching Clara through my lashes, wondering whether she would slowly fade away as people and scenes fade away in dreams. She didn't. I felt momentarily reassured that I was awake and so was Clara.

"No, we're not awake," she contradicted me, again intruding into my thoughts.

"I can speak," I said by way of validating my state of total consciousness.

"Big deal!" she cackled. "Now I am going to do something that will wake you up, so that you can continue the conversation while you are really awake." She enunciated the last word with great care, drawing it out in an exaggerated fashion.

"Wait. Wait, Clara," I pleaded. "Give me time to adjust to all this." I preferred my uncertainty to what she might do to me.

Impervious to my pleading, Clara rose and reached for the pitcher of water standing on a low table nearby. Still giggling, she hovered over me, holding the pitcher over my head. I tried to roll to the side, but I was not able to do so. My body wouldn't obey me; it seemed to be glued to the mat. Before she actually poured the water over me, I felt a cold, soft sprinkle on my face. The coldness rather than the wetness produced a most peculiar sensation. It first blurred Clara's face looming over me the way ripples distort the surface of water; then the coldness centered itself on my stomach and pulled me inward, like a sleeve that's pulled inside out. My last thought was that I was going to drown in a pitcher of water. Bubbles upon bubbles of darkness spun me around until everything went black.

When I came to myself again I was no longer lying on the mat on the floor but on the couch in the living room. Two women were standing at the foot of the couch, staring at me with wide, curious eyes. Florinda, the tall, white-haired woman with the husky voice, was sitting beside me, humming an old lullaby—or so it seemed to me—and caressing my hair, my face, my arms, with great tenderness.

Her touch and the sound of her voice held me down. I just lay there, my unblinking eyes fixed on hers, certain I was having one of my vivid dreams, which always began as dreams and ended up as nightmares. Florinda was speaking to me. She was telling me to look into her eyes. Her words moved soundlessly, like the wings of butterflies. But whatever I saw in her eyes filled me with a familiar feeling—the irrational, abject terror I experienced in my nightmares. I jumped up and bolted straight for the door. It was the automatic, animal's reaction I had always had in a nightmare.

"Don't be frightened, my darling," the tall woman said, coming after me. "Relax. We are all here to help you. There is no need to be so upset. You'll hurt your little body by subjecting it to unnecessary fright."

119

I had stopped by the door, not because she had persuaded me to stay but because I couldn't open the damn thing. Frantically, I pulled and pushed the door; it didn't budge. The tall woman was just behind me. My trembling increased. I shook so hard that my body ached, and my heart beat so loudly and erratically I knew it would burst through my chest.

"Nagual!" the tall woman called out, turning her head over her shoulder. "You'd better do something. She's going to die of fright."

I didn't see to whom she was talking, but in my wild search for an escape, I saw a second door at the other end of the room. I was certain I had enough energy left in me to make a dash for it, but my legs gave in on me. As if life had already abandoned my body, I sank to the floor. My last breath escaped from me. The woman's long arms swooped down on me like a great eagle's wings. She held me, put her mouth to mine, and breathed air into me.

Slowly, my body relaxed; my heartbeat returned to normal. I was filled with a strange peace that quickly turned into a wild excitement. It wasn't fear that filled me with wildness but her breath. It was hot; it scorched my throat, my lungs, my stomach, my groin, moving all the way to my hands and my feet. In a flash, I knew that the woman was exactly like me only taller, as tall as I would have liked to be. I felt such love for her that I did something outlandish: I kissed her passionately.

I felt her lips widen into a smile. Then she threw her head back and laughed. "This little rat kissed me," she said, turning to the others.

"I'm dreaming!" I exclaimed, and they all laughed with child-like abandon.

At first I couldn't help but laugh, too. Within moments, however, I was my usual self—embarrassed after one of my impulsive acts and angry at having been caught.

The tall woman embraced me. "I'm Florinda," she said, and she lifted me up and cradled me in her arms, as if I were a baby. "You and I are the same," she went on. "You're as petite as I would have liked to be. It's a great disadvantage to be tall. No one can ever cradle you. I'm five ten."

"I'm five two," I confessed, and we both laughed because we understood each other to perfection. I was short on the second inch but always rounded it up. I was certain Florinda was closer to five eleven but rounded it down to ten. I kissed her cheeks and her eyes. I loved her with a love that was incomprehensible to me; it was a feeling untainted by doubt or dread or expectation. It was the love one feels in dreams.

Seemingly in complete agreement with me, Florinda chuckled softly. The elusive light in her eyes, the ghostly whiteness of her hair, was like some forgotten memory. I felt as if I had known her from the day I was born. It occurred to me that children who liked their mothers must be lost children. Filial love coupled with admiration for the mother's physical being must result in a sense of total love, like the love I felt for this tall, mysterious woman.

She put me down. "This is Carmela," she said, turning me toward a beautiful, dark-eyed, dark-haired woman. Her features were delicate, and her skin was flawless; she had the smooth, creamy pallor of someone who stays much indoors.

"I only take moon baths," she whispered in my ear as she embraced me. "You ought to do the same. You're too fair to be out in the sun; you're ruining your skin."

It was her voice, more than anything else, that I recognized. She was the same woman who had asked me all those direct, personal questions at the picnic. I remembered her in a sitting position; she had seemed small and frail. To my surprise, she was three or four inches taller than I. Her powerful, muscular body made me feel insignificant in comparison.

With her arm draped around my shoulder, Florinda guided me toward the second woman who had been standing beside the couch when I awoke. She was muscular and tall but not as tall as Florinda. She wasn't conventionally beautiful—her features were too strong for that—yet there was something striking, thoroughly attractive about her, including the faint shadow of fine hair on her upper lip, which she obviously didn't bother to wax or bleach. I sensed a tremendous force in her, an agitation that was completely under control yet still there.

"This is Zoila," Florinda said to me.

Zoila made no motion to either shake my hand or to embrace me. Carmela laughed and spoke for Zoila: "I'm very happy to see you again."

Zoila's mouth curved in the loveliest of smiles, showing white, large, even teeth. As her long, slender hand, glinting with jeweled rings, brushed my cheek, I realized she was the one whose face had been hidden under a mass of scraggly hair. She was the one who had sewn the Belgian lace around the canvas cloth we had sat on during the picnic.

The three women surrounded me and made me sit on the couch.

"The first time we met you, you were dreaming," Florinda said. "So we really didn't have time to interact. This time, however, you're awake, so tell us about yourself."

I was about to interrupt her and say that this was a dream and that during the picnic, whether asleep or awake, I had told them everything worth knowing about myself.

"No, no. You're wrong," Florinda said, as if I had spoken my thoughts out loud. "You're completely awake now. And what we want to know is what you've done since our last meeting. Tell us specifically about Isidoro Baltazar."

"You mean this is not a dream?" I asked timidly.

"No. This is not a dream," she assured me. "You were dreaming a few minutes ago, but this is different."

"I don't see the difference."

"That's because you're a good dreamer," she explained. "Your nightmares are real; you said that yourself."

My whole body tensed up. And then, as though it knew that it couldn't withstand another attack of fright, it gave up. My body abandoned itself to the moment. I repeated to them what I had already told and retold Mariano Aureliano and Mr. Flores earlier. This time, however, I remembered details I had altogether overlooked before, such as the two sides of Isidoro Baltazar's face, the two simultaneous moods he showed that were plainly revealed in his eyes. The left one was sinister, menacing; the right one was friendly, open.

"He's a dangerous man," I maintained, carried away by my observations. "He has a peculiar power to move events in whatever direction he pleases, while he remains outside, watching you squirm."

The women were enthralled by what I was saying. Florinda signaled me to continue.

"What makes people so vulnerable to his charm is that he is a generous man," I went on. "And generosity is perhaps the only virtue that none of us can resist, because we are dispossessed, regardless of our background." Realizing what I had said, I stopped abruptly and gazed at them, aghast.

"I don't know what has come upon me," I muttered in an attempt to apologize. "I truly don't know why I said that when I haven't thought about Isidoro Baltazar in those terms myself. It's not me talking. I'm not even capable of making those kinds of judgments."

"Never mind, child, where you get these thoughts," Florinda said. "Obviously you're plugging into the source itself. Everybody does that—plugs into the source itself—but it takes a sorcerer to be aware of it."

I didn't understand what she was trying to tell me. I restated that I had no intention of shooting off my big mouth.

Florinda giggled and regarded me for a few moments thoughtfully. "Act as if you were in a dream. Be daring and don't apologize," she said.

I felt stupid, incapable of analyzing what I felt. Florinda nodded, as if in agreement, then turned to her companions and said, "Tell her about us."

Carmela cleared her throat and without looking at me said, "The three of us and Delia make a unit. We deal with the daily world."

I hung on her every word, but I didn't understand her at all.

"We're the unit of sorceresses who deal with people," Carmela clarified. "There is another unit of four women who don't deal with people at all." She took my hand in hers and examined my palm—as if she were to read my fortune—then closed it gently into a fist and added, "You're just like us in general. That is, you can deal with people. And you're like Florinda in particular." Again she paused, and with a dreamy look on her face she repeated what Clara had already told me. "It was Florinda who found you," she said. "Therefore, while you remain in the world of sorcerers, you belong to her. She'll guide you and look after you." Her tone carried such a great certainty that it threw me into genuine worry.

"I don't belong to anyone," I said. "And I don't need anyone to look after me." My voice was strained, unnatural, uncertain.

Silently, the women watched me, bemused smiles on their faces.

"Do you think I need guidance?" I asked defiantly, gazing from one to the other. Their eyes were half closed, their lips parted in those same contemplative smiles. The imperceptible nods of their chins clearly indicated that they were waiting for me to finish what I had to say. "I think I do very well in life on my own," I finished lamely.

"Do you remember what you did at the party where I found you?" Florinda asked me.

As I stared at her in amazement, Carmela whispered in my ear, "Don't worry, you can always find a way to explain anything." She waved a finger at me, not in the slightest disturbed. Panic crept over me at the thought that they might know that I had walked naked in that party in front of dozens of people.

Until that moment, I had been, if not proud of my outlandish behavior, at least acceptant of it. To my way of thinking, what I did at that party was a manifestation of my spontaneous personality. First, I had taken a long horseback ride with the host, in my evening gown and without a saddle, to show him—after he dared me and bet I couldn't do it—that I was as good on horseback as any cowboy. I had an uncle in Venezuela who had a stud farm, and I had been on a horse since I was a toddler. Upon winning the bet, dizzy from the exertion and alcohol, I took a plunge in his giant pool—in the nude.

"I was there by the pool when you went in naked," Florinda said, obviously privy to my recollection. "You brushed me with your naked buttocks. You shocked everyone, including me. I liked your daring. Above all, I liked that you walked naked all the way from the other side of the pool just to brush against me. I took that as an indication that the spirit was pointing you out to me."

124

"It can't be true," I mumbled. "If you had been at that party, I would have remembered you. You're too tall and striking-looking to be overlooked." It wasn't meant as a compliment. I wanted to convince myself that I was being tricked, manipulated.

"I liked the fact that you were killing yourself just to show off," Florinda went on. "You were a clown, eager to draw attention to yourself at any cost, especially when you jumped on a table and danced for a moment, shaking your buttocks shamelessly, while the host yelled his head off."

Instead of embarrassing me, her remarks filled me with an incredible sense of ease and delight. I felt liberated. The secret was out, the secret I had never dared to admit, that I was a show-off who would do anything to get attention. A new mood overtook me, definitely more humble, less defensive. I feared, however, that such a mood wouldn't last. I knew that any insights and realizations I had arrived at in dreams had never survived. But perhaps Florinda was right and this was no dream, and my new frame of mind would endure.

Seemingly cognizant of my thoughts, the three women nodded emphatically. Instead of feeling encouraged by their agreement, it only revived my uncertainties. As I had feared, my insightful mood was short-lived. Within moments I was burning with doubts. And I wanted a respite.

"Where is Delia?" I asked.

"She's in Oaxaca," Florinda said then added pointedly, "She was here just to greet you."

I had thought that if I changed the subject, I would get a respite and have a chance to recuperate my strength. Now I was facing something I had no resources to deal with. I couldn't accuse Florinda outright—as I would normally have done with anybody—of telling lies in order to manipulate me. I couldn't tell her that I suspected they had made me groggy and had taken me from room to room while I was unconscious.

"What you say is really preposterous, Florinda," I chided. "I can't believe that you expect me to take you seriously." Chewing the inside of my lip, I stared at her long and hard. "I know that Delia is hiding in one of the rooms."

125

Florinda's eyes seemed to tell me she understood my quandary. "You have no other option except to take me seriously," she said. Though her tone was mild, it was final.

I turned to the other two women, hoping for some kind of an answer, anything that would ease my growing apprehension.

"If someone else guides you, it's actually very easy to dream," Carmela confided. "The only drawback is that that someone else has to be a nagual."

"I've been hearing all along about a nagual," I said. "What is a nagual?

"A nagual is a sorcerer of great power who can lead other sorcerers through and out of the darkness," Carmela explained. "But the nagual himself told you all that a while ago. Don't you remember?"

Florinda interceded as my body contorted in an effort to remember. "Events we live in everyday life are easy to recall. We have plenty of practice in doing that. But events lived in dreams are another story. We have to struggle very hard to bring them back, simply because the body stores them in different places.

"With women who don't have your somnambulist brain," she pointed out, "dreaming instructions begin by making them draw a map of their bodies—a painstaking job that reveals where the visions of dreams are stored in their bodies."

"How do you draw this map, Florinda?" I asked, genuinely intrigued.

"By systematically tapping every inch of your body," she said. "But I can't tell you more. I'm your mother, not your dreaming teacher. Now, she recommends a small wooden mallet for the actual tapping. And she also recommends to tap only the legs and hips. Very rarely, the body stores those memories in the chest or belly. What's stored in the chest, back, and belly are the memories of everyday life. But that's another matter.

"All that concerns you now is that remembering dreams has to do with physical pressure on the specific spot where that vision is stored. For instance, if you push your vagina by putting pressure on your clitoris, you'll remember what Mariano Aureliano told you," she finished with a kind of simple cheerfulness.

I stared at her aghast, then burst into nervous, fitful giggles. I wasn't going to push anything.

Florinda laughed, too, gleefully, seemingly enjoying my embarrassment. "If you won't do it," she threatened, "then I will simply have Carmela do it for you."

I turned to Carmela. With a half smile about to break into a laugh, she assured me that indeed she would push my vagina for me.

"There is no need to!" I cried out in dismay. "I remember everything!" And indeed I did. And not only what Mariano Aureliano had said but also other events.

"Is Mr. Aureliano . . ."

"Clara told you to call him the nagual Mariano Aureliano," Carmela cut me off in midsentence.

"Dreams are doors into the unknown," Florinda said, stroking my head. "Naguals lead by means of dreams. And the act of dreaming with purpose is the art of sorcerers. The nagual Mariano Aureliano has helped you to get into dreams that all of us dreamed."

I blinked repeatedly. I shook my head, then fell back against the cushions of the couch, shocked by the absurdity of all I was remembering.

I remembered that I had dreamed of them a year ago in Sonora, a dream that had lasted, I thought, forever. In that dream, I met Clara, Nélida, and Hermelinda. The other team, the dreamers. They told me that the leader of that team was Zuleica but that I couldn't dream of her yet.

As the memory of that dream became clear in my mind, it also became clear that among those women no one was more, no one was less than the other. That one woman in each group was the leader was in no way a matter of power, of prestige, of accomplishment, but simply a matter of efficiency. I didn't know why, but I was convinced that all that mattered to them was the deep affection they had for each other.

In that dream everyone had said to me that Zuleica was my dreaming teacher. That was all I could remember. Just as Clara had told me, I needed to see them or dream of them one more time in order to solidify my knowledge of them. As it was, they were but disembodied memories.

I vaguely heard Florinda say that after a few more tries I would fare much better in shifting from my memory of dreams to the dream I was dreaming and then to the normal state of awakeness.

I heard Florinda giggle, but I was no longer in the room. I was outside, walking across the chaparral. I walked slowly along an invisible path, a little uneasy, for there was no light, no moon, no stars in the sky.

Pulled by some invisible force, I stepped into a large room. It was dark inside except for the lines of light crisscrossing from wall to wall over the faces of the people sitting in two circles—an inner and an outer circle. The light got bright and then became dim, as if someone in the circle were playing with the electric switch, turning it on and off.

I recognized Mariano Aureliano and Isidoro Baltazar sitting, back to back, in the middle of the inner circle. It wasn't so much that I recognized their faces but rather their energy. It wasn't that their energy was brighter than or different from anyone else's. There was simply more of it; it was massive. It was one splendid, great lump of inexhaustible brilliance.

The room shone white. There was a vividness to things, a hardness to every edge and corner. There was such a clarity in that room that everything stood out separately, by itself, especially those lines of light that were tied to the people sitting in the circle—or that emanated from them. The people were all connected by lines of light, and they looked as if they were the suspension points of a giant spider web. They all communicated wordlessly, through the light. I was pulled to that silent, electric tension until I, too, was a point in that web of luminosity.

"What's going to happen?" I asked, looking up at Florinda. I was stretched out on the couch, my head resting in her lap.

She didn't answer; neither did Carmela or Zoila, who were sitting by her with their eyes closed. I repeated my question several times, but all I heard was the gentle breathing of the three women. I was certain they were asleep, yet I felt their quiet, keen eyes on me. The darkness and the silence moved about the house like something alive, bringing with them an icy wind and the scent of the desert.

9

SHIVERING with cold, I wrapped the blanket tightly around me and sat up. I was in a strange bed, in a strange room furnished only with the bed and a night table, yet everything around me exuded familiarity. However, I couldn't decide why it was all so well known to me. Perhaps I am still asleep, I thought. How do I know this isn't a dream? I sank back into my pillows. I lay there with my arms behind my head and let the bizarre events I had witnessed and lived—half dream, half memory—run through my mind.

It had all begun, of course, the year before, when I drove with Delia Flores to the healer's house. She had claimed that the picnic I had had with everyone there had been a dream. I had laughed at her and discarded her statements as preposterous.

She had been right, though. I knew now that the picnic had been a dream. Not my dream, but a dream dreamt by others and to which I had been invited; I was a participating guest. My mistake all along had been to try doggedly to deny it, to discard it as a fake, without knowing what I meant by fake. All I succeeded in doing was to block that event from my mind so completely that I was never aware of it.

What I needed to do was to accept that we have a track for dreams, a groove where only dreams run. Had I set up myself to remember the dream I had had in Sonora, as nothing else but a dream, I would have succeeded in retaining the wonder of what had occurred while the dream was being dreamt.

The more I speculated about it, and about all the things that were happening to me now, the greater my discomfort. But what surprised me the most was that I wasn't really scared of all these people who, although supportive, were a scary bunch by any count. And it suddenly dawned on me that the reason why I wasn't scared was that I knew them very well. The proof to me was that they themselves had voiced the strange yet comforting feeling I had had: that I was coming home.

I discarded all these thoughts as soon as I had formulated them and honestly wondered whether perhaps I was mentally unbalanced and they had found a way to focus on it and thus enhance it. In a serious, systematic fashion I reviewed the history of my family in an effort to recall everything I might have heard about mental illness.

There was a story of a maternal great-uncle who, Bible in hand, would preach at street corners. Then both my great-grandfather and my grandfather, at the onset of the First and the Second World Wars, respectively, committed suicide upon realizing that everything was lost to them. One of my grandmothers blew her brains out when she realized that she had lost her beauty and sex appeal.

I liked to believe that I had inherited my feeling of detachment from being the true granddaughter of all those nuts. I had always believed that this feeling of detachment gave me my daring.

Those morbid thoughts caused me such anxiety that I jumped out of bed. With nervous, jerky movements I pulled my body out of the blanket. To my utter bafflement I found myself bundled in a heavy flannel nightshirt. I had on thick, knee-length wool socks, mittens, and a cardigan sweater. "I must be ill," I mumbled to myself in dismay. "Why else would I be cold with all these clothes on?" Normally, I slept in the nude, regardless of the climate.

Only then did I notice the sunlight in the room; it came through the thick, semi-opaque window. I was certain that the light shining in my eyes had awakened me. And I really needed to find the bathroom. Worried that the house didn't have inside plumbing, I stepped toward the sliding door at the other end of the room, which was open, and sure enough, it was a water closet with a lidded chamber pot in it.

"Damn it! I can't go to the bathroom in a water closet!" I yelled.

The door opened and Florinda walked in. "It's all right," she said, embracing me. "There's an outhouse. The water closet is a relic from the past."

"How fortunate it's already morning," I laughed. "No one will ever know that I'm too fainthearted to go to the outhouse in the dark."

Florinda gave me a strange look, then turned her gaze away, and at last said in a whisper, "What makes you think it's morning?"

"The sun woke me up a little while ago," I said, moving toward the window. Uncomprehendingly, I stared at the darkness outside.

Florinda's face brightened. She seemed to control herself, but then her shoulders shook with laughter as she pointed to the light bulb in the lamp standing behind the bed. I had mistaken the bright bulb for the sunlight.

"What makes you so sure you're awake?" she asked.

I turned to look at her and said, "My unbearable urge to go to the bathroom."

She took me by the arm and said, "Let me take you to the outhouse before you disgrace yourself."

"I'm not going anywhere until you tell me whether I'm awake or dreaming," I yelled.

"What a temper!" Florinda exclaimed, lowering her head until her forehead touched mine. Her eyes were wide. "You're dreaming-awake," she added, enunciating each word carefully.

In spite of my growing apprehension, I began to laugh. The sound of my laughter, which reverberated around the room like a distant echo, dispelled my anxiety. At that moment I was no longer concerned about whether I was awake or dreaming. All my attention was focused on reaching the toilet.

"Where is the outhouse?" I growled.

"You know where it is," Florinda said, folding her arms over her chest. "And you'll never reach it in time, unless you will yourself to be there. But don't bring the outhouse to your bed. That's called

131

lazy dreaming, the surest way to soil your bed. Go to the outhouse yourself in a flick of an eyelid."

To my utter horror, I couldn't reach the door when I tried to. My feet lacked the confidence to walk. Slowly and uncertainly, as if they were unable to decide which way to go, they moved, one foot ahead of the other. Resisting to accept that my feet were no longer under my command, I tried to speed up my movements by lifting, with my hands, one foot after the other.

Florinda didn't seem to care what was happening to me. Tears of frustration and self-pity welled up in my eyes as I stood rooted to the spot. My lips shaped the word *help*, but no sound came out of my mouth.

"What's the matter?" she asked as she took hold of one of my arms and gently pulled me down to the floor. She removed my heavy woolen socks and examined my feet; she now seemed genuinely concerned. I wanted to explain that my inability to move was due to my being emotionally exhausted. But hard as I tried, I couldn't formulate my thoughts into words. As I struggled to utter a sound, I noticed that something was wrong with my vision: my eyes were no longer able to focus. Florinda's face remained blurry and fuzzy no matter how hard I squeezed my eyes, regardless of how close I moved my face to hers.

"I know what's the matter with you," Florinda whispered in my ear. "You have to go to the outhouse. Do it! Will yourself there!"

I nodded emphatically. I knew that I was indeed dreaming-awake, or rather, that I was living in another reality that didn't yet fully belong to me but to which I had access through these people. Then I felt inexplicably at ease. And suddenly I was in the outhouse, not in a dreamed outhouse but in a real one.

It took me a long time to test my surroundings, to make sure this was the real thing. It was.

Then I was back in the room, but I didn't know how. Florinda said something flattering about my dreaming capacity. I paid little attention to her remarks, for I was distracted by the pile of blankets stacked against the wall. I hadn't noticed them upon awakening, yet I was certain I had seen them before.

My feeling of ease vanished quickly as I tried to recall where I had seen those blankets. My anguish grew. I didn't know any longer whether I was still in the same house I had arrived at earlier in the evening with Isidoro Baltazar or whether I was someplace else.

"Whose room is this?" I asked. "And who bundled me up with all these clothes?" It terrified me to hear my own voice.

Florinda stroked my hair and in a kind, soft voice said that for the time being this was my room. And that she had bundled me up so I wouldn't get cold. She explained that the desert is deceiving, especially at night.

She regarded me with an enigmatic expression, as though she were hinting at something else. And it disturbed me because her words gave me no clues about what she might be referring to. My thoughts reeled aimlessly. The key word, I decided, was *desert*. I hadn't known the witches' place was in the desert. We had arrived at it in such a roundabout way, I had failed to ascertain where exactly the house was located.

"Whose house is this, Florinda?" I asked.

She seemed to be wrestling with some deep problem, her expression changing from thoughtful to worried several times. "You're home," she finally said, her voice deep with emotion. Before I could remind her that she hadn't answered my question, she gestured for me to be silent and pointed a finger at the door.

Something whispered in the darkness outside. It could have been the wind and the leaves, but I knew it was neither. It was a soothing, familiar sound; it brought back to me the memory of the picnic. In particular, it brought back Mariano Aureliano's words: "I will blow you, as I blew the others, to the one person who now holds the myth in his hands."

The words rang in my ears; I turned to look, wondering if Mariano Aureliano had perhaps come into the room and was repeating them out loud this very instant.

Florinda nodded. She had read my mind. And her eyes, fixed on mine, were forcing me to acknowledge my understanding of his claim. At the picnic I hadn't given much thought to his statement; it had simply been too preposterous. Now I was so curious to find out who "the others" really were that I couldn't afford to let the topic of the conversation slip by.

"Isidoro Baltazar talked about some people who work with him," I began cautiously. "He said that they had been entrusted to him and that it was his sacred duty to help them. Are they the ones who . . . blew to him?" I asked hesitantly.

Florinda nodded her head affirmatively, a faint smile curling her lips as if she found my reluctance to mention the word *blew* amusing. "Those are the ones the old nagual blew to the new nagual; they are women, and they are like you."

"Like me?" I asked uncertainly. I wished I hadn't been so absorbed with my own puzzling changes of moods and feelings toward Isidoro Baltazar during the trip and had paid closer attention to all he had revealed about his world.

"In what way are those women like me?" I asked and then added, "Do you know them?"

"I've seen them," she said noncommittally.

"How many women have been blown to Isidoro Baltazar?" I asked with ill-concealed displeasure. Yet the mere thought of them was both exciting and alarming.

Florinda was positively gleeful at my reaction. "A few. And they don't resemble you physically, yet they are like you. What I mean is that they resemble one another the way my fellow sorceresses and I resemble one another," Florinda explained. "Weren't you, yourself, surprised at how much alike we looked when you first met us?"

Acknowledging my nod, she went on to say that what made her and her cohorts so alike—in spite of the obvious physical differences—was their unbiased commitment to the sorcerers' world. "We are drawn together by an affection that is as yet incomprehensible to you."

"I bet it is," I stated as cynically as I could. Then my curiosity and excitement about the women who had been blown to Isidoro Baltazar got the better of me. "When will I meet them?"

"When you find them," Florinda said. Her voice, though low, had an extraordinary force that all but silenced me for a moment.

"How can I find them if I don't know them? It's impossible."

"Not for a witch," she remarked casually. "As I already said, you don't resemble them physically, but the glow inside you is as bright as the glow inside them. You will recognize them by that glow." Her eyes were fixed on me intently, as if she could indeed see the glow inside me. "It's the glow of sorcerers." Her face was grave, her voice unusually low.

I wanted to make some impudent remark, but something in her manner alarmed me. "Can I see that glow?" I asked.

"We need the nagual for that," Florinda said and pointed to the nagual Mariano Aureliano, who was standing in the shadowy corner of the room. I hadn't noticed him at all, but I didn't find his sudden appearance in any way alarming.

Florinda told him what I wanted. He motioned me to follow him to the middle of the room. "I'll show you that glow," he said then squatted and, holding up both hands, gestured for me to get on his back.

"We are going for a piggyback ride?" I made no effort to conceal my disappointment. "Aren't you going to show me the glow of sorcerers?" Although I clearly remembered his words that true sorcery was not bizarre behavior, rituals, drugs, or incantations, I nevertheless expected a show, some demonstration of his power, such as mixing spells and simples over the fire.

Ignoring my disillusionment, Mariano Aureliano urged me to put my arms around his neck, lightly so as not to choke him.

"Don't you think I am a little too old to be carried around?" I cautioned him.

Mariano Aureliano's laughter gurgled up inside him, exploding with outrageous delight. In one swift motion he sprang to his feet. Tucking his arms behind my knees, he shifted me into a comfortable position and stepped out into the hall, but my head didn't hit the door frame.

He walked so fast and effortlessly I had the distinct sensation of floating down the long dark corridor. Curious, I glanced all around me. However, we moved too fast to catch any but brief glimpses of the house. A soft yet persistent scent permeated everything: a fragrance of orange blossoms and the freshness of cold air.

Outside, the yard was blurred by mist. All I was able to see was a uniform mass of dark silhouettes. Swirls of fog transformed every space, revealing and then blotting out strange shapes of trees and stones. We were not at the witches' house. I was sure of that.

I heard nothing except a rhythmical breathing. I couldn't tell if it was the nagual Mariano Aureliano's breathing or my own. The sound spread all over the yard. It made the leaves tremble, as if a wind were rustling through the branches. The trembling seeped into my body with every breath I took. It made me so dizzy I wrapped my arms tightly around his shoulders lest I lose consciousness. Before I had a chance to tell him what I was experiencing, the fog closed in around me, and I felt myself dissolve into nothingness.

"Rest your chin on the top of my head." The nagual Mariano Aureliano's voice came as if from a great distance. The words jolted me, for I had quite forgotten that I was riding on his back.

"Whatever you do, don't let go of me," he added with great urgency as he pushed me up on his back so my head was above his.

"What could possibly happen if I let go?" I asked in a tone that betrayed my growing apprehension. "I would just fall onto the ground, wouldn't I?" My voice had gotten terribly screechy.

Mariano Aureliano laughed softly but didn't answer. Leisurely, he walked up and down the extensive yard with light, soft steps, almost in a kind of dance. And then, for an instant, I had the distinct impression that we rose in the air; we became weightless. I felt that we actually traveled through the darkness for a fleeting moment, then I felt the solid ground through Mariano Aureliano's body. Whether the fog had lifted or whether we were in a different yard, I couldn't determine, but something had changed. Perhaps it was only the air; it was heavier, harder to breathe.

There was no moon, and the stars were faint, yet the sky shone as if it were lit from some faraway spot. Slowly, as if someone were outlining them in the air, the contours of trees became clear.

About five feet away, in front of a particularly tall and bushy zapote tree, Mariano Aureliano came to an abrupt halt. At the foot of that tree stood a group of people, perhaps twelve or fourteen. The long leaves, weighed down by the mist, shadowed their faces. A strange green light emanating from the tree made each person unnaturally vivid. Their eyes, their noses, their lips, all of their features gleamed in that green light, yet I could make out nothing of their faces. I didn't recognize any of them. I couldn't even determine whether they were males or females; they were simply people. "What are they doing?" I whispered into Mariano Aureliano's ear. "Who are they?"

"Keep your chin on the top of my head," he hissed.

I pressed my chin firmly against his head, fearing that if I pushed too hard my whole face would sink into his skull.

Hoping to recognize someone by his or her voice, I said good evening to them.

Fleeting smiles parted their lips. Instead of returning my greeting, they averted their faces. An odd sound came from amidst them. A sound that energized them, for they, too, like the tree, began to glow. Not a green light, but a golden brilliance that coalesced and shimmered until they all fused into one big golden ball that just hovered there under the tree.

Then the golden ball dissolved into patches of luminosity. Like giant glowworms they appeared and disappeared among the trees, sowing light and shadow in their passing.

"Remember that glow," Mariano Aureliano murmured. His voice echoed in my head. "It's the glow . . . of the surem."

A sudden gust of wind scattered his words. The wind was alive; it glowed against the darkness of the sky. It blew with great violence, with a strange ripping sound. Then the wind turned against me; I was certain it meant to annihilate me. I cried out in pain as a particularly icy gust seared my lungs. A coldness spread through my body until I felt myself grow stiff.

Whether it was Mariano Aureliano who had spoken or the wind itself, I couldn't tell. The wind roared in my ears, blotting out everything around me. Then it was inside my lungs. It wriggled like a living thing, eager to devour every cell in my body. I could feel myself collapse, and I knew I was going to die. But the roaring stopped. The silence was so sudden I heard it. I laughed out loud, thankful that I was still alive.

10

THE bed was big and comfortably soft. A golden radiance filled the room. Hoping to prolong this moment of well-being a bit longer, I closed my eyes and buried myself in sleepy bliss amidst fragrant linen sheets and subtly scented lavender pillow cases.

I could feel every muscle, every bone in my body tense as I remembered the night's events, disconnected fragments of some god-awful dream. There was no continuity, no linear sequence to all I had experienced during those interminable hours. I had awoken twice during the night, in different beds, in different rooms, even in a different house.

As if they had a life of their own, these disconnected images piled up and expanded, all at once, into a labyrinth that somehow I was able to comprehend all at once. That is, I perceived every event simultaneously. The sensation of those images growing out of my skull into an enormous, fanciful headdress was so real I jumped out of bed and dashed across the room to the steel and glass dresser. The three-paneled mirror was covered with rice paper. I tried to peel off a corner, but the paper clung to the glass like a skin.

The sight of the silver-backed hairbrush with its matching comb, the bottles of perfume, and the jars of cosmetics on the dresser had a soothing effect on me; I, too, would have arranged the bottles and jars by size, in a row, like tools. Somehow I knew that I was in Florinda's room, in the witches' house; this knowledge restored my sense of equilibrium.

Florinda's room was enormous; the bed and the dresser were the only pieces of furniture in it. They stood in opposite corners, away from the walls and at an angle, leaving a triangular space behind them. I pondered the arrangement of the bed and the dresser for quite some time but couldn't figure out whether it followed some kind of esoteric pattern, the significance of which eluded me, or whether it was merely the result of Florinda's aesthetic whim.

Curious as to where the three doors in the room led, I tried them all. The first one was locked from the outside. The second one opened to a small, rectangular-shaped walled-in patio. Puzzled, I stared at the sky, until it finally dawned on me that it was not morning, as I had assumed upon awakening, but late afternoon. I wasn't disturbed that I had slept the whole day; on the contrary, I was elated. Convinced that I am an insomniac, I am always overjoyed by my oversleeping spells.

The third door opened into the corridor. Anxious to find Isidoro Baltazar, I made my way to the living room; it was empty. There was something forbidding about the neat and straight manner in which the furniture was arranged. Nothing revealed that anyone had sat on the couch and the armchairs the night before. Even the cushions stood stiffly, as if at attention.

The dining room across the corridor looked equally forsaken, equally austere. Not a chair was out of place. Not a crumb, not a stain in the polished surface of the mahogany table, nothing betrayed that I had sat there last night with the nagual Mariano Aureliano and Mr. Flores and eaten dinner.

In the kitchen, separated from the dining room by an arched vestibule and a narrow hall, I found a jug, half filled with champurrado, and a covered plate with some sweet tamales. I was too hungry to bother with heating them. I poured myself a mugful of the thick chocolate and ate the three corn cakes directly from their corn-husk wrappings. Stuffed with pieces of pineapple, raisins, and slivered almonds, they were delicious.

It was inconceivable to me that I had been left alone in the house. Yet I couldn't ignore the stillness around me. It wasn't the comforting peace one is conscious of when people are purposely being quiet, but rather, it was the overwhelming soundlessness of a deserted place. The possibility that, indeed, I had been abandoned there made me choke on a piece of tamale.

On my way back to Florinda's room, I paused in front of every door I passed. "Anybody home?" I called out as I knocked repeatedly. There was no answer.

I was about to step outside when I distinctly heard someone ask, "Who is calling?" The voice was deep and raspy, but I couldn't tell whether it was a man or a woman who had spoken. I couldn't determine from which direction, let alone from which room, the voice had come.

I retraced my steps and called out again at the top of my voice whether anybody was home. Upon reaching the far end of the corridor, I hesitated for a moment in front of a closed door. I turned the doorknob, then quietly opened it a crack and sidled in.

With my eyes tightly shut, I reclined against the wall and waited for my heartbeat to normalize. Suppose someone caught me in here, I thought guiltily. But my curiosity outweighed any sense of wrongdoing as I breathed in the air of mystery, of enchantment, that permeated the room.

The heavy, dark curtains were drawn, and the only light came from a tall reading lamp. Its huge shade, fringed with tassels, cast a circle of yellow light on the chaise lounge by the window. At the very center of the room stood a four-poster bed; canopied and curtained, it dominated the space as if it were a throne. The bronze and wood-carved oriental figurines, ensconced on the four round tables in each corner, appeared to stand guard over the room like some celestial deities.

Books, papers, and magazines were piled on the drop-front French desk and on the chest of drawers. There was no mirror on the kidney-shaped dresser, and instead of a comb and brush, or bottles of perfume and cosmetics, a set of fragile-looking demitasses stood on the glass-topped surface. Strands of pearls, gold chains, rings, and brooches spilled from the delicate gold-rimmed cups like some abandoned treasure. I recognized two of the rings; I had seen them on Zoila's hand.

The inspection of the bed I reserved for last. Almost reverentially, as if indeed it were a throne, I pulled back the curtain and gasped with delight: the brightly colored pillows on the silky green bedspread made me think of wild flowers in a meadow.

And yet an involuntary shiver shook my body as I stood in the middle of the room. I couldn't help but feel that the warmth, the mystery, and the enchantment this room exuded were but an illusion.

The sensation of having stepped into some kind of a mirage was even more pronounced in the third room. It, too, seemed warm and friendly at first. The very air was tender and loving. Echoes of laughter seemed to bounce off the walls. However, this atmosphere of warmth was only a tenuous, fleeting impression, like the fading sunlight streaking through the glassless, gauze-curtained windows.

As in the other room, the bed dominated the space. It too was canopied and decorated with brightly colored pillows that had been tossed about with absentminded abandon.

Against one wall stood a sewing machine; it was an old one, a hand-painted treadle machine. Next to it was a tall bookcase. Instead of books, the shelves were stacked with bolts of the finest cottons, silks, and wool gabardine cloth, all neatly arranged by color and fabric.

Six different colored wigs, all stretched over staked gourds, were displayed on a low table under the window. Among them was the blond one I had seen Delia Flores wear and the dark, curly one Mariano Aureliano had pulled over my head outside the coffee shop in Tucson.

The fourth room was a bit further down from the others and across the hall. Compared to the other two, it gave the impression of being empty. The last afternoon sun rays, filtering through a latticed wall, lay on the floor like a carpet of light and shadows, a wavering square of rectangular patterns.

The few pieces of furniture were so artfully placed it made the space seem larger than it actually was. Low bookshelves with glass doors lined the walls. At the far end, in an alcove, stood a narrow bed. The white-and-grey-checkered blanket hung low and matched the shadows on the floor. The dainty rosewood secretaire with its delicate chair of ebonized rosewood with ormolu didn't detract from the overall sense of starkness of the room but rather enhanced it. I knew that it was Carmela's room.

I would have liked to check the titles of the books behind the glass panels, but my anxiety was too great. As if someone were chasing me, I dashed out into the corridor and down to the inside patio. I sat on one of the rush chairs; I was trembling and perspiring, yet my hands were icy cold. It wasn't guilt that had me shaking—I wouldn't have minded getting caught snooping around—but the alien, other-worldly quality these beautifully furnished rooms exuded. The stillness that clung about the walls was an unnatural stillness. It had nothing to do with the absence of its inhabitants but with the absence of feelings and emotions that usually permeate lived-in spaces.

Every time someone had referred to the women as sorceresses and witches, I had inwardly laughed; they neither acted nor looked as I expected witches to look and act—flamboyantly dramatic and sinister. But now I knew for certain that they were indeed different from other human beings. It frightened me that they were different in ways I couldn't understand, in ways I couldn't even conceive.

A soft, rasping sound put an end to my disturbing thoughts. Following the distinctly eerie noise, I tiptoed down the corridor, away from the bedrooms, toward the other end of the house. The rasping sound came from a room at the back of the kitchen. I crept up softly, only to have the sound die down the instant I pressed my ear against the door. It resumed as soon as I moved away. Puzzled, I once more pressed my ear to the door, and the rasping sound promptly ceased. I moved back and forth several times, and, as if the rasping sound were dependent on my doings, it either started or stopped.

Determined to find out who was hiding—or worse, who was purposely trying to frighten me—I reached for the doorknob. Unable to open the door, I fumbled for several minutes before I realized that it was locked and that the key had been left in the lock.

That someone dangerous might have been confined in that room, for a very good reason, only came to me once I was inside. An oppressive semidarkness clung about the heavy drawn curtains, like something alive that was luring the shadows of the entire house to this enormous room. The light grew dimmer; the shadows thickened around what appeared to be discarded pieces of furniture and peculiar-looking small and enormous figures made out of wood and metal.

The same rasping sound that had drawn me to this room broke the silence. Like felines, the shadows prowled about the room as if searching for prey. In frozen horror, I watched the curtain; it pulsated and breathed like a monster of my nightmares.

All of a sudden, the sound and the movement ceased; the motionless silence was even more frightening. I turned to leave, and the pulsating, rasping sound began again. Resolutely, I crossed the room and pulled back the curtain. I laughed out loud upon discovering the broken glass pane in the French door. The wind had been alternately sucking and blowing the curtain through the jagged gap.

The fading afternoon light streaming through the half-opened curtain rearranged the shadows in the room and revealed an oval-shaped mirror on the wall, half hidden by one of the odd-looking metal figures. I squeezed myself between the sculpture and the wall and gazed rapturously into the old Venetian glass; it was blurry and misty with age, and it distorted my image so grotesquely that I ran out of the room.

I went outside the house, through the back door. The wide clearing behind the house was deserted. The sky was still bright, but the tall fruit trees circling the grounds had already turned the color of twilight. A flock of crows passed overhead; their black flapping wings extinguished the brightness in the sky, and night swiftly descended into the yard.

With a feeling of utter dejection and despair, I sat on the ground and wept. The harder I cried, the more pleasure I felt from lamenting at the top of my voice.

The sound of a rake jolted me out of my self-pity. I looked up and saw a slight person raking leaves toward a small fire in the back of the clearing.

"Esperanza!" I cried out, rushing toward her, only to stop abruptly upon realizing that it wasn't her but a man. "I'm sorry," I mumbled apologetically. "I mistook you for someone else." I held out my hand and introduced myself. I tried not to stare at him, but I couldn't help it; I wasn't quite sure that he wasn't Esperanza disguised as a man.

He put his hand in mine, pressing it softly, and said, "I'm the caretaker." He didn't tell me his name.

His hand felt as brittle as a bird's wing in mine. He was a thin, ancient-looking man. His face was birdlike, too, aquiline and keeneyed. His white hair was tufted and feathery. It wasn't only his slight frame and birdlike appearance that reminded me of Esperanza but also the wrinkled, expressionless face and the eyes, shiny and limpid as those of a child, and the teeth, small and square and very white.

"Do you know where Florinda is?" I asked. He shook his head and I added, "Do you know where any of the others are?"

He was silent for a long moment, and then as though I hadn't asked him anything, he repeated that he was the caretaker. "I take care of everything."

"You do?" I asked, eyeing him suspiciously. He was so frail and puny-looking he didn't seem capable of taking care of anything, including himself.

"I take care of everything," he repeated, smiling sweetly as if thus he could erase my doubts. He was about to say something else, but instead he chewed his lower lip thoughtfully for a moment, then turned around and went on raking the leaves into a little pile with neat, deft, quick movements.

"Where is everyone?" I asked.

Resting his chin on his hand, cupped over the end of the rake handle, he glanced at me absently. Then grinning inanely, he looked all around him, as though at any moment someone might materialize from behind one of the fruit trees.

Sighing loudly and impatiently, I turned to leave.

He cleared his throat, and in a voice that was wavering and hoarse with old age said, "The old nagual took Isidoro Baltazar to the mountains." He didn't look at me; his eyes were focused somewhere in the distance. "They'll be back in a couple of days."

"Days!" I screeched indignantly. "Are you sure you heard them correctly?" Dismayed that my worst fear had come true, I could only mumble, "How could he have left me here all by myself?"

"They left last night," the old man said, pulling back a leaf that the wind had blown away from the pile in front of him.

"That's impossible," I contradicted him forcefully. "We only got here last night. Late last night," I stressed.

Indifferent to my assertively rude tone and to my presence, the old man set fire to the little pile of leaves in front of him.

"Didn't Isidoro Baltazar leave a message for me?" I asked, squatting beside him. "Didn't he leave me a note or something?" I felt an impulse to shout, but for some reason I didn't dare. Some mystifying aspect of the old man's appearance disconcerted me. The thought that he was Esperanza in disguise still nagged me.

"Did Esperanza go with them to the mountains?" I asked. My voice trembled because suddenly I was seized by a desperate desire to laugh. Short of pulling down his pants and showing me his genitals, there was nothing he could do to convince me that he was indeed a man.

"Esperanza is in the house," he murmured, his attention fixed on the little pile of burning leaves. "She's in the house with the others."

"Don't be ridiculous; she's not in the house," I contradicted him rudely. "No one is in the house. I've been searching for them the whole afternoon. I checked every room."

"She's in the little house," the old man repeated obstinately, watching me as intently as he had watched the burning leaves. The glint of mischief in his eyes made me want to kick him.

"What little . . ." My voice faded as I remembered the other house, the one I had seen upon our arrival. It actually caused me an intense physical pain to think of that place.

"You could have told me right away that Esperanza is in the little house," I said peevishly. Surreptitiously, I glanced all around me, but I couldn't see the place. The tall trees and the wall beyond hid it from view. "I'm going to see if Esperanza is indeed there as you claim," I said, rising.

The old man rose, too, and turning toward the nearest tree, he reached for an oil lamp and a burlap sack hanging from a low branch. "I'm afraid I can't let you go there by yourself," he said.

"I don't see why not," I countered, piqued. "Perhaps you're not aware of it, but I'm Florinda's guest. I was taken to the little house last night." I paused for a moment, then added for good measure, "I was there for sure."

He listened carefully, but his face looked doubtful. "It's tricky to get there," he warned me at last. "I have to prepare the path for you. I have to . . ." He seemed to catch himself in the middle of a thought he didn't want to express. He shrugged, then repeated that he had to prepare the path for me.

"What's there to prepare?" I asked irritably. "Do you have to cut through the chaparral with a machete?"

"I'm the caretaker. I prepare the path," he repeated obstinately and sat on the ground to light the oil lamp. For an instant it guttered in the air, then burned strongly. His features appeared almost fleshless, unwrinkled, as if the light had smoothed away the mark of time. "As soon as I'm done with burning these leaves, I'll take you there myself."

"I'll help you," I offered. Clearly, the man was senile and needed to be humored. I followed him around the clearing and helped him gather the leaves into little piles, which he promptly burned. As soon as the ashes had cooled, he swept them into the burlap sack. The sack was lined with plastic. It was this particular detail—the plastic lining—that brought back a half-forgotten childhood memory.

As we swept the heaps of ashes into the sack, I told him that as a small child, living in a village near Caracas, I was often awakened by the sound of a rake. I used to sneak out of bed and, cat-footed, creep down the corridor, past my parents' and brothers' rooms into the parlor, which faced the plaza. Heedful of the creaking hinges, I used to open the wooden panels covering the windows and squeeze through the wrought iron bars. The old man in charge of keeping the plaza clean was always there to greet me with a toothless smile, and together we used to rake into little piles the leaves that had fallen during the night—any other kind of refuse was put into trash cans. We burned these piles, and as soon as the ashes had cooled, we swept them into a silk-lined burlap sack. He claimed that the water fairies, dwelling in a sacred stream in the nearby mountains, turned the ashes into gold dust.

"Do you also know of fairies who change ashes into gold dust?" I asked, seeing how delighted the caretaker was with my story.

He didn't answer but giggled with such pleasure and abandon I couldn't help but laugh, too. Before I knew it, we had reached the last little pile of ashes, next to a recessed, arched doorway built into the wall; the narrow wooden gate stood wide open.

Across the chaparral, almost hidden in shadows, was the other house. No light shone through the windows, and it appeared to be shifting away from me. Wondering whether the house was but a figment of my imagination, a place remembered in a dream, I blinked repeatedly and rubbed my eyes. Something was wrong, I decided as I recalled walking up to the witches' house the night before with Isidoro Baltazar. The smaller house had stood to the right of the larger one. How then, I asked myself, could I now see the place from the witches' backyard? In an effort to orient myself, I moved this way and that, but I couldn't get my bearings. I bumped into the old man, who was squatting before the pile of ashes, and fell over him.

With astounding agility he rose and helped me up. "You're full of ashes," he said, wiping my face with the folded cuff of his khaki shirt.

"There it is!" I cried out. Sharply focused, silhouetted against the sky, the elusive house appeared to be only a few steps away. "There it is," I repeated, jumping up and down, as if by doing so I could hold the house in place, detain it in time. "That's the true house of the witches," I added, standing still in front of the old man so he could proceed with wiping the ashes off my face. "The big house is but a front."

"The house of the witches," the old man said slowly, savoring his words. Then he cackled, seemingly amused. He swept the last of the ashes into his burlap sack, then motioned me to follow him through the gate.

Two orange trees grew on the other side of the gate, away from the wall. A cool breeze rustled through the blooming branches, but the flowers didn't stir; they didn't fall to the ground. Against the dark foliage, the blossoms looked carved, as though they had been made of milky quartz. Like sentinels, the two trees stood guard over the narrow path. The path was white and very straight, like a line that had been drawn on the landscape with a ruler.

The old man handed me the oil lamp, then scooped out a handful of ashes from his burlap sack and poured them from one hand to the other—as though he were weighing them—before he sprinkled them onto the ground.

"Don't ask any questions and do as I say," he said. His voice was no longer hoarse; it had an airy quality; it sounded energetic and convincing. He bent slightly, and walking backwards, he let the rest of the ashes trickle directly from his burlap sack onto the narrow trail. "Keep your feet on the line of ashes," he admonished. "If you don't, you'll never reach the house."

I coughed to hide my nervous laughter. Holding out my arms, I balanced on the narrow line of ashes as if it were a tightrope. Each time we stopped for the old man to catch his breath, I turned to look at the house we had just left; it seemed to be receding into the distance. And the one in front of us didn't seem to get any closer. I tried to convince myself that it was merely an optical illusion, yet I had the vague certainty that I would never make it on my own to either house.

As if sensing my discomfort, the old man patted my arm reassuringly. "That's why I'm preparing the path." He looked into his burlap sack and added, "It won't be long now before we'll get there. Just remember to keep your feet on the line of ashes. If you do, you'll be able to move back and forth safely, anytime."

My mind told me that the man was a lunatic. My body, however, knew that I was lost without him and his ashes. I was so absorbed in keeping my feet on the faint line, it took me by surprise when we finally stood in front of the door.

The old man took the oil lamp from my hand, cleared his throat, then rapped lightly on the carved panel with his knuckles. He didn't wait for an answer but pushed the door open and went inside.

"Don't go so fast!" I cried out, afraid to be left behind. I followed him into a narrow vestibule. He left the oil lamp on a low table. Then without a word or a backward glance, he opened a door at the far end and disappeared into the darkness.

Guided by some vague memory, I stepped into the dimly lit room and went directly to the mat on the floor. There was no doubt in my mind now that I had been there the night before, that I had slept on that very mat. What I wasn't so sure of was how I got to that room in the first place. That Mariano Aureliano had carried me on his back across the chaparral was vivid in my mind. I also was certain that I had woken up in that room—before being carried over by the old nagual—with Clara sitting beside me on the mat.

Confident that within moments all would be explained to me, I sat on the mat. The light in the oil lamp flickered and then went out. I sensed, rather than saw, things and people moving around me. I heard a murmur of voices, intangible sounds coming from every corner. Out of all these noises, I recognized a familiar rustling of skirts and a soft giggle.

"Esperanza?" I whispered, "God! I am so glad to see you!" Although it was her I expected to see, I was nevertheless stunned when she sat beside me on the mat. Timidly, I touched her arm.

"It's me," she assured me.

Only after hearing her voice was I convinced that it was indeed Esperanza and not the caretaker who had exchanged his khaki pants and shirt for the rustling petticoats and the white dress. And once I felt the soothing touch of her hand on my face, all thoughts of the caretaker vanished.

"How did I get here?" I asked.

"The caretaker brought you here," she laughed. "Don't you remember?" She turned toward the low table and relit the oil lamp.

"I'm talking about last night," I clarified. "I know I was here. I woke up on this mat. Clara was here with me. And then Florinda was here, and the other women . . ." My voice trailed off as I remembered that I had awoken afterward in the living room of the other house and then again on a bed. I shook my head, as if I could thus bring some order to my memories. Forlornly, I gazed at Esperanza, hoping she would fill in the gaps. I told her of the difficulties I was having remembering the night's events in sequential order.

"You shouldn't have any problems," she said. "Get in the track of dreams; you're dreaming-awake now."

"You mean that I am asleep now, this very instant?" I asked mockingly. I leaned toward her and asked, "Are you asleep, too?"

"We are not asleep," she repeated, enunciating her words carefully. "You and I are dreaming-awake." She held up her hands in a helpless gesture. "I told you what to do last year. Remember?"

A rescuing thought suddenly occurred to me, as if someone had just whispered it in my ear: when in doubt, one must separate the two tracks, the track for ordinary affairs and the track for dreams, since each has a different state of awareness. I felt elated, for I knew that the first track one should test is the track of dreams; if the situation at hand doesn't fit that track, then one is not dreaming.

My elation quickly vanished when I tried to test the track for dreams. I had no inkling of how to go about it or of what the track for dreams was, for that matter. And worse, I couldn't remember who had told me about it.

"I did," Esperanza said just behind me. "You have moved a great deal in the realm of dreams. You nearly remembered what I told you last year, the day after the picnic. I said to you then that, when in doubt about whether you are in a dream or whether you are awake, you should test the track where dreams run on—meaning the awareness we have in dreams—by feeling the thing you are in contact with. If you are dreaming, your feeling comes back to you as an echo. If it doesn't come back, then you are not dreaming."

Smiling, she pinched my thigh and said, "Try it on this mat you're lying on. Feel it with your buttocks; if the feeling returns, then you're dreaming."

There was no feeling returning to my numbed buttocks. In fact, I was so numb that I didn't feel the mat. It seemed to me I was lying on the rough tiles of the floor.

I had a strong urge to point out to her that it should be the opposite—if the feeling returns, then one is awake—but I controlled myself in time. For I knew without any doubt that what she meant by "the feeling returning to us" had nothing to do with our known, agreed-upon knowledge of what feeling is. The distinction between being awake and dreaming-awake still eluded me, yet I was certain that its meaning had nothing to do with our ordinary way of understanding awareness.

Right then, however, words came out of my mouth without any control on my part. I said, "I know that I am dreaming-awake, and that's that." I sensed that I was near a new, deeper level of understanding, and yet I could not quite grasp it. "What I would like to know is, when did I fall asleep?" I asked.

"I've already told you, you're not asleep. You are dreaming-awake."

I began to laugh involuntarily, in a quiet, utterly nervous manner. She didn't seem to notice or to care. "When did the transition occur?" I asked.

"When the caretaker was making you cross the chaparral and you had to concentrate on keeping your feet on the ashes."

"He must have hypnotized me!" I exclaimed, in a not altogether pleasant voice. I began to talk incoherently, entangling myself in words without quite succeeding in making sense, until finally I was weeping and denouncing them all.

Esperanza watched me silently, her eyebrows lifted, her eyes wide open with surprise.

I was immediately ashamed of my outburst, but at the same time I was glad I had spoken, for a momentary relief, the kind that comes after a confrontation, washed over me.

"Your confusion," she continued, "originates with your facility to move from one state of awareness into the other with great ease. If you had struggled, like everybody else does, to attain smooth transitions, then you would know that dreaming-awake is not just hypnosis." She paused for an instant, then finished softly, "Dreaming-awake is the most sophisticated state humans can attain."

She stared off into the room as if a clearer explanation might suddenly be brought to her by someone hiding in the shadows. Then she turned to me and asked, "Did you eat your little food?"

Her change of subject took me by surprise, and I began to stammer. Once I recovered, I told her that I had indeed eaten the sweet tamales. "I was so hungry, I didn't bother to heat them up; they were delicious."

Idly playing with her shawl, Esperanza asked me to give her an account of what I had done since I awoke in Florinda's room.

As if I had been given a truth-telling potion, I blurted out more than I intended to reveal. But Esperanza didn't seem to mind my snooping around the women's rooms. She wasn't impressed with my knowing to whom each room belonged.

What interested her to no end, however, was my encounter with the caretaker. With a smile of unmistakable glee on her face, she listened as I told my tale of confusing the man with her. When I mentioned that at one point I considered asking him to pull down his pants so I could check his genitals, she doubled up on the mat, shrieking with laughter.

She leaned against me and whispered suggestively in my ear, "I'll put you at ease." There was a wicked gleam in her eyes as she added, "I'll show you mine."

"There is no need to, Esperanza," I tried to ward her off. "I don't doubt that you are a woman."

"One can never be too sure what one is," she casually dismissed my words. Oblivious to my embarrassment—caused not so much by her imminent nudity but by the thought that I had to look at her old, wrinkled body—she lay down on the mat and with great finesse slowly lifted her skirts.

My curiosity won out over my embarrassment. I stared at her, open-mouthed. She had no panties on. She had no pubic hair. Her body was incredibly young, the flesh strong and firm, the muscles delicately delineated. She was all one color, an even, copperish pink. There were no stretch marks on her skin, no ruptured veins: nothing marred the smoothness of her stomach and legs.

I reached out to touch her, as if needing to reassure myself that her silky, smooth-looking skin was real, and she opened the lips of her vagina with her fingers. I averted my face, not so much from embarrassment as from my conflicting emotions. Nudity, whether male or female, wasn't the issue. I had grown up quite freely at home; no one was particularly careful to avoid being seen naked. While in school in England, I had been invited one summer to spend

152

a couple of weeks in Sweden at a friend's house by the sea. The whole family belonged to a nudist colony, and they all worshiped the sun with every bit of their naked skin.

Seeing Esperanza naked before me was different. I was aroused in a most peculiar manner. I had never really focused on a woman's sexual organs. Of course, I had examined myself thoroughly in the mirror and from every possible angle. I had also seen pornographic movies, which I had not only disliked but had found offensive as well. Seeing Esperanza so intimately was a shattering experience, for I had always taken my sexual responses for granted. I had thought that as a woman I could only get aroused with a male. My overwhelming desire to jump on top of her took me completely by surprise and was counterbalanced by the fact that I didn't have a penis.

When Esperanza suddenly rose from the mat and took off her blouse I gasped out loud, then stared at the floor until the feverish, tingling sensation in my face and neck subsided.

"Look at me!" Esperanza demanded impatiently. Her eyes were bright; her cheeks were flushed. She was completely naked. Her body was slight, yet bigger and stronger looking than when dressed. Her breasts were full and pointed.

"Touch them!" she commanded in a soft, alluring tone.

Her words echoed around the room like a disembodied sound, a mesmerizing rhythm that swelled into a throb in the air, a pulse of sound felt rather than heard, which little by little tightened and quickened until it beat fast and hard, like the rhythm of my own heart.

Then all I heard and felt was Esperanza's laughter.

"Is the caretaker hiding in here, by any chance?" I asked when I could talk. I was suddenly suspicious and guilty about my daring.

"I hope not!" she cried out with such an air of dismay that it made me laugh.

"Where is he?" I asked.

Her eyes opened wide, then she grinned as though she were going to laugh. But she wiped the mirth from her face and in a serious tone said that the caretaker was somewhere on the grounds and that he took care of both houses, but he didn't go around spying on anybody.

"Is he really the caretaker?" I asked, trying to sound skeptical. "I don't want to malign him, but he really doesn't look capable of taking care of anything."

Esperanza giggled then said that his frailness was deceptive. "He is very capable," she assured me. "You have to be careful with him; he likes young girls, especially blond ones." She leaned closer and, as if afraid we might be overheard, whispered in my ear, "Did he make a pass at you?"

"Heavens no!" I defended him. "He was exquisitely polite and helpful. It's just that . . ." My voice trailed off into a whisper, and my attention began to wander in an odd sort of way to the furniture in the room, which I couldn't see because the low-burning oil lamp cast more shadows than light on my surroundings.

When I finally managed to focus my attention back on her, I was no longer concerned with the caretaker. All I could think of, with a persistence I couldn't shake off, was why Isidoro Baltazar had left for the mountains without letting me know, without leaving me a note.

"Why would he leave me like that?" I asked, turning to Esperanza. "He must have told someone when he'll return." Seeing her all-knowing smirk, I added belligerently, "I'm sure you know what's going on."

"I don't," she insisted, quite incapable of understanding my plight. "I don't concern myself with such things. And neither should you. Isidoro Baltazar is gone, and that's that. He'll be back in a couple of days, in a couple of weeks. Who knows? It all depends on what happens in the mountains."

"It all depends?" I shrieked. I found her lack of sympathy and understanding abominable. "What about me?" I demanded. "I can't stay here for weeks."

"Why not?" Esperanza inquired innocently.

I regarded her as if she were demented, then blurted out that I had nothing to wear, that there was nothing for me to do here. My list of complaints was endless; they came pouring out until I was exhausted.

"I simply have to go home, be in my normal milieu," I finished. I felt the inevitable tears and did my best to suppress them.

"Normal?" Esperanza repeated the word slowly, as though she were tasting it. "You can leave any time you wish. No one is holding you back. It can easily be arranged to get you to the border where you can catch a Greyhound bus bound for Los Angeles."

I nodded, not trusting myself to speak. I didn't want that either. I didn't know what I wanted, but the thought of leaving was unbearable. I somehow knew that if I left I would never find these people again, not even Isidoro Baltazar in Los Angeles. I began to weep uncontrollably. I wouldn't have been able to put it into words, but the bleakness of a life, of a future without them, was unbearable to me.

I didn't notice Esperanza leaving the room, and I didn't notice her coming back. I wouldn't have noticed anything if it wasn't for the delicious aroma of hot chocolate wafting under my nose.

"You'll feel better after eating," she assured me, placing a tray in my lap. Smiling slowly and affectionately, she sat beside me and confided that there is nothing like chocolate to take away one's sadness.

I couldn't agree with her more. I took a few hesitant sips and ate several of the buttered, rolled tortillas. I told her that although I didn't really know her or any of her friends, I couldn't conceive of not ever seeing them again. I confessed that I felt a freedom and an ease with her and her group that I had never encountered anywhere else before. It was a strange feeling, I explained, part physical, part psychological, and wholly defiant of analysis. I could describe it only as a sense of well-being or a certainty that I had finally found a place where I belonged.

Esperanza knew exactly what it was I was trying to express. She said that having been part of the sorcerers' world even for a short time was addictive. It wasn't the amount of time, she stressed, but the intensity of the encounters that mattered. "And your encounters have been very intense," she said.

"They have?" I asked.

Esperanza lifted her eyebrows with sincere surprise, then rubbed her chin in an exaggerated attitude, as though she were deliberating on a problem that had no solution. After a long silence, she finally pronounced, "You will walk lighter after you fully realize that there is no going back to your old life." Her voice, though low, had an extraordinary force. Her eyes held mine for a moment, and I knew in that instant what her words meant.

"Nothing will ever be the same for me again," I said softly.

Esperanza nodded. "You'll return to the world, but not to your world, to your old life," she said, rising from the mat with the abrupt majesty small people command. She rushed toward the door, only to come to a sudden halt. "It's wildly exciting to do something without knowing why we are doing it," she said, turning to look at me. "And it's even more exciting to set out to do something without knowing what the end result will be."

I couldn't disagree with her more. "I need to know what I'm doing," I declared. "I need to know what I'm getting into."

She sighed and held up her hands in comical deprecation. "Freedom is terribly frightening." She spoke harshly, and before I had a chance to respond, she added gently, "Freedom requires spontaneous acts. You have no idea what it is to abandon yourself spontaneously . . ."

"Everything I do is spontaneous," I interjected. "Why do you think I am here? Do you think I deliberated much whether I should come or not?"

She returned to the mat and stood looking down at me for a long moment before she said, "Of course you didn't deliberate about it. But your acts of spontaneity are due to a lack of thought rather than to an act of abandon." She stomped her foot to prevent me from interrupting her again. "A real spontaneous act is an act in which you abandon yourself completely but only after profound deliberation," she went on. "An act where all the pros and cons have been taken into consideration and duly discarded, for you expect nothing, you regret nothing. With acts of that nature, sorcerers beckon freedom."

"I'm not a sorcerer," I mumbled under my breath, pulling at the hem of her dress to prevent her from leaving. But she made it clear that she had no interest in continuing our conversation.

I followed her outside, across the clearing, to the path that led to the other house.

As the caretaker had done earlier, she, too, urged me to keep my feet on the line of ashes. "If you don't," she admonished, "you'll fall into the abyss."

156

"Abyss?" I repeated uncertainly, glancing all around me at the mass of dark chaparral extending on either side of us.

A light breeze sprung up. Voices and whispers rose from a dark mass of shadows. Instinctively, I held on to Esperanza's skirt.

"Can you hear them?" she asked, turning to face me.

"Who am I supposed to hear?" I murmured hoarsely.

Esperanza moved closer, then, as if afraid we might be overheard, she whispered in my ear, "Surems of another time; they use the wind to wander across the desert, forever awake."

"You mean ghosts?"

"There are no ghosts," she said with finality and started walking again.

I made sure that my feet stayed on the line of ashes, and I didn't let go of her skirt until she came to an abrupt halt in the middle of the patio of the big house. For an instant she hesitated, as though she couldn't decide to which part of the house she ought to take me. Then she went up and down the various corridors and turned corners until finally we stepped into an immense room that had escaped my earlier exploration of the house. The walls were lined to the ceiling with books. At one end of the room stood a sturdy, long, wooden table; at the other end hung a white, flouncy, handwoven hammock.

"What a magnificent room!" I exclaimed. "Whose is it?"

"Yours," Esperanza offered graciously. She went to the wooden chest standing by the door and opened it. "The nights are cold," she warned, handing me three thick woolen blankets.

"You mean I can sleep in here?" I asked excitedly. My whole body shivered with pleasure as I matted the hammock with the blankets and lowered myself into it. As a child, I had often slept in one. Sighing with contentment, I rocked myself back and forth, then pulled in my legs and stretched out luxuriously. "Knowing how to sleep in a hammock is like knowing how to ride a bicycle; one never forgets how," I said to her. But there was no one to hear me. She had left without my noticing it.

11

I TURNED off the light and lay very still in my hammock, lulled by the noises of the house, strange creaking sounds and the trickling of water from an earthenware filter standing outside my door.

Abruptly, I sat up as the unmistakable sound of footsteps echoed along the corridor. "Who could it be at this hour?" I thought. I tiptoed across the room and pressed my ear against the door. The footsteps were heavy. My heart beat fast and loud as the footsteps came closer. They stopped in front of my door. The knock was urgent, and although I was expecting it, it nonetheless startled me. I jumped back, knocking over a chair.

"Did you have a nightmare?" Florinda asked, stepping into the room. She left the door half open, and the light from the corridor shone inside. "I thought you would be happy to hear the sound of my steps," she said mockingly, smiling at me. "I didn't want to sneak up on you." She straightened up the chair and draped a pair of khaki pants and a shirt over the backrest. "Compliments of the caretaker. He says you can keep them."

"Keep them?" I repeated, eyeing the garments suspiciously. They looked clean and ironed. "What's wrong with my jeans?"

"You'll be more comfortable in these pants during the long drive to Los Angeles," Florinda said.

"But I don't want to leave!" I cried out in alarm. "I'm staying here until Isidoro Baltazar returns."

Florinda laughed, then, seeing that I was about to weep, she said, "Isidoro Baltazar is back, but you're welcome to stay longer if you wish."

"Oh, no, I don't," I blurted out. The anxiety I had felt for the past two days was all but forgotten. So were all the questions I had wanted to ask Florinda. All I could think of was that Isidoro Baltazar was back. "Can I see him now?" I asked.

"I'm afraid you can't." Florinda stopped me from leaving the room.

For a moment her statement didn't register. I stared at her un-comprehendingly, and she repeated that it wasn't possible to see the new nagual tonight.

"Why not?" I asked, bewildered. "I'm sure he would want to see me."

"I'm sure he would," she readily agreed. "But he is sound asleep, and you can't wake him up." It was such a fierce refusal that all I could do was stare at her, speechless.

Florinda looked at the floor for a long time, then gazed up at me. Her expression was sad. For an instant I believed she would relent and take me to see Isidoro Baltazar. Instead, she repeated with sharp finality, "I'm afraid you can't see him tonight." Hastily, as if afraid she might still change her mind, she embraced and kissed me, and then left the room. She switched off the light outside, then turned from the shadows of the corridor to look at me and said, "Go to sleep now."

Tossing and turning, I lay awake for hours. Close to dawn I finally got up and put on the clothes Florinda had brought me. They fit me well, except for the pants, which I had to cinch in at the waist with a piece of string—I had no belt with me.

Shoes in hand, I stole down the corridor, past the caretaker's room, to the back entrance. Mindful of the creaking hinges, I opened the door carefully and only a crack. It was still dark outside, yet a soft, radiant blue was spreading across the eastern sky. I ran to the arched doorway built into the wall, stopping momentarily by the two trees outside it that guarded the path. The air was heavy with the fragrance of orange blossoms. Whatever lingering doubts I might have had about crossing the chaparral were dispelled as I discovered that fresh ashes had been strewn on the ground. Without another thought I dashed to the other house.

The door was ajar. I didn't go in right away. I crouched beneath a window and waited for some kind of a sound. I didn't have to wait long before I heard a loud snoring. I listened for a while and then went inside. Guided by that distinct snoring sound, I went directly to the room at the back of the house. In the darkness, I could hardly make out the sleeping form on the straw mat, yet I had no doubt that it was Isidoro Baltazar. Fearing that he might be startled if I were to wake him too suddenly, I returned to the front room and sat on the couch. I was so excited I could not sit still. I was beside myself with joy thinking that any moment now he would wake up. Twice I tiptoed back into the room and looked at him. He had turned in his sleep and was no longer snoring.

I must have dozed off on the couch. I sensed through my fitful sleep that someone stood in the room. I half roused to murmur, "I'm waiting for Isidoro Baltazar to wake up," but I knew I had made no sound. I made a conscious effort to sit up. I swayed dizzily before I could focus my eyes on the man standing beside me. It was Mariano Aureliano. "Is Isidoro Baltazar still asleep?" I asked him.

The old nagual gazed at me for a long time. Wondering whether I was dreaming, I boldly reached for his hand, only to drop it abruptly. It burnt as if it were on fire.

He raised his brows, seemingly surprised by my actions. "You won't be able to see Isidoro Baltazar until the morning." He spoke slowly, as if it cost him a great effort to enunciate the words.

Before I had a chance to say that it was almost morning, that I would wait for Isidoro Baltazar on the couch, I felt Mariano Aureliano's burning hand on my back, pushing me across the threshold.

"Go back to your hammock."

There was a sudden rush of wind. I turned around to protest, but Mariano Aureliano was no longer there. The wind reverberated in my head like a deep gong. The sound grew softer and softer until it was but a bare vibration. I opened my mouth to prolong the last faint echoes.

It was midmorning when I awoke in my hammock, wearing the clothes Florinda had brought me. Automatically, almost without thought, I went outside, across the clearing to the little house. The door was locked. I knocked repeatedly. I called out, but there was no answer. I tried to force the windows open but they too were locked. I was so shaken I was on the verge of tears. I ran down the hill to the small clearing beside the road, the only spot where a car could be parked. Isidoro Baltazar's van was not there. I walked along the dirt road for quite some time, looking for fresh tire tracks. There were none.

More confused than ever, I returned to the house. Knowing that it would be useless to look for the women in their rooms, I stood in the middle of the inside patio and yelled for Florinda at the top of my voice. There was no sound, except for the echo of my own voice settling around me.

No matter how many times I reviewed what Florinda had said, I couldn't come up with a satisfying answer. The only thing I could be sure of was that Florinda had come to my room in the middle of the night to bring me the clothes I was wearing. Her visit, and her statement that Isidoro Baltazar was back, must have triggered a vivid dream in me.

To stop myself from speculating why I was alone in the house— not even the caretaker seemed to be about—I began to mop the floors. Cleaning always had a soothing effect on me. I was done with all the rooms, including the kitchen, when I heard the distinct sound of a Volkswagen engine. I ran down the hill and flung myself at Isidoro Baltazar even before he got out of the van, almost jerking him to the ground.

"I still can't get over it," he laughed, putting his arms around me in a tight embrace. "You were the one the nagual told me so much about. Do you know that I nearly passed out when they greeted you?"

He didn't wait for my comment but hugged me again and, laughing, lifted me off the ground. Then, as if some restraint had broken free within him, he began to talk nonstop. He said that he had known about me for a year; the nagual had told him that he was entrusting a weird girl to him. The nagual described that girl metaphorically as "twelve o'clock in the morning of a clear day which is neither windy nor calm, neither cold nor hot, but alternates between all those, driving one nuts."

Isidoro Baltazar confessed that being the pompous ass that he was, he knew instantaneously that the nagual was referring to his girlfriend.

"Who is your girlfriend?" I cut him short.

He made a sharp movement with his hand, positively displeased by my words. "This is not a story of facts," he snapped. "This is a story of ideas. So you would see how idiotic I am." His annoyance quickly gave way to a brilliant smile. "I actually believed I could find out for myself who that girl was." He paused for an instant, then added softly, "I've even involved a married woman with children in my search."

He heaved a deep sigh then grinned and said, "The moral of my story is that in the sorcerers' world one has to cancel out the ego or it is curtains for us, for in that world, there is no way for average persons like ourselves to predict anything."

Then, seeing that I was weeping, he held me off at arm's length and gazed at me anxiously. "What is the matter, nibelunga?"

"Nothing really," I laughed in between my sobs, drying my tears. "I don't have an abstract mentality that can worry about the world of abstract stories," I added cynically and in as hard a tone as I could muster. "I worry about the here and now. You've got no idea what I've been through in this house."

"Of course, I have a very good idea," he retorted with deliberate harshness. "I've been at it for years." He regarded me with an inquisitor's eye and asked, "What I want to know is, why didn't you tell me you had been with them already?"

"I was about to, but I didn't feel it was important," I mumbled in confusion. Then my voice acquired a firm and steady ring as words poured involuntarily out of me. "It turns out that meeting them was the only important thing I have ever done." To hide my surprise, I immediately began to complain that I had been left in the house all by myself.

"I didn't have a chance to let you know that I was off to the mountains with the nagual," he whispered with a sudden irrepressible smile.

"I forgot all about that," I assured him. "I'm talking about today. This morning when I awoke, I expected you to be here. I was certain you had spent the night in the little house, sleeping on a straw mat. When I couldn't find you, I panicked."

Seeing his puzzled face, I told him of Florinda's midnight visit, of my subsequent dream, of finding myself alone in the house upon awakening this morning. I sounded incoherent. My thoughts and words were all mixed up. However, I couldn't stop talking.

"There are so many things I cannot accept," I said, finally putting an end to my diatribe. "Yet I cannot refute them either."

Isidoro Baltazar didn't say a word. He kept staring at me as if expecting me to continue, his eyebrows raised in an inquiring, mocking arch. His face was thin and drawn and the color of smoke. His skin exuded a strange coolness and a faint scent of earth, as if he had spent his days underground in a cave.

All thought of my turmoil vanished as I gazed into his ominous left eye, with its terrible, merciless gaze. At that moment it no longer mattered what was the authentic truth and what was the illusion, the dream within a dream. I laughed out loud, feeling as light as the wind. I could feel an unbearable weight being lifted off my shoulders as I kept staring into his wizard's eye. I recognized it. Florinda, Mariano Aureliano, Esperanza, and the caretaker all had such an eye. Preordained for all time to be without feeling, without emotion, that eye mirrors emptiness. As if it had revealed enough, an inside lid—as in a lizard's eye—shut over the left pupil.

Before I had a chance to comment on his wizard's eye, Isidoro Baltazar closed both eyes for an instant. When he opened them again they were exactly alike, dark and shiny with laughter, the wizard's eye but an illusion. He put one arm around my shoulders and walked with me up the hill.

163

"Get your things," he said just before reaching the house. "I'll wait for you in the car."

I thought it odd that he wouldn't come in with me, but at the moment I didn't think of asking him why. Only as I was gathering my few belongings did it occur to me that perhaps he was afraid of the women. The possibility made me laugh out loud, for I suddenly knew, with a certainty that astonished me, that the only thing Isidoro Baltazar was not afraid of was women.

I was still laughing when I reached the van at the bottom of the hill. I opened my mouth to explain to Isidoro Baltazar the cause of my mirth, when a strange, fierce emotion flooded me. A stab so strong I couldn't speak. What I felt wasn't sexual passion. Neither was it a platonic affection. It wasn't the feeling I felt for my parents or brothers or friends. I simply loved him with a love that was untainted by any expectation, doubts, or dread.

As if I had spoken out loud, Isidoro Baltazar embraced me so fiercely I could hardly breathe.

We drove off very slowly. I craned my neck out the window, hoping to catch a glimpse of the caretaker amidst the fruit trees. "It feels odd to leave like this," I mused, slumping back in my seat. "In a way, Florinda said goodbye to me last night. But I wish I could have thanked Esperanza and the caretaker."

The dirt road wound around the hill, and as we reached a sharp bend, the back of the little house came into view. Isidoro Baltazar stopped the car and turned off the engine. He pointed to the frail old man sitting on a crate in front of the house. I wanted to get out of the car and run up the hill, but he held me back. "Just wave at him," he whispered.

The caretaker rose from the crate. The wind made his loose jacket and pants flap against his limbs, as if they were wings. He laughed out loud, then bent backwards and, seemingly with the wind's momentum, did a double back flip. For a moment he appeared to be suspended high in the air. He never landed on the ground but vanished, as if the wind had sucked him away.

"Where did he go?" I whispered in awe.

"To the other side," Isidoro Baltazar giggled with childlike delight. "That was his way of saying good-bye to you." He set the car in motion again. As if he were baiting me, he glanced at me mockingly from time to time. "What is it that's troubling you, nibelunga?" he finally asked.

"You know who he is, don't you?" I said accusingly. "He isn't the caretaker, is he?"

Isidoro Baltazar frowned slightly, then after a long silence he reminded me that, for me, the nagual Juan Matus was Mariano Aureliano. He assured me that there must be a good reason that I knew him under that name. "I'm sure there is an equally sound justification for the old man not to reveal his name to you."

I argued that, since I knew who Mariano Aureliano was, I didn't see the purpose of the old man's pretension. "And," I stressed smugly, "I do know who the caretaker is." I glanced sideways to see Isidoro Baltazar's reaction. His face revealed nothing.

"Like all the people in the sorcerers' world, the caretaker is a sorcerer," he said. "But you don't know who he is." He turned to me briefly, then fixed his attention again on the road. "After all these years, I don't know who any of them really is, including the nagual Juan Matus. As long as I am with him, I think I know who he is. The moment his back is turned, however, I am at a loss."

Almost dreamily, Isidoro Baltazar went on to say that in the world of everyday life, our subjective states are shared by all our fellow men. For this reason, we know at all times what our fellow men would do under given circumstances.

"You're wrong, you're deadly wrong," I shouted. "Not to know what our fellow men would do under given circumstances is what's exciting about life. That's one of the few exciting things left. Don't tell me you want to do away with it."

"We don't know what our fellow men would exactly do," he explained patiently, "but we could write down a list of possibilities which would hold true. A very long list, I grant you, yet a finite list. In order to write down this list, we don't have to ask our fellow men for their preferences. All we have to do is place ourselves in their position and write down the possibilities pertinent to us. They'll be true to everybody, because we share them. Our subjective states are shared by all of us." He said that our subjective knowledge of the world is known to us as common sense. It might be slightly different from group to group, from culture to culture, yet in spite of all these differences, common sense is sufficiently homogeneous to warrant the statement that the everyday world is an intersubjective world.

"With sorcerers, however, the common sense we are accustomed to is no longer in operation," he stressed. "They have another kind of common sense, because they have other kinds of subjective states."

"You mean that they are like beings from another planet?" I asked.

Isidoro Baltazar laughed. "Yes. They are like beings from another planet."

"Is that why they are so secretive?"

"I don't think secretive is the right term," he remarked thoughtfully. "They deal differently with the everyday world. Their behavior appears secretive to us because we don't share the same meaning, and since we don't have any standards to measure what is common sense to them, we opt for believing that their behavior is secretive."

"They do whatever we do: they sleep, they cook their meals, they read," I interjected. "Yet I could never catch them in the act. Believe me, they are secretive."

Smiling, he shook his head. "You saw what they wished you to see," he insisted. "And yet they weren't hiding anything from you. You couldn't see. That's all."

I was about to contradict him, but I didn't want him to dislike me. It wasn't so much that he was right, for I didn't really understand what he was talking about; rather, I felt that all my snooping around had not given me a clue as to who these people were or what they did. Sighing, I closed my eyes and leaned my head against the backrest.

As we drove, I told him again of my dream. How real it was to have seen him asleep, snoring on the straw mat. I told him of my conversation with Mariano Aureliano, the heat on his hand. The more I spoke, the more I was convinced that it hadn't been a dream at all. I drove myself into such a state of agitation I ended up weeping.

"I don't know what they did to me," I said. "I'm not quite sure whether I'm awake or dreaming even now. Florinda kept telling me that I was dreaming-awake."

Isidoro Baltazar nodded, then said softly, "The nagual Juan Matus refers to it as heightened awareness."

"Heightened awareness," I repeated.

The words rolled easily off my tongue even though they sounded exactly the opposite of dreaming-awake. I vaguely remembered hearing them before. Either Florinda or Esperanza had used the term, but I couldn't recall in what connection. The words were on the verge of suggesting some meaning, albeit vague, but my brain was already too dulled by my unsuccessful attempts to recount my daily activities at the witches' house.

Regardless of how hard I tried, there were certain episodes I could not recall. I fumbled for words that somehow paled and died away in front on my very eyes, like a vision half seen and half remembered. It wasn't that I had forgotten anything, but rather, images came to me fragmented, like pieces in a puzzle that didn't quite fit. This forgetfulness was a physical sensation, as if a fog had settled over certain parts of my brain.

"So dreaming-awake and heightened awareness are the same?" More than a question, it was a statement whose meaning escaped me. I shifted in my seat and, pulling my legs under me, sat facing Isidoro Baltazar. The sun outlined his profile. The black curly hair falling over his high forehead, the sculpted cheekbones, the strong nose and chin, and finely chiseled lips gave him a Roman appearance.

"I must be still in heightened awareness," I said, "I never noticed you before."

The car swayed on the road as he threw his head back and laughed. "You are definitely dreaming-awake," he stated, slapping his thigh. "Don't you remember that I'm short, brown, and homely looking?"

I giggled. Not because I agreed with his description but because it was the only thing I remembered him saying in the lecture he gave the day I formally met him. My merriment was quickly replaced by an odd anxiety. It seemed that months had passed, instead of only two days, since we came to the house of the witches.

"Time passes differently in the sorcerers' world," Isidoro Baltazar said as if I had spoken out loud. "And one experiences it differently." He went on to say that one of the most difficult aspects of his apprenticeship was to deal with sequences of events in terms of time. Often they were all mixed up in his mind, confused images that sank deeper whenever he tried to focus on them. "Only now, with the nagual's help, do I remember aspects and events of his teachings that took place years ago," he said.

"How does he help you?" I asked. "Does he hypnotize you?"

"He makes me shift levels of awareness," he said. "And when he does, it is not only that I remember past events, but I relive them."

"How does he do that?" I insisted. "I mean, make you shift."

"Until recently I believed that it was accomplished by a sharp pat on my back, between the shoulder blades," he said. "But now I'm quite certain that his mere presence makes me shift levels of awareness."

"Then he does hypnotize you," I insisted.

He shook his head and said, "Sorcerers are experts at shifting levels of awareness. Some are so adept they can shift the level of awareness of others."

I nodded. Already I had numerous questions, but he gestured for patience.

"Sorcerers," he went on, "make one see that the whole nature of reality is different from what we believe it to be; that is, from what we have been taught it to be. Intellectually, we are willing to tease ourselves with the idea that culture predetermines who we are, how we behave, what we are willing to know, what we are able to feel. But we are not willing to embody this idea, to accept it as a concrete, practical proposition. And the reason for that is that we are not willing to accept that culture also predetermines what we are able to perceive.

"Sorcery makes us aware of different realities, different possibilities, not only about the world but also about ourselves, to the extent that we no longer are able to believe in even the most solid assumptions about ourselves and our surroundings."

I was surprised that I could absorb his words so easily, when I didn't really understand them.

"A sorcerer is not only aware of different realities," he went on, "but he uses that knowledge in practicalities. Sorcerers know—not only intellectually but also practically—that reality, or the world as we know it, consists only of an agreement extracted out of every one of us. That agreement could be made to collapse, since it's only a social phenomenon. And when it collapses, the whole world collapses with it."

Seeing that I couldn't follow his argument, he tried to present it from another angle. He said that the social world defines perception to us in proportion to its usefulness in guiding us through the complexity of experience in everyday life. The social world sets limits to what we perceive, sets limits to what we are capable of perceiving. "To a sorcerer, perception can go beyond these agreed-upon parameters," he stressed. "These parameters are constructed and buttressed by words, by language, by thoughts. That is, by agreement."

"And sorcerers don't agree?" I asked tentatively, in an effort to understand his premise.

"They do agree," he said, beaming at me, "but their agreement is different. Sorcerers break the normal agreement, not only intellectually but also physically or practically or whatever one wants to call it. Sorcerers collapse the parameters of socially determined perception, and to understand what sorcerers mean by that, one has to become a practitioner. That is, one has to be committed; one has to lend the mind as well as the body. It has to be a conscious, fearless surrender."

"The body?" I asked suspiciously, immediately wondering what kind of ritual might be involved. "What do they want with my body?"

"Nothing, nibelunga," he laughed. Then, in a serious yet kind tone, he added that neither my body nor my mind was yet in any condition to follow the arduous path of the sorcerer. Seeing that I was about to protest, he quickly allowed that there was nothing wrong with either my mind or my body.

"Wait a minute now!" I interjected forcefully.

169

Isidoro Baltazar ignored my interruption and went on to say that the world of sorcerers is a sophisticated world, that it wasn't enough to understand its principles intuitively. One also needed to assimilate them intellectually. "Contrary to what people believe," he explained, "sorcerers are not practitioners of obscure esoteric rituals but stand ahead of our times. And the mode of our time is reason. We are reasonable men as a whole. Sorcerers, however, are *men of reason,* which is a different matter altogether. Sorcerers have a romance with ideas; they have cultivated reason to its limits, for they believe that only by fully understanding the intellect can they embody the principles of sorcery without losing sight of their own sobriety and integrity. This is where sorcerers differ drastically from us. We have very little sobriety and even less integrity."

He glanced at me briefly and smiled. I had the unpleasant impression that he knew exactly what I was thinking, or rather, that I couldn't think at all. I had understood his words, but their meaning had eluded me. I didn't know what to say. I didn't even know what to ask. For the first time in my life, I felt utterly stupid. It didn't make me feel inadequate, though, for I realized that he was right. My interest in intellectual matters had always been shallow and superficial. To have a romance with ideas was a totally alien concept to me.

We were at the U.S. border in Arizona in a few hours, yet the drive was unwarrantedly exhausting. I wanted to talk, but I didn't know what to say, or rather, I couldn't find the words to express myself. I felt somehow intimidated by all that had happened. It was a new feeling for me!

Sensing my uncertainty and discomfort, Isidoro Baltazar began to talk. In a candid manner, he admitted to being baffled by the sorcerers' world even to this day, after so many years of studying and interacting with them.

"And when I say studying, I really mean studying." He laughed and slapped his thigh to emphasize his statement.

"Only this morning I was clobbered by the sorcerers' world in ways impossible to describe." He spoke in a tone that was half assertion, half complaint, yet there was such a delighted power in his voice, some wonderful inner strength in him, that I felt uplifted. He gave me the impression that he could do anything, endure anything, and allow nothing to matter. I sensed a will in him, an ability to overcome all obstacles.

"Imagine, I really thought I was gone with the nagual for only two days." Laughing, he turned to me and shook me with his free hand.

I had been so absorbed by the sound, the vitality of his voice, that I had failed to understand what he was talking about. I asked him to repeat what he had said. He did, and I still missed what he meant.

"I don't get what's exciting you so much," I finally said, suddenly irritated by my inability to grasp what he was trying to tell me. "You were gone for two days. What of it?"

"What?" His loud exclamation made me jump in my seat, and I banged my head on the roof of the van.

He peered straight into my eyes but didn't say a word. I knew he was not accusing me of anything, yet I felt that he was making fun of my moroseness, my changing moods, my lack of attention. He parked the car on the side of the road, turned off the engine, then shifted in his seat to face me.

"And now I want you to tell me all you've experienced." There was a nervous excitement in his voice, a restlessness, a vitality. He assured me that the sequential order of events didn't mean a thing.

His compelling, engaging smile was so reassuring, I told him at great length all I remembered.

He listened attentively, chuckling from time to time, urging me on with a movement of his chin every time I faltered.

"So, all this has happened to you in . . ." He paused, gazing at me with shining eyes, then casually added, "two days?"

"Yes," I said firmly.

He crossed his arms over his chest in an expansive gesture. "Well, I have news for you," he said. The merry look in his eyes belied the seriousness of his tone, the set expression of his straight lips. "I've been gone for twelve days. But I thought it was only two. I thought you were going to appreciate the irony of it, because you had kept a better count of time. You didn't, though. You're just like me. We've lost ten days."

"Ten days," I mumbled, bewildered, then turned to look out the window. I didn't say a word for the rest of the trip. It wasn't that I didn't believe him. It wasn't that I didn't want to talk. There was nothing for me to say, even after I bought the L.A. *Times* in the first newsstand that carried it and corroborated that, indeed, I had lost ten days. But were they really lost? I asked myself that question, yet I didn't wish a reply.

12

ISIDORO Baltazar's office-studio consisted of one rectangular room overlooking a parking lot, a small kitchen, and a pink-tiled bathroom. He took me there the night we returned from Sonora. Too exhausted to notice anything, I followed him up the two flights of stairs, along a darkly carpeted corridor to apartment number 8. The instant my head hit the pillow, I was asleep and dreamt that we were still on the road. We had driven nonstop all the way from Sonora, alternating with each other at the wheel and pausing only to eat or fill up the gas tank.

The apartment was sparsely furnished. Beside the twin bed, he had a long, masonite folding picnic table that served as his desk, a folding chair, and two metal filing cabinets in which he kept his field notes. Several suits and half a dozen shirts hung in the two big closets in the hall. The rest of the space was taken up by books. They were stacked up in piles. There were no bookcases. The books appeared to have never been touched, let alone read. The cupboards in the kitchen were also crammed with books, except for one shelf, which had been set aside for a plate, a mug, a knife, a fork, and a spoon. On the gas stove stood a kettle and a saucepan.

Within three weeks I found myself a new apartment, about a mile down the street from the UCLA campus, right around the corner from his office-studio. Yet I continued to spend most of my time at his place. He had set up a second twin bed for me, a card table, and a folding chair—identical to his—at the other end of the room.

In the six months that followed, Sonora became a mythological place for me. Having no longer any desire to block away my experiences, I juxtaposed the memories of the two times I had been there. But hard as I tried, I couldn't remember a thing about the eleven days I had lost: one during the first trip, ten during the second.

Isidoro Baltazar plainly refused even to mention the idea of having lost those days. At times, I was in total agreement with him; the absurdity of considering those days lost simply because I couldn't remember them became so plain to me that I was filled with gratitude toward him for attaching no importance to the matter. It was clear that he was protecting me. At other times, however, for no reason at all, I nursed a deep resentment. It was his duty to help me, to clarify the mystery for me, I repeated to myself, until I was convinced he was purposely hiding things from me.

"You'll drive yourself nuts if you keep harping on it," he finally said one day. "And all your turmoil will be for nothing, because it will resolve nothing." He hesitated for a moment, as if reluctant to voice what he was about to say next, then shrugged and added in a challenging tone, "Why don't you use the same energy in a more practical manner, like lining up and examining your bad habits."

Instead of admitting to such a notion, I immediately counterattacked with the other complaint that had been brewing inside me. I still hadn't met the other young women who had been entrusted to him by the old nagual.

He had told me so much about them that I felt I already knew them. Whenever I had asked him about them, he had answered my questions at great length. He spoke rapturously about them. With profound and obviously sincere admiration, he had said that an outsider would describe them as attractive, intelligent, accomplished— they all possessed advanced university degrees—self-assured, and fiercely independent. To him, however, they were much more than that; they were magical beings who shared his destiny. They were linked to him by ties of affection and commitment that had nothing to do with the social order. They shared in common their search for freedom, he had said.

Once, I even gave him an ultimatum. "You've got to take me to them, or else."

Isidoro Baltazar laughed gaily, a deep, chuckling laugh. "All I can tell you is that nothing is as you imagine," he said. "And there is no way to tell when you will finally meet them. You'll just have to wait."

"I've waited long enough!" I shouted. Seeing no reaction on his face, I added derisively, "You're deluding yourself if you believe that I will find a bunch of women in Los Angeles. I don't even know where to start looking."

"You'll find them the way you found me," he stated, "the way you found Mariano Aureliano."

I regarded him suspiciously. I couldn't help but suspect that there was a sort of secret malice about him. "I wasn't looking for you," I pointed out peevishly. "Nor was I looking for Mariano Aureliano. Believe me, meeting you and him was purely accidental."

"There are no accidental meetings in the sorcerers' world," he noted casually. I was on the verge of telling him that I didn't need this kind of advice when he added in a serious voice, "You'll meet them when the time is right. You don't have to go looking for them."

Facing the wall, I counted to ten, then turned toward him smiling and said sweetly, "The problem with you is that you're a typical Latin. Tomorrow is always good enough for you. You've no concept of getting things done." I raised my voice to prevent him from interrupting me. "My insistence on meeting your friends is to speed things up."

"To speed things up?" he repeated uncomprehendingly. "What's there to speed up?"

"You have been telling me almost daily that there is so little time left," I reminded him. "You, yourself, are always talking about how important it is for me to meet them, and yet you act as if you had an eternity before you."

"I tell you this constantly because I want you to hurry and clean your inner being, not because I want meaningless acts done as fast as you can," he said impatiently. "It isn't up to me to introduce them to you. If it were up to me, I wouldn't be sitting here listening to your inanities." He closed his eyes and sighed exaggeratedly in mock resignation. He smiled, then mumbled softly, "You're too dumb to see what's happening."

"Nothing is happening," I retorted, stung by his insult. "I'm not as stupid as you think. I've noticed this air of ambivalence about your reactions toward me. Sometimes I have the distinct impression that you don't know what to do with me."

"I know exactly what to do," he contradicted me.

"Then why do you always appear undecided when I propose something?" The words had escaped me as if of their own accord.

Isidoro Baltazar looked sharply at me. For a moment I expected that he would attack me with those quick, harsh words he could use, demolish me with some sharp criticism. But his voice was surprisingly gentle when he said that I was quite right in my assessment.

"I always wait till events make a choice for me," he affirmed. "And then I move with speed and vigor. I will leave you behind if you don't watch out."

"I'm already far behind," I said in a self-pitying tone. "Since you won't help me find these women, I'm doomed to remain behind."

"But this is not the real pressing problem," he said. "You haven't yet made your decision, that's the trouble." He lifted his brows expectantly, as if waiting for my impending outburst.

"I don't know what you mean. What is it I have to decide?"

"You haven't decided to join the sorcerers' world. You're standing at the threshold, looking in, waiting to see what's going to happen. You're waiting for something practical that will make it worth your while."

Words of protest rose in my throat. But before I could give vent to my profound indignation, he said that I had the mistaken idea that moving into a new apartment and leaving my old life-style behind was a change.

"What is it then?" I asked sarcastically.

"You haven't left anything behind, except your belongings," he said, ignoring my tone. "For some people that is a gigantic step. For you, though, it's nothing. You don't care about possessions."

"No, I don't," I agreed, then insisted that regardless of what he believed, I had made my decision to join the sorcerers' world a long time ago. "Why do you think I'm sitting here if I haven't joined yet?"

"You have certainly joined it in body," he stated, "but not in spirit. Now you are waiting for some kind of map, some comforting blueprint before you make your final decision. Meanwhile, you'll go on humoring them. The main problem with you is that you want to be convinced that the sorcerers' world has something to offer."

"Doesn't it?" I blurted out.

Isidoro Baltazar turned to me, his face crinkling with delight. "Yes, it has something very special to offer. It's called freedom. However, there's no guarantee that you'll succeed in attaining it. That any of us, for that matter, will succeed."

I nodded thoughtfully, then asked him what I had to do to convince him that I had indeed joined the sorcerers' world.

"You don't have to convince me. You have to convince the spirit. You have to close the door behind you."

"What door?"

"The one you still keep open. The door that will permit you to escape if things are not to your liking or don't fit your expectations."

"Are you saying that I will leave?"

He regarded me with an enigmatic expression, then shrugged his shoulders and in a voice that was but a mere murmur said, "That's between you and the spirit."

"But if you yourself believe that—"

"I don't believe anything," he cut me short. "You came into this world the way everybody else did. It was none of anybody's doing. And it will be none of anybody's doing if you or anyone else decides to leave."

I gazed at him in confusion. "But surely you'll try to convince . . . if I . . . ," I stammered.

He shook his head before I finished speaking. "I will not convince you or anyone else. There will be no power in your decision if you need to be propped up every time you falter or doubt."

"But who will help me?" I asked, stricken.

177

"I will. I'm your servant." He smiled, not cynically but shyly and sweetly. "But I serve the spirit first. A warrior is not a slave but a servant of the spirit. Slaves have no choice; servants do. Their choice is to serve impeccably.

"My help is exempt from calculation," he continued. "I cannot invest in you, and neither, of course, can you invest in me or in the sorcerers' world. This is the basic premise of that world: nothing is done in it that might be construed as useful; only strategic acts are permitted. This is what the nagual Juan Matus taught me and the way I live: a sorcerer practices what he or she preaches. And yet nothing is done for practical reasons. When you get to understand and practice this, you will have closed the door behind you."

A long, breathless silence settled between us. I changed positions on the bed where I was sitting. Thoughts swarmed into my mind. Perhaps none of the sorcerers would believe me, but I had certainly changed, a change that had been almost imperceptible at first. I noticed it because it had to do with the most difficult thing some of us women can encounter: jealousy and the need to know.

My fits of jealously were a pretense, not necessarily a conscious one, but nevertheless there was something of a posturing about them. Something in me demanded that I be jealous of all the other women in Isidoro Baltazar's life. But then something in me was keenly aware that the new nagual's life wasn't the life of an ordinary man, not even one who might have many wives. Our relation, if it could be called that, did not fit into any kind of habitual, known mold, no matter how I tried to make it fit into that mold. In order for jealousy and possessiveness to have a grasp, it needs a mirror, not only one's own but one's partner's as well. And Isidoro Baltazar no longer mirrored the drives, needs, feelings, and emotions of a man.

My need to know about Isidoro Baltazar's life was an overpowering need; it simply consumed me that he never allowed me a real entry into his private world. And yet I did nothing about it. It would have been quite simple to follow him or to snoop through his papers and find out once and for all who he really was, I often reminded myself. But I couldn't do it. Something in me knew that I could not proceed with him as I normally would have done. What stopped me, more than any sense of propriety, was the trust he had

178

bestowed on me. He had given me complete access to his belongings, and that made him, not only in practice but even in my thoughts, inviolable.

I laughed out loud. I did understand what a warrior's strategic act was. Isidoro Baltazar was wrong. He was taking my lifelong habit of moodiness and Germanic finickiness as lack of commitment. It didn't matter. I knew that I had at least begun to understand and practice the warrior's strategy, at least when he was present—not necessarily present in the studio but present in Los Angeles. In his absence, however, I often began to falter, and when I did, I usually went to sleep in his studio.

One night, as I was inserting my key in the lock, I felt an arm reach out and pull me in. I screamed in terror. "What . . . what . . . ," I stammered as the hand that was holding my arm let go of me. Trying to regain my balance, I leaned against the wall. My heart thumped wildly. "Florinda!" I stared at her, bewildered. She had on a long robe, gathered at the waist. Her hair hung loose down the sides and back. I wondered whether she was real or merely a shadowy apparition, rimmed by the faint light behind her shoulders. I moved toward her and surreptitiously touched her sleeve.

"Is that you, Florinda? Or am I dreaming?"

"It's the real thing, dear. The real me."

"How did you get here? Are you all by yourself?" I was well aware of the futility of asking her that.

"Had I known that you would come, I would have started earlier with my cleaning," I said, trying to smile. My lips stuck to my teeth. "I love to clean Isidoro Baltazar's studio at night. I always clean at night."

Instead of making any remark, Florinda turned sideways, so the light hit her face. A wicked smile of delight dawned in her eyes. "I told you never to follow any one of us or come uninvited. You're lucky," she said. "You're lucky it wasn't someone else who pulled you in here tonight."

"Who else could have pulled me in?" I asked with a bravado I was far from feeling.

Florinda gazed at me for a moment longer, then turned around and said over her shoulder, "Someone who wouldn't have cared if you had died of fright." She moved her head slightly, so her profile was outlined by the faint light. She laughed softly, and, waving her hand in the air as if to brush away the words, she traveled the length of the room to the small kitchen. She seemed not to walk but to glide in a sort of undeliberate dance. It made her long white hair, hanging unbraided down her back, shimmer like a silvery curtain in the uncertain light.

Trying to imitate her graceful walk, I followed behind her. "I do have a key, you know," I said. "I've been coming here every day, at any hour, since we returned from Sonora. In fact, I practically live here."

"Didn't Isidoro Baltazar tell you not to come here while he's in Mexico?" Florinda's tone was even, almost casual. She was not accusing me, yet I felt she was.

"He might have mentioned something," I remarked with studied indifference. Seeing that she frowned, I felt compelled to defend myself. I told her that I was often there by myself and that I didn't think it would make any difference whether Isidoro Baltazar was five miles or five hundred miles away. Emboldened by her repeated nods, I confided that besides doing my schoolwork there, I spent hours rearranging the books in the closets. I had been restacking them by author and subject matter. "Some of the books are so new the pages are still uncut," I explained. "I've been separating them. In fact, that's what I came here to do tonight."

"At three in the morning?" she exclaimed.

Blushing, I nodded. "There are plenty of pages still to cut. It takes forever in that one has to be very careful not to damage the pages. It's soothing work, though. It helps me sleep."

"Extraordinary," Florinda said softly.

Encouraged by her obvious approval, I went on talking. "I'm sure you can understand what being here does to me," I said. "In this apartment, I feel detached from my old life, from everything and everyone but Isidoro Baltazar and his magical world. The very air fills me with a sense of utter remoteness." I sighed, long and loudly. "Here I never feel alone, even though most of the time I'm here by myself. Something about the atmosphere of this apartment reminds me of the witches' house. That same coldness and lack of feeling, which at first I had found so disturbing, permeates the walls. And it's precisely this lack of warmth, this remoteness, that I seek day and night. I find it oddly reassuring. It gives me strength."

"Incredible," Florinda whispered as if in disbelief and took the kettle to the sink. She said something, which I didn't hear above the splash of water, then put the water-filled kettle on the stove.

"I'm so happy that you feel so at home here," she said, sighing dramatically. "The security you must feel in such a little nest, knowing you have a companion." She added in a most facetious tone that I should do everything I could to make Isidoro Baltazar happy and that included sexual practices, which she described with horrendous directness.

Stupefied to hear such things, I stared at her open-mouthed. With the assuredness and efficiency of someone familiar with the peculiar setup of the kitchen, she produced the two mugs, my special teapot, and the bag of chocolate chip cookies I kept hidden in the cupboards behind the thick German and French Cassels' dictionaries.

Smiling, Florinda turned to me and asked abruptly, "Whom did you expect to find here tonight?"

"Not you!" I blurted out, realizing too late that my answer had given me away. I went into a lengthy and elaborate elucidation of why I believed I might find there, if not all of them, then at least one of the other young women.

"They will cross your path when the time is right," Florinda said. "It isn't up to you to force an encounter with them."

Before I knew what I was saying, I found myself blaming her, as well as Mariano Aureliano and Isidoro Baltazar, for my sneakiness. I told her that it was impractical—not to mention impossible—for them to expect me to wait until some unknown women crossed my path and to believe that I would actually recognize them by something so inconceivable as their inner glow. As usual, the more I complained, the better I felt.

Florinda ignored me. "One, two spoonfuls, and one for the pot," she chanted in an exaggerated British accent as she measured

181

out the tea. Then in a most casual manner she remarked that the only capricious and impractical thing was for me to think of and treat Isidoro Baltazar as a man.

"I don't know what you mean," I said defensively.

She gazed at me intently until I blushed. "You know exactly what I mean," she stated, then poured the tea into the mugs. With a quick gesture of her chin she indicated which of the two I should take. With the bag of cookies in her hand she sat on Isidoro Baltazar's bed, the one nearest to the kitchen. Slowly, she sipped her tea. I sat beside her and did the same.

"You haven't changed at all," she said all of a sudden.

"That's pretty much what Isidoro Baltazar said to me some days ago," I retorted. "I know, however, that I've changed a great deal."

I told her that my world had been turned upside down since my return from Sonora. At great length I explained about finding a new apartment, about moving and leaving everything I owned behind. She did not so much as nod but sat there silent and stiff like a stone.

"Actually, I can't take much credit for disrupting routines or becoming inaccessible," I conceded, laughing nervously and faltering on through her silence. "Anyone in close contact with Isidoro Baltazar will forget that there are boundaries between night and day, between weekdays and holidays." I glanced at her sideways, pleased with my words. "Time just flows by and gives way to some . . ." I couldn't finish the sentence. I had been hit by a strange thought. Nobody, in my memory, had ever told me about disrupting routines or becoming inaccessible. I regarded Florinda intently, then my glance wavered involuntarily. Was it her doing? I asked myself. Where did I get these ideas? And what was even more baffling, I knew exactly what these ideas meant.

"This should be a warning that something is just about to pop out of you," Florinda said, as if she had followed my train of thoughts. She went on to say that whatever I had done so far in dreams hadn't imbued my waking hours with the necessary hardness, the necessary self-discipline needed to fare in the sorcerers' world.

"I've never done anything like this in my life," I said. "Give me a break. I am new at it."

"Of course," she readily agreed. She reclined her head against the pillows and closed her eyes. She was silent for so long I thought she had fallen asleep, and thus I was startled when she said, "A real change is not a change of mood or attitude or outlook. A real change involves a total transformation of the self."

Seeing that I was about to interrupt her, she pressed her fingers against my lips and added, "The kind of change I'm talking about cannot be accomplished in three months or in a year or in ten. It will take a lifetime." She said that it was extraordinarily difficult to become something different than what one was raised to be.

"The world of sorcerers is a dream, a myth, yet it is as real as the everyday world," Florinda proceeded. "In order to perceive and to function in the sorcerers' world, we have to take off the everyday mask that has been strapped to our faces since the day we were born and put on the second mask, the mask that enables us to see ourselves and our surroundings for what we really are: breathtaking events that bloom into transitory existence once and are never to be repeated again.

"You'll have to make that mask yourself." She settled more comfortably on the bed and, cupping her hands around the mug, which I had refilled, took noisy little sips.

"How do I make this mask?" I asked.

"By dreaming your other self," she murmured. "Certainly not by just having a new address, new clothes, new books." She glanced at me sideways and grinned mockingly. "And certainly not by believing you have a new man."

Before I could deny her brutal accusation, she said that outwardly I was a fluid person, capable of moving at great speed. But inside I was rigid and stiff. As Isidoro Baltazar had remarked already, she, too, maintained that it was fallacious for me to believe that moving into a new apartment and compulsively giving away all I possessed was a change.

I bowed my head, accepting her criticism. I had always had an urge to get rid of things. And as she had pointed out, it was basically a compulsion. To my parents' chagrin, I had periodically disposed of my clothes and toys since early childhood. My joy at seeing my room and closets neatly arranged and nearly empty surpassed the joy of having things.

Sometimes my compulsion was so overpowering that I thinned out my parents' and brothers' closets as well. Hardly ever were these items missed, for I always made sure to get rid of clothes I hadn't seen anyone wear for a while. Quite a few times, nevertheless, the whole household would explode in sudden and total confusion as my father went from room to room, opening wardrobes and yelling, searching for a specific shirt or a pair of pants.

Florinda laughed, then got to her feet and moved to the window overlooking the alley. She stared at the black-out curtain as though she could see through it. Glancing backward over her shoulder, she said that for a woman it is a great deal easier than for a man to break ties with family and past.

"Women," she maintained, "are not accountable. This lack of accountability gives women a great deal of fluidity. Unfortunately, women rarely, if ever, make use of this advantage." She moved about the room, her hand trailing over the large metal filing cabinet and over the folding card table. "The hardest thing to grasp about the sorcerers' world is that it offers total freedom." She turned to face me and added softly, "But freedom is not free."

"What does freedom cost?"

"Freedom will cost you the mask you have on," she said. "The mask that feels so comfortable and is so hard to shed off, not because it fits so well but because you have been wearing it for so long." She stopped pacing about the room and came to stand in front of the card table.

"Do you know what freedom is?" she asked rhetorically. "Freedom is the total absence of concern about yourself," she said, sitting beside me on the bed. "And the best way to quit being concerned with yourself is to be concerned about others."

"I am," I assured her. "I constantly think of Isidoro Baltazar and his women."

"I'm sure you do," Florinda readily agreed. She shook her head and yawned. "It's time for you to begin to shape your new mask.

The mask that cannot have anyone's imprint but your own. It has to be carved in solitude. Otherwise it won't fit properly. Otherwise there will always be times when the mask will feel too tight, too loose, too hot, too cold . . ." Her voice trailed off as she went on enumerating the most outlandish discomforts.

A long silence ensued, and then in that same sleepy voice she said, "To choose the sorcerers' world is not just a matter of saying you have. You have to act in that world. In your case, you have to dream. Have you dreamt-awake since your return?"

In a thoroughly morose mood, I admitted that I hadn't.

"Then you haven't made your decision yet," she observed severely. "You are not carving your new mask. You are not dreaming your other self.

"Sorcerers are bound to their world solely through their impeccability." A definite gleam appeared in her eyes as she added, "Sorcerers have no interest to convert anyone to their views. There are no gurus or wise men among sorcerers, only naguals. They are the leaders, not because they know more or because they are in any way better sorcerers, but simply because they have more energy. I'm not necessarily referring to physical strength," she qualified, "but to a certain configuration of their being that permits them to help anyone break the parameters of perception."

"If sorcerers are not interested in converting anyone to their views, why then is Isidoro Baltazar the old nagual's apprentice?" I interrupted her.

"Isidoro Baltazar appeared in the sorcerers' world the same way you did," she said. "Whatever it was that brought him could not be ignored by Mariano Aureliano. It was his duty to teach Isidoro Baltazar all he knew about the sorcerers' world." She explained that no one had been looking for Isidoro Baltazar or for me. Whatever had brought us into their world had nothing to do with anyone's doing or volition. "There is nothing any one of us would do to keep you against your will in this magical world," she said, smiling. "And yet we would do any imaginable or unimaginable thing to help you stay in it."

Florinda turned sideways, as if she wanted to hide her face from me. An instant later she looked back over her shoulder. Something cold and detached showed in her eyes, and the change of expression was altogether so remarkable that I was frightened. Instinctively, I moved away from her.

"The only thing I cannot and will not do, and neither will Isidoro Baltazar, for that matter, is to help you be your old ugly, greedy, indulgent self. That'd be a travesty."

As if to soften the insult, she put her arm around my shoulders and hugged me. "I'll tell you what you need," she whispered, then was silent for so long I thought she had forgotten what she was going to say.

"You need a good night's sleep," she finally murmured.

"I'm not in the least tired," I retorted. My response was automatic, and I realized that most of my responses were contradictions of what was being said. For me, it was a matter of principle to be right.

Florinda laughed softly, then embraced me again. "Don't be so Germanic," she murmured. "And don't expect everything to be spelled out clearly and precisely to you." She added that nothing in the sorcerers' world was clear and precise; instead, things unfolded slowly and vaguely. "Isidoro Baltazar will help you," she assured me. "However, do remember that he won't help you in the way you expect to be helped."

"What do you mean?" I asked, disentangling myself from her arms so I could look at her.

"He will not tell you what you want to hear. He will not tell you how to behave, for, as you already know, there are neither rules nor regulations in the sorcerers' world." She giggled gleefully, seemingly enjoying my growing frustration. "Always remember, there are only improvisations," she added, then, yawning widely, she stretched out fully on the bed and reached for one of the neatly folded blankets stacked on the floor. Before she covered herself, she rose up on her elbow and looked at me closely. There was something hypnotic about her sleepy voice as she told me that I should always bear in mind that I traveled on the same warrior's path as Isidoro Baltazar.

She closed her eyes, and in a voice that was almost too faint to be heard said, "Never lose sight of him. His actions will guide you in so artful a manner that you won't even notice it. He's an impeccable and peerless warrior."

I urgently shook her arm. I was afraid she would fall asleep before she finished talking.

Without opening her eyes, Florinda said, "If you watch him carefully, you'll see that Isidoro Baltazar doesn't seek love or approval. You'll see that he remains impassive under any conditions. He doesn't demand anything, yet he is willing to give anything of himself. He avidly seeks a signal from the spirit in the form of a kind word, an appropriate gesture, and when he gets it, he expresses his thanks by redoubling his efforts.

"Isidoro Baltazar doesn't judge. He fiercely reduces himself to nothing in order to listen, to watch, so that he can conquer and be humbled by his conquest or be defeated and enhanced by his defeat.

"If you watch carefully, you'll see that Isidoro Baltazar doesn't surrender. He may be vanquished, but he'll never surrender. And above all, Isidoro Baltazar is free."

I was dying to interrupt her, to cry out that she had already told me all that, but before I could ask her anything else, Florinda was sound asleep.

Afraid I might miss her in the morning if I returned to my apartment, I sat down on the other bed.

Strange thoughts rushed into my awareness. I relaxed. I let myself go completely as I realized that they were disconnected from the rest of my normal thoughts. I saw them like beams of light, flashes of intuition.

Following one of those flashes of intuition, I decided to feel with my seat the bed I was sitting on. And to my dumbfounded surprise, my buttocks felt as if they had sunk into the bed itself. For an instant, I was the bed, and the bed was reaching out to touch my buttocks. I relished this sensation for quite some time. I knew then that I was dreaming, and I understood with complete clarity that I had just felt what Esperanza had described as "my feeling being thrown back at me." And then my whole being melted, or better yet, it exploded.

I wanted to laugh out loud for the sheer joy of it, but I didn't want to wake Florinda. I had remembered it all! Now I had no difficulty whatsoever in recalling what I had done in the witches' house in those ten lost days. I had dreamt! Under Esperanza's watchful eye, I had dreamt on and on of waking up in the witches' house or in Esperanza's place or sometimes in other places I couldn't quite see at the moment.

Clara had insisted that before any particular thing I saw in dreams could be fixed permanently in my memory, I needed to see it twice. I had seen all the women more than twice; they were permanently etched in my memory. As I sat there on the bed watching Florinda sleep, I remembered the other women of the sorcerers' party with whom I had interacted in a dreamlike state during those forgotten days. I saw them clearly, as if they had conjured themselves up before me, or rather as if I had been transported, bodily, back to those events.

The most striking to me was Nélida, who looked so much like Florinda that at first I believed she was her twin. Not only was she as tall and thin as Florinda, but she had the same color eyes, hair, and complexion; even their expressions were the same. Temperamentally, they were alike, too, except that Nélida came across as more subdued, less forceful. She seemed to lack Florinda's wisdom and energetic force. And yet there was a patient, silent strength to Nélida that was very reassuring.

Hermelinda could have easily passed as Carmela's younger sister. Her thin, five-foot two-inch body was delicately rounded and so were her exquisite manners. She appeared to be less self-assured than Carmela. She was soft-spoken and moved in quick jerks that somehow meshed into gracefulness. Her companions told me that her shyness and quietness brought out the best in others and that she could not handle a group or even two people at the same time.

Clara and Delia made a stupendous team of pranksters. They weren't really as big as they first appeared. It was their robustness, their vigor and energy, that made one think they were large, indestructible women. And they did play the most delightful competitive games. They paraded their outlandishly eccentric outfits at the slightest opportunity. Both played the guitar very well and had beautiful voices to match; they sang, one trying to outdo the other, not only in Spanish, but in English, German, French, and Italian as well. Their repertoire included ballads, folk songs, every conceivable popular song including the latest pop songs. I only had to hum or recite the first line of a song and either Clara or Delia would immediately finish the whole song for me. And then they had their poem writing contests, writing verse to the occasion.

They had written written poems to me and slipped them under my door, unsigned. I had to guess who had written the poem. Each claimed that if I truly loved her, as she loved me, I would intuitively know the author.

What made their competitiveness delightfully appealing was the fact that there was no edge to it. It was meant to entertain, not to put each other down. Needless to say, Clara and Delia had as much fun as their audience.

If they took a liking to someone, as they seemed to have done with me, there was no limit to their affection and loyalty. Both of them defended me with an astonishing perseverance, even when I was in the wrong. In their eyes, I was perfect and could do no wrong. From them I learned that it was a dual responsibility to uphold that trust. It wasn't that I was afraid of disappointing them and tried to live up to their expectations, but rather, it was the most natural thing for me to believe that I was perfect and to behave with them in an impeccable manner.

The strangest among all the women sorcerers was my dreaming teacher, Zuleica, who never taught me anything. She didn't even speak to me or perhaps hadn't noticed that I existed.

Zuleica was, just like Florinda, very beautiful; perhaps not as striking, but beautiful in a more ethereal way. She was petite; her dark eyes with the winged eyebrows and the small, perfect nose and mouth were framed by wavy dark hair that was turning grey. It accentuated her aura of other-worldliness.

Hers was not an average beauty, but a sublime one, tempered by her relentless self-control. She was keenly aware of the comic element of being beautiful and appealing in the eyes of others.

189

She had learned to recognize it and used it as if it were a prize she had won. She was, therefore, totally indifferent to anything or anyone.

Zuleica had learned to be a ventriloquist and had turned it into a superior art. According to her, words voiced by moving the lips become more confusing than they really are.

I was delighted by Zuleica's habit of talking, as a ventriloquist, to walls, tables, china, or any other object in front of her, and so I kept on following her around whenever she made an appearance. She walked through the house without seeming to touch the ground, without seeming to stir the air. When I asked the other sorcerers whether this was an illusion, they explained that Zuleica abhorred leaving footprints.

After I had met and interacted with all the women, they explained to me the difference between the dreamers and the stalkers. They called it the two planets. Florinda, Carmela, Zoila, and Delia were stalkers: forceful beings with a great deal of physical energy; go-getters; inexhaustible workers; specialists on that extravagant state of awareness they called dreaming-awake.

The other planet—the dreamers—was composed of the other four women: Zuleica, Nélida, Hermelinda, and Clara. They had a more ethereal quality. It was not that they were less forceful or less energetic; it was rather that their energy was simply less apparent. They projected a sense of otherworldliness even when engaged in the most mundane activities. They were the specialists on another peculiar state of awareness they called "dreaming in worlds other than this world." I was told that this was the most complex state of awareness women could reach.

When the dreamers and the stalkers worked together, the stalkers were like a protective, hard, outer layer that hid a deep core. The dreamers were that deep core; they were like a soft matrix that cushioned the hard, outer layer.

During those days in the witches' house, I was taken care of as if I were their most precious concern; they cossetted and fussed over me as if I were a baby. They cooked me my favorite foods; they made me the most elegant and well-fitting clothes I had ever had. They showered me with presents, outright silly things and valuable jewels, which they put away, waiting for the day I would wake up, they said.

There were two more women in the sorcerers' world. They were both stalkers: two fat girls, Martha and Teresa. Both were lovely to look at and had glorious appetites to match. Not that they fooled anyone, but they kept a cache of cookies, chocolates, and assorted candies hidden in a secret compartment in the pantry. To my great delight, they made me privy from the very beginning to their secret cache and encouraged me to dip freely into it, which, of course, I did.

Martha was the older of the two. She was in her mid-twenties, an exotic blend of German and Indian blood. Her color, if not altogether white, was pale. Her luxurious black hair was soft and wavy and framed a high-cheeked, broad face. Her slanted eyes were a brilliant green-blue, and her ears were small and delicate, like a cat's, soft and almost rosily transparent.

Martha was given to long, sorrowful sighs—Germanic, she claimed—and to moody silences, a heritage of her Indian soul. She had recently begun to take lessons on the violin, which she would practice at any hour of the day. Instead of anyone criticizing her or getting angry, they unanimously agreed that Martha had a great ear for music.

Teresa was barely five feet tall, but her bulk made her seem much taller. Rather than looking Mexican, she looked like an Indian from India. Her flawless skin was a rich, creamy light brown. Her almond-shaped eyes, liquid and dark, were framed by long, curly lashes, so heavy they kept her lids low, giving her a dreamy, far-away expression. Her gentleness and sweet disposition made one want to protect her.

Teresa was artistic, too. She painted watercolors late in the afternoon. With her easel before her, her brushes and tray with paint and water at the ready, she would sit for hours in the yard, waiting for the light and shadows to be just right. Then, with Zen-like control and fluidity, she would dash across the page with her paint-dipped brushes.

191

The bulk of my hidden memories had surfaced. I was exhausted. The rhythm of Florinda's faint snoring, rising and falling across the room like a distant echo, was mesmerizing.

When I opened my eyes, the first thing I did was to call out her name. She didn't answer. The bed was empty. The yellow sheet, tucked tightly under the mattress, showed no evidence that anyone had sat, let alone slept, there. The two pillows were back to their usual position—plopped against the wall—and the blanket she had used was stacked with the others on the floor.

Eagerly, I searched the apartment for a clue, some indication that she had indeed been there. I found nothing, not even a long grey hair in the bathroom.

13

WHENEVER I was fully awake, I didn't quite remember about those lost days, except that I knew,
with absolute certainty, that they were not lost.
Something had happened to me during that time, something with
an inward meaning that escaped me. I didn't make a conscious effort
to recapture all those vague memories; I simply knew they were
there, half hidden, like people one knows slightly but whose names
one can't exactly recall.

I have never been a good sleeper, but from that night on—since
Florinda's appearance at Isidoro Baltazar's studio—I went to sleep
at all hours just to dream. I simply passed out every time I lay down,
and slept for inordinately long stretches of time. I even put on
weight, which unfortunately didn't go to the right places. Yet I never
dreamt with the sorcerers.

One afternoon I awoke abruptly to a loud clatter. Isidoro
Baltazar had dropped the kettle in the sink. My head hurt, my eyes
were blurred. I had the immediate memory of a terrible dream that
just as quickly escaped recall. I was sweating heavily.

"It's all your fault," I yelled at him. "If you would only help
me, I wouldn't be sleeping my life away." I wanted to rant, to give
in to my frustration and impatience. But it suddenly flashed through
my mind that I couldn't do that because I could no longer enjoy my
complaining as I used to.

His face was radiant with pleasure, as though I had spoken my thoughts out loud. He grabbed his chair, sat astride it, and said, "You know that I cannot help you. Women have a different dreaming avenue. I can't even conceive what women do to dream."

"You ought to know, with so many women in your world," I retorted churlishly.

He laughed; nothing seemed to alter his good spirits. "I can't even begin to conceive what women do to dream," he went on. "Males have to struggle incessantly to arrange their attention in dreams; women don't struggle, but they do have to acquire inner discipline." His smile was brilliant as he added, "There is one thing that might help you. Don't approach dreaming in your usual compulsive manner. Let it come to you."

I opened and closed my mouth, then quickly my astonishment turned to rage. My former insight forgotten, I put on my shoes and stomped out in a huff, making sure to bang the door behind me. His laughter followed me all the way to my car in the parking lot below.

Dejected, feeling utterly unloved, alone, and above all, sorry for myself, I drove to the beach. It was deserted. It was raining at the beach. There was no wind, and the rain fell very gently, very straight.

There was something peaceful about the hushed sound of the lapping waves and the rain hitting the water. I took off my shoes, tucked up my pants, and walked until I was washed clean of my indulgent moods.

I knew that I was rid of them because I heard from the whispering, lapping waves Florinda's words, "It's a solitary fight." I wasn't threatened; I simply accepted that I was indeed alone. And it was this acquiescence that brought me the conviction of what I had to do. And since I am not one to wait, I acted immediately.

After leaving a note under Isidoro Baltazar's door—I didn't want him to talk me out of it—I set out for the witches' house. I drove all night, all the way to Tucson. I checked in at a motel, slept most of the day, then late in the afternoon set out again, taking the same route Isidoro Baltazar had followed on our return trip.

My sense of direction is poor, yet that route is imprinted deep within me. With a baffling assurance, I knew exactly what roads to take, where to turn. I reached the witches' house in no time at all. I didn't bother to check my watch, for I didn't want to lose the feeling that no time had elapsed between the time I got into my car in Tucson and my arrival at the witches' house.

That there was no one at the house didn't bother me in the least. I was aware that no direct, formal invitation had been extended to me. But I remembered clearly that Nélida had told me, as she hid in a drawer a small basket with the gifts they had all given me, that I should come back any time I wished. "Day or night, this basket will pull you safely in." Her words rang in my ears.

With an assurance that ordinarily only comes from practice, I went directly to the room Esperanza had given me. The white, flouncy hammock was ready, as if waiting for me. A vague uneasiness finally took hold of me, but I wasn't nearly as scared as I should have been. Not quite relaxed, I lowered myself in the hammock, one leg outside to rock myself back and forth.

"To hell with my fears," I cried out and pulled my leg in and stretched out luxuriously like a cat until all my joints cracked.

"Oh, you've made it back safely," a voice said to me from the corridor.

I didn't see her, I didn't necessarily recognize her voice, yet I knew it was Nélida. I waited expectantly for her to come in, but she didn't.

"Your food is in the kitchen," I heard her say. Her steps moved away from my door, down the corridor.

I jumped up and dashed after her. "Wait, wait, Nélida!" I shouted. There was no one in the hall, in the rooms I passed on my way to the kitchen. There was no one in the whole house, for that matter. Yet, I was sure they were there. I heard their voices, their laughter, the clatter of dishes, of pots and pans.

I spent the next few days in a perpetual state of anticipation, waiting for something significant to occur. I couldn't imagine what was supposed to happen, but I knew that it had to be connected with the women.

For some unfathomable reason, the women didn't want to be seen. Their astoundingly furtive behavior kept me in the corridors at all hours, prowling noiselessly, like a shadow. Regardless of the ingeniously sneaky schemes I devised to surprise the women, I never caught so much as a glimpse of them. They glided in and out of their rooms, in and out of the house, as if in between worlds, leaving in their wake the sound of their voices and laughter.

Sometimes I wondered whether the women were indeed there, whether the sounds of footsteps, of murmurs and giggles, were but figments of my imagination. Whenever I was about to believe it was my imagination, I would hear one of them tinkering on the patio. Then, seized by renewed fervor, expectation, and excitement, I would run to the back of the house, only to discover that once again I had been outwitted. At those times I was convinced that the women, being real witches, had some kind of a bat-like internal echo location system that alerted them to my sounds.

My disappointment at not being able to catch them in front of the stove always vanished at the sight of the exotic little meals they left behind for me; the deliciousness of the dishes amply compensated for the meagerness of the portions. With great gusto I ate their wonderful food. Yet I was still hungry.

One day just before twilight, I heard a man's voice softly calling my name from the back of the house. I jumped out of my hammock and ran down the corridor. I was so glad to see the caretaker, I nearly jumped on him like a dog does. Unable to contain my joy, I kissed him on the cheeks.

"Watch out, nibelunga." He said this in the same voice and manner of Isidoro Baltazar. I sprang back, my eyes wide with surprise. He winked at me and added, "Don't get carried away, because the next thing you know, you'll be taking advantage of me."

For an instant I didn't know what to make of his words. But when he laughed and patted my back reassuringly, I completely relaxed.

"It's good to see you," he said softly.

"It's wonderful to see you!" I giggled self-consciously, then asked him where everybody else was.

"Oh, they are around," he said vaguely. "At the moment they are mysteriously inaccessible, but ever present." Seeing my disappointment he added, "Have patience."

"I know they are around," I murmured. "They leave food for me." I glanced over my shoulder to ham it up and confided, "But I'm still hungry. The portions are too little."

According to the caretaker, this was the natural condition of power food: One could never get enough of it. He said that he cooked his own food—rice and beans with either chunks of pork, beef, or chicken—and ate only once a day but never at the same hour.

He took me then to his quarters. He lived in the large, cluttered room behind the kitchen, amidst the odd wood and iron sculptures, where the air, thick with the scents of jasmine and eucalyptus, hung heavy and motionless around the drawn curtains. He slept on a cot, which he kept folded in the armoire when it was not in use, and ate his meal at a small chippendale table with spindly legs.

He confided that he, like the mysterious women, disliked routines. Day or night, morning or afternoon, was all the same to him. He swept the patios and raked the leaves outside the clearing whenever he felt like doing so; whether there were blossoms or leaves on the ground was immaterial.

In the days that followed, I had a hellish time trying to adjust to this seemingly unstructured way of life. Out of compulsion, rather than out of any desire to be useful, I helped the caretaker with his chores. Also, I invariably accepted his invitations to share his meals. His food was as delicious as his company.

Convinced that he was more than the caretaker, I did my best to get him off-guard with my devious questions; a useless technique, for I never got any satisfactory answers.

"Where do you come from?" I bluntly asked him one day while we were eating.

He looked up from his plate, and as if he had been expecting an outright interrogation, he dutifully pointed to the mountains toward the east, framed by the open window like a painting.

"The Bacatete Mountains?" My voice betrayed my disbelief. "But you're not an Indian," I mumbled disconcertedly. "The way I see it, only the nagual Mariano Aureliano, Delia Flores, and Genaro Flores are Indians." Emboldened by the surprised, expectant look on his face, I added that, in my opinion, Esperanza transcended racial categories. I leaned across the table and in a secretive tone confided to him what I had already told Florinda. "Esperanza wasn't born like a human being. She was established by an act of witchcraft. She is the very devil."

Leaning back in his chair, the caretaker shrieked with joy. "And what do you have to say about Florinda? Did you know she's French? Or rather, her parents were French. They were from the families that came to Mexico with Maximilian and Carlota."

"She's very beautiful," I murmured, trying to remember when, exactly, in the eighteen hundreds the Austrian prince was sent by Napoleon to Mexico.

"You haven't seen her when she's all dolled up," the caretaker gushed. "She's something else. Age means nothing to her."

"Carmela told me that I am like Florinda," I said in a fit of vanity and wishful thinking.

Propelled by the laughter bubbling up inside him, the caretaker sprang up from his chair. "That'll be the day." He said the words with no particular feeling, as though he didn't care in the least how they would be received.

Irritated by his remark, his lack of feeling, I glared at him with ill-concealed animosity. Then, eager to change the subject, I asked him about the nagual Mariano Aureliano. "Where exactly does he come from?"

"Who knows where naguals come from?" he muttered, moving toward the window. For a long while he gazed at the distant mountains, then he turned toward me once again and said, "Some people say that naguals come from hell itself. I believe it. Some people say that naguals are not even human." Again he paused, and I wondered if the long silence was to be repeated. As if sensing my impatience, he came to sit beside me and added, "If you ask me, I'd say that naguals are superhuman. That's the reason they know everything about human nature. You can't lie to a nagual. They see through you. They see through anything. They even see through space, to other worlds in this world and to others out of this world."

I moved uneasily in my chair, wishing he would stop talking. I regretted engaging him in this conversation. There was no doubt in my mind that the man was insane.

"No, I'm not insane," he assured me, and I let out a loud shriek. "I'm saying things that you've never heard before, that's all."

I blinked repeatedly, put oddly on the defensive. But my uneasiness gave me a surge of courage, and I asked him point blank, "Why are they hiding from me?"

"It's obvious," he shot back, then seeing that it wasn't at all obvious to me, he added, "You should know it. You and your kind are the crew, not me. I'm not one of them. I'm merely the caretaker. I oil the machine."

"You're getting me more confused than I was," I muttered, irritated. Then a momentary flash of insight hit me. "Who are the crew you are referring to?"

"All the women you met the last time you were here. The dreamers and the stalkers. They told me that the stalkers are your kind. And you are one of them."

He poured himself a glass of water and went with it to the window. He took a few sips then informed me that the nagual Mariano Aureliano had tried out my stalking abilities in Tucson, Arizona, when he sent me into the coffee shop to put a cockroach in my food. The caretaker turned his back to the window, looked straight into my face, and added, "You failed."

"I don't want to hear about that nonsense," I cut him short. I had no desire to hear the rest of the story.

His face crinkled with mischief. "But then, after your failure, you exonerated yourself by kicking and yelling at the nagual Mariano Aureliano without shame or regard. Stalkers," he stressed, "are people who have a knack for dealing with people."

I opened my mouth to say that I didn't understand a word he was saying, but quickly shut it again.

"What has been baffling," he went on, "is that you are a great dreamer. If it wouldn't be for that, you'd be like Florinda—less the height and the looks, of course."

Smiling venomously, I cursed the old creep silently.

"Do you remember how many women were there at the picnic?" he asked all of a sudden.

I closed my eyes to better visualize the picnic. I clearly saw six women sitting on the canvas cloth, spread out under the eucalyptus trees. Esperanza wasn't there, but Carmela, Zoila, Delia, and Florinda were.

"Who were the other two?" I asked, more mystified than ever.

"Ah," he murmured appreciatively, a brilliant smile creasing his face. "Those two were dreamers from another world. You saw them clearly, but then they disappeared, and your mind didn't acknowledge their vanishing because it was simply too outlandish."

I nodded absentmindedly, unable to conceive that I had actually seen only four women, when I knew that there had been six.

The thought must have seeped through to him, for he said that it was only natural to have focused on the four. "The other two are your source of energy. They are incorporeal and not from this world."

Lost and bewildered, all I could do was stare at him; I had no more questions to ask.

"Since you are not in the planet of the dreamers," he clarified, "your dreams are nightmares, and your transitions between dreams and reality are very unstable and dangerous to you and to the other dreamers. So Florinda has taken it upon herself to buffer and protect you."

I rose with such impetus my chair turned over. "I don't want to know anything else!" I cried out. Just in time, I stopped myself from blurting out that I was better off not knowing about their mad ways and rationales.

The caretaker took me by the hand and walked with me outside, across the clearing, across the chaparral to the back of the small house.

"I need you to help me with the generator," he said. "It needs fixing."

I laughed out loud and told him that I didn't know anything about generators. Only when he opened the trap door of a concrete encasement did I realize that the electric current for the lights in the house was generated there. I had completely taken for granted that the electrical lights and appliances of rural Mexico were like those I was familiar with.

From that day on, I tried not to ask him too many questions. I felt that I was not prepared for his answers. Our meetings acquired the nature of a ritual in which I did my best to match the old man's exquisite usage of the Spanish language. I spent hours pouring over the various dictionaries in my room, searching for new and often archaic words with which to impress him.

One afternoon, as I was waiting for the caretaker to bring in the food—it was the first time since I discovered his room that I was alone in it—I remembered the old, strange mirror. I carefully examined its spotty, misty surface.

"You'll get trapped in the mirror if you look at yourself too much," a voice behind me said.

Expecting to see the caretaker, I turned around, but there was no one in the room. In my eagerness to reach the door, I almost knocked over the wood and iron sculpture behind me. Automatically, I reached out to steady it, but before I so much as touched it, the figure seemed to spin away from me in an odd circular motion, then came to its original position with an astonishingly human sigh.

"What's the matter?" the caretaker asked, stepping into the room. He placed a large tray on the rickety table and, looking up into my ashen face, asked once more what was wrong with me.

"Sometimes, I've the feeling that these monstrosities are alive, watching me," I said, gesturing with my chin toward the nearby sculpture. Noticing his grave, unsmiling face, I hastened to reassure him that I didn't mean monstrous in terms of ugliness but rather in terms of being big. I took several deep, shuddering breaths and repeated that his sculptures gave me the impression of being alive.

Glancing furtively around himself and lowering his voice to a barely audible whisper, he said, "They are alive."

I felt so uncomfortable that I began to babble about the afternoon I first discovered his room, how I had been lured to it by an eerie-sounding murmur that turned out to be the wind pushing the curtain through a broken window. "Yet at the time I believed it to be a monster," I confided, giggling nervously. "An alien presence feeding on the twilight shadows."

Chewing his lower lip, the caretaker regarded me with keen eyes. Then his gaze drifted unfocused around the room. "We better sit down to eat," he finally said. "We don't want to let our food get cold." He held out the chair for me, and as soon as I was comfortably seated, he added in a vibrant tone, "You're quite right to call them presences, for they are not sculptures. They are *inventions*." He confided in a conspiratorial tone, "They were conceived from patterns glimpsed at in another world, by a great nagual."

"By Mariano Aureliano?" I asked.

He shook his head and said, "By a much older nagual, named Elías."

"Why are these inventions in your room?" I asked. "Did this great nagual make them for you?"

"No," he said. "I only take care of them." Rising, he reached into his pocket and pulled out a neatly folded white handkerchief and proceeded to dust the nearby invention with it. "Since I'm the caretaker, it falls upon me to take care of them. One day, with the help of all these sorcerers you've already met, I will deliver these inventions where they belong."

"And where is that?"

"Infinity, the cosmos, the vacuum."

"How do you propose to take them there?"

"Through the same power that got them here in the first place: the power of dreaming-awake."

"If you dream like these sorcerers dream," I began cautiously, trying hard to conceal the triumph in my voice, "then you must also be a sorcerer yourself."

"I am, but I am not like them."

His candid admission confused me. "What's the difference?"

"Ah!" he exclaimed knowingly. "All the difference in the world. But I can't explain it now. If I do, you'd get even more morose and angry. Someday, though, you'll know all about it by yourself, without anyone having to tell you."

I could feel the wheels churning in my head as I desperately tried to come up with something else to say, another question to ask.

"Can you tell me how the nagual Elías came to have the inventions?"

"He saw them in his dreaming and captured them," the caretaker confided. "Some of them are copies, done by him, of inventions he couldn't cart away. Others are the real thing. Inventions transported by that great nagual all the way to here."

I didn't believe a word he said, yet I couldn't help but add, "Why did the nagual Elías bring them?"

"Because the inventions themselves asked him to."

"Why did they?"

The caretaker dismissed my probings with a wave of his hand and urged me to eat my food. His unwillingness to satisfy my curiosity only piqued my interest. I couldn't imagine why he didn't want to talk about the contraptions when he was so good at evasive answers; he could have told me anything.

The instant we finished our meal, he asked me to retrieve his cot from the armoire. Knowing his preference, I unfolded it for him in front of the curtained French door. Sighing contentedly, he lay down, resting his head on the rectangular little pillow that was attached to one end of the cot. It was filled with dried beans and maize kernels. According to him, the pillow ensured sweet dreams.

"I'm ready for my nap now," he said, loosening the belt on his pants. It was his polite way of dismissing me.

Peeved by his refusal to talk about the inventions, I piled our plates on the tray and stormed out of the room. His snores followed me all the way to the kitchen.

That night I awoke to the strumming of a guitar. Automatically, I reached for the flashlight I kept beside my low-hanging hammock and checked my watch. It was a bit past midnight. I wrapped my blanket tightly around me and tiptoed out into the corridor that led to the inside patio.

On the patio, sitting on a rush chair, was a man playing a guitar. I couldn't see his face, but I knew it was the same man Isidoro Baltazar and I had seen and heard the first time I was there. As he did then, the man stopped playing the moment he saw me; he got up from his chair and went inside the house.

As soon as I was back in my room, his plucking resumed. I was about to doze off when I heard him sing in a clear, strong voice. He sang to the wind, beckoning it to come from across miles of silence and emptiness.

As if responding to his haunting invocation, the wind gathered force. It whistled through the chaparral. It tore the withered leaves from the trees and swept them into rustling heaps against the walls of the house.

On an impulse, I opened the door to the patio. The wind filled the room with an unspeakable sadness, not the sadness of tears but the melancholic solitariness of the desert, of dust and ancient shadows. The wind circled around the room like smoke. I inhaled it with every breath. It sat heavy in my lungs, yet the deeper I breathed, the lighter I felt.

I went outside and, squeezing between the tall bushes, made my way to the back of the house. The white-washed walls caught the moonlight and reflected it brightly onto the windswept ground of the wide clearing. Afraid I might be seen, I darted from fruit tree to fruit tree, hiding in the dark shadows cast by the moonlight until I reached the two blooming orange trees outside the wall guarding the path to the little house.

The wind brought the sound of giggles and dim murmurings from across the chaparral. Daringly, I dashed along the path, only to lose my nerve once I reached the front door of the small, dark house. Quivering with excitement, I inched my way to an open window. I recognized Delia's and Florinda's voices, but the window was too high for me to see what the women were doing.

I listened, expecting to hear something profound, to be transported by some mind-shattering revelation that would help me resolve what I had come there for—my inability to dream. But I only heard gossip. I became so engrossed in their malicious insinuations that I laughed out loud several times, forgetting that I was eavesdropping.

At first I thought they were gossiping about outsiders, but then I realized they were talking about the women dreamers, and their most insidious remarks were directed against Nélida.

They said that she had so far been unable, after so many years, to break away from the grip of the world. Not only was she vain—they claimed she spent all day in front of the mirror—but she was lusty as well. She did everything in her power to be a sexually desirable woman in order to entice the nagual Mariano Aureliano. Someone pointed out, cattily, that, after all, she was the only one who could accommodate his enormous, intoxicating organ.

Then they talked about Clara. They called her a pompous elephant who believed that it was her duty to bestow blessings on everyone. The recipient of her attention was, at the moment, the nagual Isidoro Baltazar, and the treat was her naked body. He wasn't to have it, only to see it. Once in the morning and again once at night she would regale him with the sight of her nakedness. She was convinced that by doing this, she would ensure the young nagual's sexual prowess.

The third woman they talked about was Zuleica. They said that she had delusions of being a saint and the Virgin Mary. Her so-called spirituality was nothing but craziness. Periodically she would lose her marbles. And whenever she had one of her fits of insanity, she would clean the house from top to bottom, even the rocks in the patio or around the grounds.

Then there was Hermelinda. She was described as being very sober, very proper, the paragon of middle-class values. As Nélida, she was incapable, after so many years, of stopping herself from seeking to be the perfect woman, the perfect homemaker. Although she couldn't cook or sew or embroider or play the piano to entertain her guests, Hermelinda wanted to be known, they said in between fits of giggles, as the paragon of good femininity, just as Nélida wanted to be known as the paragon of naughty femininity.

If the two of them would only combine their talents, one voice remarked, then they would have the perfect woman to please the master: perfect in the kitchen and in the living room, wearing an apron or an evening dress, and perfect in bed with her legs up whenever the master wanted it.

When they grew silent, I ran back to the house, to my room and into my hammock. But hard as I tried, I could no longer go back to sleep. I felt that some kind of a protective bubble had burst around me, obliterating my sense of delight, of enchantment at being at the witches' house. All I could think of was that, by my own doings this time, I was stuck there in Sonora with a bunch of crazy old women who did nothing else but gossip, when I could have been in Los Angeles having fun.

I had come looking for advice. Instead, I was ignored, reduced to the company of a senile old man who I believed to be a woman.

By the time I sat down to eat with the caretaker in the morning, I had driven myself into such a state of righteous indignation that I couldn't swallow a bite.

"What's the matter?" the old man asked, gazing at me intently. Normally, he avoided direct eye contact. "Aren't you hungry?"

I glared back at him. Giving up any attempt at self-control, I unburdened all my pent-up anger and frustration. As I went on complaining, I had a flash of sobriety; I told myself that I shouldn't blame the old man, that I should be grateful, for he had shown me nothing but kindness. But it was too late to stop myself. My petty grievances had acquired a life of their own. My voice became shriller still as I magnified and deformed the events of the past few days. With malicious satisfaction, I told him that I had eavesdropped on the women.

"They don't want to help me in the least," I asserted with resonant authority. "All they do is gossip. They said horrible things about the women dreamers."

"What did you hear them say?"

With great relish I told him everything. I surprised myself with my extraordinary power to recollect every detail of the women's wicked remarks.

"Obviously, they were talking about you," he declared the moment I finished my account. "In a symbolic fashion, of course." He waited for the words to sink in, and before I could protest, he asked innocently, "Aren't you quite a bit like all this?"

"Like hell I am!" I exploded. "And don't give me any psychological shit; I won't take this kind of crap, not even from an educated man, much the less from you, you fucking peon."

The caretaker's eyes opened wide in bewilderment and his frail shoulders sagged. I felt no sympathy for him, only pity for myself. I had wasted my time telling him what I had heard.

I was about to say what a mistake it had been for me to make that long, arduous journey and all for nothing, when the caretaker looked at me with such contempt that I felt ashamed of my outburst.

"If you hold your temper, you'll understand that nothing these sorcerers do is just to entertain themselves or to impress someone or to give way to their compulsiveness," he said with great equanimity. "Everything they do or say has a reason, a purpose." He stared at me with an intensity that made me want to move away, but I couldn't. "Don't go around thinking that you're here on a vacation," he stressed. "For the sorcerers you've fallen prey to, there are no holidays."

"What are you trying to tell me?" I demanded angrily. "Don't beat around the bush, just say it."

"How can anyone be more clear?" His voice was deceptively mellow and loaded with more meaning than I could fathom. "The witches already told you last night what you are. They used the four women of the dreamers' planet as a false front to describe to you, the eavesdropper, what you really are: a slut, with delusions of grandeur."

So great was my shock, I was momentarily stunned. Then anger, hot as lava, shot through my whole body. "You miserable, insignificant piece of shit," I yelled and kicked him in the groin. Before my kick had landed I already had a flash image of the little old bastard on the ground, wriggling with pain, except that my kick never landed anywhere but in the air. With the speed of a prize fighter he had jumped out of the way.

He smiled with his mouth, but his eyes were flat and cold as he watched me puffing and groaning. "You are playing on the nagual Isidoro Baltazar all those tricks the witches talked about. You were trained for it. Think about it. Don't just get angry."

I opened my mouth to say something, but no sound emerged. It wasn't so much his words that had left me speechless as his devastatingly indifferent, icy tone. I would have preferred he had yelled at me, for then I would have known how to react: I would have yelled louder.

There was no point in fighting him. He wasn't right, I assured myself. He was simply a senile man with a bitter tongue. No, I wasn't going to get mad at him, but I wasn't going to take him seriously either.

"I hope you're not going to weep," he warned me before I recovered from my shock.

Despite my determination not to get mad at the senile bastard, my face grew red with anger. "Of course, I'm not," I snapped. Before I tried another kick, I yelled at him that since he was only a chicken-shit servant he deserved to be beaten for his impertinence, but the hard, relentless expression in his eyes made me lose my momentum. Somehow he managed to convince me, without the faintest change in his courteous yet inexpressive tone, that I should apologize to him.

"I'm sorry," I finally said, and truly meant it. "My bad temper and bad manners always get the best of me."

"I know it; they all warned me about you," he said seriously, then added, smiling, "Eat your food."

I was ill at ease all through the meal. Chewing slowly, I watched him surreptitiously. Although he didn't make the slightest effort to be friendly, I knew that he wasn't angry with me. I tried to comfort myself with that thought, but I didn't find it very comforting. I sensed that his lack of concern wasn't deliberate or studied. He wasn't punishing me. Nothing of what I had said or done would have had any effect on him.

I swallowed the last bite and said the first thing that entered into my head with an assurance that astonished me, "You're not the caretaker."

He looked at me and asked, "And who do you think I am?" His face relaxed into an amused grin.

His smile made me lose all caution. A tremendous recklessness came over me. I blurted out—and naturally as an insult—that he was a woman, that he was Esperanza. Relieved that I had finally gotten it off my chest, I sighed loudly and added, "That's why you're the only one who has a mirror; you need to look convincing as either a man or a woman."

"The Sonoran air must have affected you," he mused. "It's a known fact that the thin desert air affects people in the most peculiar manner." He reached for my wrist and held it in a tight grip as he added, "Or it is perhaps your nature to be mean and onerous and blurt out, with an air of absolute authority, anything that enters your head?"

Chuckling, the caretaker leaned closer toward me and suggested that I take a nap with him. "It'll do us a lot of good. We're both onerous," he said.

"So that's it!" I exclaimed, uncertain whether I should take offense or laugh at his suggestion. "You want me to sleep with you, eh?" I added that Esperanza had already warned me about him."

"Why do you object to taking a nap with me if you believe me to be Esperanza?" he asked, rubbing the nape of my neck. His hand was warm and soothing.

"I don't object," I defended myself feebly. "I simply hate naps. I never take a nap. I was told that even as a baby I hated naps." I spoke rapidly and nervously, tripping over my words, repeating myself. I wanted to get up and leave, but the slight pressure of his hand on my neck kept me pinned down to the chair. "I know that you're Esperanza," I insisted rashly. "I recognize her touch; it has the same soothing effect as yours." I could feel my head sway, and my eyes closed against my will.

"So it has," he agreed gently. "It'll do you good to lie down, even if only for a moment." Taking my silence for acquiescence, he went to the armoire and pulled out his cot and two blankets. He gave me one.

It was a time of endless surprises for me. Without knowing why, I lay down without protest. Through half-closed lids, I watched him stretch until all his joints cracked. He shook off his boots, unfastened his belt, then lowered himself on the cot next to me. Under the cover of his thin cotton blanket, he wiggled out of his pants, casually dropping them on the floor, next to his boots.

209

He lifted his blanket and showed himself to me. Blushing, I stared at him with wild curiosity and wonder. His naked body, like Esperanza's, was the antithesis of what I had taken it to be. His body was supple, hairless, and smooth. He was thin as a reed and yet muscular. And he was definitely a male and young!

I didn't even pause to think, but holding my breath, I gingerly lifted my blanket.

The sound of a woman's faint giggle made me close my eyes and pretend I was asleep. But knowing that she wasn't going to come into the room, I relaxed. Putting my arms behind my head I became absorbed in an uncanny sense that the caretaker and the faint giggles coming from the corridor had restored a balance, had renewed the magic bubble all around me. What exactly I meant by this, I didn't know, except that the more my body relaxed, the closer I was getting to an answer.

14

AFTER my return from the witches' house I never needed any more coaxing or encouragement. The women sorcerers had succeeded in giving me a strange coherence, a sort of emotional stability I never had before. It wasn't that I was suddenly a changed person, but rather there was a clear purpose to my existence. My fate was delineated for me: I had to struggle to free my energy. And that was that. Simplicity itself.

But I didn't remember, clearly or even vaguely, all that had transpired in the three months I spent at their house. The task of remembering it took me years, a task into which I plunged with all my might and determination.

The nagual Isidoro Baltazar, nevertheless, warned me about the fallaciousness of clear-cut goals and emotionally charged realizations. He said that they were worthless, because the real arena of a sorcerer is the day-to-day life, and there, superficial rationales do not withstand pressure.

The women sorcerers had said more or less the same but in a more harmonious way. They explained that since women are used to being manipulated, they agreed easily, and that their agreements are simply empty adaptations to pressure. But if it is really possible to convince women of the need to change their ways, then half the battle is won; even if they don't agree, their realization is infinitely more durable than that of men.

I had the two opinions to weigh. I thought that both were right. From time to time, all my sorcery rationales crumbled under the pressures of the everyday world, but my original commitment to the sorcerers' world was never in need of revision.

Little by little I began to acquire enough energy to dream. This meant that I finally understood what the women had told me: Isidoro Baltazar was the new nagual. And he was no longer a man. This realization also gave me enough energy to return periodically to the witches' house.

That place, known as the witches' house, belonged to all the sorcerers of the nagual Mariano Aureliano's group. A big and massive house from the outside, it was indistinguishable from other houses in the area, hardly noticeable in spite of the exuberantly blooming bougainvillea hanging over the wall that encircled the grounds. What made people pass the house without noticing it, the sorcerers said, was the tenuous fog that covered it, thin as a veil, visible to the eye, but unnoticeable to the mind.

Once inside the house, however, one was acutely and inescapably aware of having stepped into another world. The three patios, shaded by fruit trees, gave a dreamlike light to the dark corridors and the many rooms that opened on these corridors. What was most arresting about the house were the brick and tile floors which were laid out in the most intricate designs.

The witches' house was not a warm place, yet it was friendly. It was not a home by any stretch of the imagination, for there was something crushing about its impersonality, its relentless austerity. It was the place where the old nagual Mariano Aureliano and his sorcerers conceived their dreams and realized their purpose. Since the concern of those sorcerers had nothing to do with the daily world, their house reflected their otherworldly preoccupations; their house was the true gauge of their individuality, not as persons but as sorcerers.

At the witches' house, I interacted with all the sorcerers of the nagual Mariano Aureliano's party. They didn't teach me sorcery or even dreaming. According to them, there was nothing to teach. They said that my task was to remember everything that had transpired

212

between all of them and me during those initial times that we were together. In particular, I was to remember everything that Zuleica and Florinda did or said to me—but Zuleica had never talked to me.

Whenever I tried to ask any of them for help, they outright refused to have anything to do with me. They all argued that, without the necessary energy on my part, all they would do would be to repeat themselves, and that they didn't have time for that.

At first, I found their refusal ungenerous and unfair. After a while, however, I gave up every attempt to probe them, and I simply enjoyed their presence and their company. And I realized that they were, of course, totally right in refusing to play our favorite intellectual game, that of pretending to be interested by asking so-called soul-searching questions, which usually have no meaning to us whatsoever. And the reason they have no meaning to us is that we don't have the energy to do anything about the answer we might hear, except to agree or disagree with it.

Via our daily interaction, however, I realized scores of things about their world. The dreamers and the stalkers embodied two modes of behavior among women, as different as they could be.

Initially, I wondered whether the group that was described to me as the dreamers—Nélida, Hermelinda, and Clara—were the actual stalkers. For as far as I could ascertain, my interaction with them was on a strictly everyday, worldly level. Only later did I fully realize that their mere presence elicited—without even any hint of it—a new modality of behavior on my part. That is, I felt no need to reassert myself with them. There were no doubts, there were no questions on my part whenever I was with them. They had the singular ability to make me see—without ever having to state it verbally—the absurdity of my existence. And yet I felt no need to defend myself.

Perhaps it was this lack of forcefulness, of directness, that made me acquiesce, accept them without any resistance. It wasn't long before I realized that the women dreamers, by interacting with me on a worldly level, were giving me the necessary model to rechannel my energies. They wanted me to change the manner in which I focused on mundane matters such as cooking, cleaning, laundering, staying in school, or earning a living. These were to be done, they told me, under different auspices; they were not to be mundane chores but artful endeavors, one as important as the other.

Above all, it was their interaction with each other and with the women stalkers that made me aware of how special they were. In their humanness, their ordinariness, they were devoid of ordinary human failings. Their total awareness coexisted easily with their individual characteristics, be it short-temperedness, moodiness, rude forcefulness, madness, or cloying sweetness.

In the presence and company of any of those sorceresses, I experienced the most peculiar feeling that I was on a perpetual holiday. But that was but a mirage. They were on a perpetual warpath. And the enemy was the idea of the self.

At the witches' house, I also met Vicente and Silvio Manuel, the other two sorcerers in the nagual Mariano Aureliano's group.

Vicente was obviously of Spanish descent. I learned that his parents had come from Catalonia. He was a lean, aristocratic-looking man with deceptively frail-looking hands and feet. He shuffled around in slippers and preferred pajama tops, which hung open over his khaki pants, to shirts. His cheeks were rosy, but otherwise he was pale. His beautifully cared for goatee added a touch of distinction to his otherwise absentminded demeanor.

Not only did he look like a scholar, but he was one. The books in the room I slept in were his, or rather, it was he who collected them, who read them, who cared for them. What made his erudition so appealing—there was nothing he didn't know about—was that he conducted himself as though he was always the learner. I felt sure that this could seldom be the case, for it was obvious that he knew more than the others. It was his generous spirit that made him give his knowledge away with a magnificent naturalness and without ever shaming anyone for knowing less.

Then there was Silvio Manuel. He was of medium height, corpulent, beardless, and brown skinned. A mysterious, sinister-looking Indian, he was the perfect image of what I expected an evil-looking *brujo* to look like. His apparent moodiness frightened me, and his sparse answers revealed what I believed to be a violent nature.

Only upon knowing him did I realize how much he enjoyed cultivating this image. He was the most open, and for me, delightful, of all the sorcerers. Secrets and gossip were his passion; whether they were truths or falsehoods didn't matter to him. It was his recounting of them that was priceless to me, and to everyone else, for that matter. He also had an inexhaustible supply of jokes, most of them downright dirty. He was the only one who enjoyed watching TV and thus was always up to date on world news. He would report it to the others with gross exaggerations, salting it with a great deal of malice.

Silvio Manuel was a magnificent dancer. His expertise in the various indigenous, sacred dances was legendary. He moved with rapturous abandon and would often ask me to dance with him. Whether it was a Venezuelan joropo, a cumbia, a samba, a tango, the twist, rock and roll, or a cheek-to-cheek bolero, he knew them all.

I also interacted with John, the Indian I had been introduced to by the nagual Mariano Aureliano in Tucson, Arizona. His round, easygoing, jovial appearance was but a facade. He was the most unapproachable of all the sorcerers. He drove around in his pickup truck on errands for everyone else. He also fixed whatever needed to be mended in and around the house.

If I didn't bother him with questions or comments and kept silent, he would take me with him on his errands and show me how things were fixed. From him I learned how to change washers and adjust a leaking faucet or toilet tank; how to fix an iron, a light switch; how to change the oil and spark plugs in my car. Under his guidance, the proper use of a hammer, a screwdriver, a saw, an electric drill became quite natural to me.

The only thing none of them did for me was answer my questions and probes about their world. Whenever I tried to engage them, they referred me to the nagual Isidoro Baltazar. Their standard rebuff was to say, "He's the new nagual. It's his duty to deal with you. We are merely your aunties and uncles."

At the beginning, the nagual Isidoro Baltazar was more than a mystery to me. Where he actually lived was not clear to me. Oblivious to schedules and routines, he appeared at and disappeared from the studio at all hours. Day and night were all the same to him. He slept when he was tired—hardly ever—and ate when he was hungry—almost always. Between his frantic comings and goings, he worked with a concentration that was astounding. His capacity to stretch or compress time was incomprehensible to me. I was certain that I spent hours, even entire days, with him, when in reality it could have been only moments, snatched here and there, either during the day or the night, from something else he did— whatever it might have been.

I had always considered myself an energetic person. However, I could not keep up with him. He was always in motion—or so it appeared—agile and active, ever ready to undertake some project. His vigor was simply incredible.

It was much later that I fully understood that the source of Isidoro Baltazar's boundless energy was his lack of concern with himself. It was his unwavering support, his imperceptible yet masterful machinations, that helped me stay on the right track. There was a lighthearted-edness in him, a pure delight in his subtle yet forceful influence, that made me change without my noticing that I was being led along a new path, a path on which I no longer had to play games or needed to pretend or use my womanly wiles to get my way.

What made his guidance so tremendously compelling was that he had no ulterior motive; he wasn't in the least possessive, and his guidance wasn't adulterated with promises or sentimentality.

He didn't push me in any particular direction. That is, he didn't advise me on what courses I should take or what books I should read; that was left entirely up to me.

There was only one condition he insisted upon: I was to work for no particular goal other than the edifying and pleasurable process of thinking. A startling proposition! I had never considered thinking in those terms or in any others. Although I didn't dislike going to school, I had certainly never thought of schoolwork as particularly pleasurable. It was simply something I had to do, usually in a hurry and with the least possible effort.

I couldn't help but agree with what Florinda and her cohorts had so bluntly pointed out to me the first time I met them: I went to school not to pursue knowledge but to have a good time. That I had good grades was more a matter of luck and loquaciousness than studiousness. I had a fairly good memory. I knew how to talk. And I knew how to convince others.

Once I got past my initial embarrassment over having to admit and to accept the fact that my intellectual pretensions were a sham, that I didn't know how to think except in the most shallow manner, I felt relieved. I was ready to put myself under the sorcerers' tutelage and to follow Isidoro Baltazar's study plan. To my great disappointment, he didn't have one. All he did was insist that I stop studying and reading outdoors. He believed that the thinking process was a private, almost secret rite and could not possibly occur outdoors in public view. He compared the process of thinking with leavened dough. It can only rise inside a room.

"The best way to understand anything, of course, is in bed," he said to me once. He stretched out on his bed, propped his head against several pillows, and crossed the right leg over the left, resting the ankle on the raised knee of the left leg.

I didn't think much of this absurd reading position, yet I practiced it whenever I was by myself. With a book propped on my chest, I would fall into the most profound sleep. Keenly sensitive to my insomniac tendencies, I was more pleased with sleep than with knowledge.

Sometimes, however, just prior to that moment of losing consciousness, I would feel as if hands were coiling around my head, pressing ever so lightly against my temples. My eyes would automatically scan the open page before I was even conscious of it and lift entire paragraphs off the paper. The words would dance before my eyes until clusters of meaning exploded in my brain like revelations.

Eager to uncover this new possibility opening up before me, I pushed on, as if driven by some relentless taskmaster. There were times, however, when this cultivation of reason and method exhausted me, physically as well as mentally. At those times, I asked Isidoro Baltazar about intuitive knowledge, about that sudden flash of insight, of understanding, that sorcerers are supposed to cultivate above all else.

He always said to me at those times that to know something only intuitively is meaningless. Flashes of insight need to be translated into some coherent thought, otherwise they are purposeless. He compared flashes of insight to sightings of inexplicable phenomena. Both wane as swiftly as they come. If they are not constantly reinforced, doubt and forgetfulness will ensue, for the mind has been conditioned to be practical and accept only that which is verifiable and quantifiable.

He explained that sorcerers are men of knowledge rather than men of reason. As such, they are a step ahead of Western intellectual men who assume that reality—which is often equated with truth—is knowable through reason. A sorcerer claims that all that is knowable through reason is our thought processes but that it is only by understanding our total being, at its most sophisticated and intricate level, that can we eventually erase the boundaries with which reason defines reality.

Isidoro Baltazar explained to me that sorcerers cultivate the totality of their being. That is, sorcerers don't necessarily make a distinction between our rational and our intuitive sides. They use both to reach the realm of awareness they call silent knowledge, which lies beyond language, beyond thought.

Again and again, Isidoro Baltazar stressed that for one to silence one's rational side one first has to understand his or her thought process at its most sophisticated and intricate level. He believed that philosophy, beginning with classical Greek thought, provided the best way of illuminating this thought process. He never tired of repeating that, whether we are scholars or laymen, we are nonetheless members and inheritors of our Western intellectual tradition. And that means that regardless of our level of education and sophistication, we are captives of that intellectual tradition and the way it interprets what reality is.

Only superficially, Isidoro Baltazar claimed, are we willing to accept that what we call reality is a culturally determined construct. And what we need is to accept at the deepest level possible that culture is the product of a long, cooperative, highly selective, highly developed, and, last but not least, highly coercive process that culminates in an agreement that shields us from other possibilities.

Sorcerers actively strive to unmask the fact that reality is dictated and upheld by our reason; that ideas and thoughts stemming from reason become regimes of knowledge that ordain how we see and act in the world; and that incredible pressure is put on all of us to make certain ideologies acceptable to ourselves.

He stressed that sorcerers are interested in perceiving the world in ways outside of what is culturally determined. What is culturally determined is that our personal experiences, plus a shared social agreement on what our senses are capable of perceiving, dictate what we perceive. Anything out of this sensorially agreed-upon perceptual realm is automatically encapsulated and disregarded by the rational mind. In this manner, the frail blanket of human assumptions is never damaged.

Sorcerers teach that perception takes place in a place outside the sensorial realm. Sorcerers know that something more vast exists than what we have agreed our senses can perceive. Perception takes place at a point outside the body, outside the senses, they say. But it isn't enough for one merely to believe this premise. It is not simply a matter of reading or hearing about it from someone else. In order for one to embody it, one has to experience it.

Isidoro Baltazar said that sorcerers actively strive, all their lives, to break that frail blanket of human assumptions. However, sorcerers don't plunge into the darkness blindly. They are prepared. They know that whenever they leap into the unknown, they need to have a well-developed rational side. Only then will they be able to explain and make sense of whatever they might bring forth from their journeys into the unknown.

He added that I wasn't to understand sorcery through reading the works of philosophers. Rather, I was to see that both philosophy and sorcery are highly sophisticated forms of abstract knowledge. Both for sorcerer and philosopher, the truth of our Being-in-the-world does not remain unthought. A sorcerer, however, goes a step further. He acts upon his findings, which are already, by definition, outside our culturally accepted possibilities.

Isidoro Baltazar believed that philosophers are intellectual sorcerers. However, their probings and their pursuits always remain mental endeavors. Philosophers cannot act upon the world they understand and explain so well except in the culturally agreed-upon manner. Philosophers add to an already existing body of knowledge. They interpret and reinterpret existing philosophical texts. New thoughts and ideas resulting from this intense studying don't change them, except perhaps in a psychological sense. They might become kinder, more understanding people—or, perhaps, the opposite. However, nothing of what they do philosophically will change their sensorial perception of the world, for philosophers work from within the social order. They uphold the social order even if intellectually they don't agree with it. Philosophers are sorcerers manqué.

Sorcerers also build upon an existing body of knowledge. However, they don't build upon this knowledge by accepting what has already been established and proven by other sorcerers. Sorcerers have to prove to themselves anew that that which already stands as accepted does indeed exist, does indeed yield to perceiving. To accomplish this monumental task, sorcerers need an extraordinary amount of energy, which they obtain by detaching themselves from the social order without retreating from the world. Sorcerers break the agreement that has defined reality, without breaking up in the process themselves.

15

UNCERTAINTY took hold of me shortly after we crossed the border at Mexicali. My justification for going to Mexico with Isidoro Baltazar, which had seemed so brilliant to me, now seemed only a shady excuse for forcing him to take me along. I doubted now that I would be able to read sociological theory at the witches' house, as I said I would.

I knew that I would do there exactly what I did on all previous occasions: sleep a great deal, dream weird dreams, and try desperately to figure out what the people in the sorcerers' world wanted me to do.

"Any regrets?" Isidoro Baltazar's voice made me jump. He was looking at me sideways and had probably been watching me for a while.

"Of course not," I hastened to assure him, wondering whether he was referring to my general feeling or to my quietness. I stammered some inanities about the heat, then turned to look out the window.

I didn't speak anymore, mainly because I was scared and morose. I could feel anxiety crawling on my skin like a swarm of ants.

Isidoro Baltazar, on the other hand, warmed up to his ebullient best. He was elated. He sang and told me inane jokes. He recited poetry in English, Spanish, and Portuguese. Even tidbits of spicy gossip about people we both knew at UCLA failed to dispel my gloom. That I wasn't a responsive audience didn't mean a thing to him. Even my yelling at him to leave me alone didn't dampen his high spirits.

"If people were watching us, they would believe that we've been married for years," he commented in between fits of laughter.

If sorcerers were watching us, I thought dejectedly, they would know that something is wrong. They would know that Isidoro Baltazar and I are not equals. I am factual and final about my actions and decisions. For him actions and decisions are fluid, whatever their outcome, and their finality is measured in that he assumes full responsibility for them, regardless of how trivial or how significant they are.

We drove straight south. We didn't meander, as we usually did in order to get to the witches' house. When we left Guaymas—never before had we been that far south on our way to the witches' house—I asked him, "Where are you taking me?"

He casually responded, "We are taking the long way. Don't worry."

That was the same answer he gave me when I asked again, during our dinner in Navojoa.

We left Navojoa behind and drove south, heading toward Mazatlán. I was beside myself with worry. Around midnight, Isidoro Baltazar veered off the main highway and turned into a narrow dirt road. The van swayed and rattled as he drove over potholes and stones. Behind us the main highway was visible only for an instant in the scant flicker of the taillights, then it disappeared altogether, swallowed by the bushes that fringed the road. After an excruciatingly long ride, we came to an abrupt halt, and he switched off the headlights.

"Where are we?" I asked, looking all around me. For a moment I saw nothing. Then, as my eyes got accustomed to the darkness, I saw tiny white specks not too far ahead of us. Tiny stars that appeared to have fallen from the sky. The exuberant fragrance of the jasmine bushes climbing up the roof and tumbling down over the ramada had been so entirely blocked out of my mind that, when I suddenly recognized it, I felt as though I had inhaled that perfumed air before only in a dream. I began to giggle. It all gave me an almost childlike sense of wonder and delight. We were at Esperanza's house.

"It was here I first came with Delia Flores," I mumbled to myself, then reached for Isidoro Baltazar's hand and asked, "But how can this be possible?" In one instant, I was nearly choking with anxiety.

"What?" he asked in a bewildered tone. He was agitated and ruffled; his hand, which was always warm, was icy cold.

"This house was in the outskirts of Ciudad Obregón, more than a hundred miles north," I yelled. "I drove here myself. And I never left the paved road." I looked all around me in the darkness, and I recalled that I had also driven from that house to Tucson, and I had never been in or near Navojoa in my life.

Isidoro Baltazar was silent for a few minutes; he seemed pre-occupied, searching in his mind for an answer. I knew there was none that would have pleased me. Shrugging, he turned to face me. There was a force, an edge to him—much like there was to the nagual Mariano Aureliano—as he said that to him there was no doubt that I had been dreaming-awake when, together with Delia, I left Hermosillo for the healer's house. "I suggest that you let it go at that," he admonished. "I know from personal experience how the mind can go in circles trying to arrange the unarrangeable."

I was about to protest when he cut me off and pointed to the light moving toward us. He smiled in anticipation, as though he knew exactly to whom that enormous, swaying shadow on the ground belonged.

"It's the caretaker," I murmured in astonishment, as he came to stand in front of us. Impulsively, I put my arms around his neck and kissed him on both cheeks. "I never expected to see you here," I muttered.

He smiled sheepishly but didn't talk to me. He embraced Isidoro Baltazar, patting him repeatedly on the back the way Latin men are wont to do when greeting each other, then mumbled something to him. Hard as I tried to listen, I couldn't understand a single word. He led us to the house.

There was something forbidding about the massive front door. It was closed. So were the barred windows. No light, no sound escaped the thick walls. We circled the house to the backyard, enclosed by a high fence, to the door that led directly to a square room. I felt reassured upon recognizing the four doors. It was the same room I had been taken to by Delia Flores. It was as sparsely furnished as I remembered it: a narrow bed, a table, and several chairs.

The caretaker placed the oil lamp on the table and then urged me to sit down. Turning to Isidoro Baltazar, he draped an arm around his shoulders and walked with him out into the dark corridor. The suddenness of their departure left me stunned. Before I fully recovered from my surprise and my indecision as to whether I should follow them, the caretaker reappeared. He handed me a blanket, a pillow, a flashlight, and a chamber pot.

"I would rather use the outhouse," I said primly.

The caretaker shrugged his shoulders, then pushed the chamber pot under the bed. "Just in case you have to go in the middle of the night." His eyes glinted with emphatic glee as he told me that Esperanza kept a big, black watchdog outside. "He doesn't take kindly to strangers wandering across the yard at night." As if on cue, I heard a loud barking.

"I'm not a stranger," I said casually, trying to ignore the ominous note in the beast's barking. "I've been here before. I know the dog."

The caretaker lifted his brows in surprise, then asked, "Does the dog know you?"

I glared at him. He sighed, and, reaching for the oil lamp on the table, he turned to the door.

"Don't take away the light," I said, stepping quickly in front of him to block his way. I tried to smile, but my lips stuck to my teeth. "Where is everybody?" I finally managed to ask. "Where are Esperanza and Florinda?"

"At the moment, I'm the only person who's here," he said.

"Where is Isidoro Baltazar?" I asked, panic-stricken. "He promised to take me to the witches' house. I've to work on my paper." My thoughts, my words were all jumbled and confused as I talked about my reasons for accompanying Isidoro Baltazar to Mexico. I was close to tears as I told the caretaker how important it was for me to finish my work.

He patted my back most reassuringly and made soothing noises, as if he were talking to a child. "Isidoro Baltazar is asleep. You

224

know how he is. The instant his head hits the pillow, he's gone out of the world." He smiled faintly and added, "I'll leave my door open in case you need me. Just call me if you have a nightmare or something, and I'll come right away."

Before I had a chance to tell him that I hadn't had one since the last time I was in Sonora, the caretaker disappeared down the dark corridor.

The oil lamp on the table began to sputter, and moments later it went out. It was pitch dark. I lay down fully clothed and closed my eyes. All was silent except for a soft, raspy breathing coming from far away. Conscious of that breathing sound and the hardness and narrowness of my bed, I soon gave up the effort to sleep.

Flashlight in hand, I crept down the corridor on noiseless feet, hoping to find Isidoro Baltazar or the caretaker. Softly, I rapped on door after door. No one answered. No sound came from any of the rooms. An odd, almost oppressive silence had settled over the house. Even the rustlings and chirpings outside had ceased. As I suspected, I had been left alone in the house.

Rather than worry about it, I decided to look into the rooms. They were bedrooms, eight of them, of the same size and disposition: rather small, perfectly square, and furnished only with a bed and a night table. The walls and the two windows in all of them were painted white, and the tile floors were of an intricate design. I opened the sliding doors of the closets by gently pushing their bottom left corners with my foot. I knew, without knowing how I knew, that a tap or gentle kick on that spot released a mechanism that opened the doors.

I moved the folded blankets stacked up on the floor in one of the closets and got to a small secret door. I released the concealed dead bolt, disguised as a wall light socket. Since I was beyond being surprised, I accepted my knowledge of the trap doors, a knowledge that was, of course, inadmissible to my conscious mind.

I opened the small, secret door, crawled through the tiny opening, and found myself in the closet of the next room. With no great astonishment—since I already knew it—I discovered that by squatting through these secret openings I could go from one to another of the seven rooms.

I swore under my breath as my flashlight went out. Hoping to revive the batteries, I took them out and screwed them back in again. It was no use; they were dead. The darkness was so intense in these rooms that I couldn't see my own hands. Afraid of hitting myself against a door or a wall, I slowly felt my way into the corridor.

The effort was so great I was gasping and shaking as I pulled myself upright and leaned against the wall. I stood in the corridor for a long time, wondering in which direction to go to find my own room.

From the distance came fragments of voices. I couldn't tell whether the sound came from inside the house or from the outside. I followed the sound. It led me to the patio. I vividly recalled that green, almost tropical patio past the stone archway, with its ferns and thick foliage, its fragrance of orange blossoms and honeysuckle vines.

I hadn't taken but a few steps when I saw the enormous silhouette of a dog shadowed against the wall. The beast growled; its blazing eyes sent a chill running up my spine.

Instead of giving in to my fear, or perhaps because of it, I felt the strangest thing happen. It was as if I had always been folded like a Japanese fan or like a folded cutout figurine. Suddenly, I unfolded. The physical sensation was almost painful.

The dog watched me, confused. It began to whine like a puppy. It flapped its ears and coiled on the ground. And I stood there glued to the spot. I wasn't afraid. I simply couldn't move. Then, as if it were the most natural thing in the world, I folded back, turned around, and left. This time I had no trouble finding my room.

I awoke with a headache and that illusion of not having slept at all, which, as an insomniac, I knew so well. The muscles of my body were disconnected. I groaned out loud as I heard a door open and light fell over my face. Feebly, I tried to turn on my other side without falling off the narrow bed.

"Good morning!" Esperanza exclaimed, stepping into the room in a sweep of skirts and petticoats. "Actually, good afternoon," she corrected herself, pointing at the sun through the open door. There was a wonderful gaiety in her, a delightful power in her voice when she told me that it was she who had thought of retrieving my books and papers from the van before Isidoro Baltazar left with the old nagual.

Abruptly, I sat up. I was fully awake. "Why didn't the nagual Mariano Aureliano come to say hello to me? Why didn't Isidoro Baltazar tell me he was leaving?" I blurted out.

I mentioned to her that now I would never be able to finish my paper and enter graduate school.

Esperanza regarded me with a curious expression and said that if writing my paper was such a mercenary act I would never be able to bring it through.

Before I had a chance to tell her that personally I didn't care if I never entered graduate school, she added, "You don't do your paper to get into graduate school. You do it because you love doing it. Because there's nothing else at the moment you would rather do."

"There is plenty I would rather do."

"Like what?" she challenged me.

I thought for a moment but couldn't come up with anything specific. I had to admit, if only to myself, that I had never enjoyed working on a paper as much as I did on this one. For once, I had started with the reading and research at the beginning of the term instead of waiting, as I usually did, until a few days before the paper was due. It was the knowledge that it was my ticket into graduate school that had spoiled my enjoyment.

Esperanza, as if again privy to my thoughts, said that I should forget about graduate school and only think of writing a good paper. "Once you're part of the sorcerers' world and begin to grasp the nature of dreams, you are on your way to understanding what sorcery is all about. And that understanding frees you."

I looked at her, puzzled. I couldn't figure out what she was trying to tell me.

"It frees you from wanting anything." Esperanza enunciated the sentence very carefully, as if I were deaf. She regarded me thoughtfully then added, "Greed is your middle name, and yet you don't need or want anything . . ." Her voice trailed off as she began to arrange my books, papers, and stacks of index cards on the table. Her face was radiant as she turned to look at me. In her hands, she held several pencils. "I sharpened them for you with a razor blade," she said. "I'll sharpen them for you whenever they get dull." She placed the pencils beside my legal-sized writing pad and then flung her arms wide, as if to encompass the whole room. "This is a wonderful place for you to work. No one will bother you here."

"I'm sure of that," I said. Seeing that she was about to leave, I asked her where Isidoro Baltazar had slept last night.

"On his straw mat. Where else?" Giggling softly, she gathered up her skirts and petticoats and stepped out into the yard. I watched her until she disappeared behind the stone arch. My eyes hurt, dazzled from staring into the light.

Moments later, there was a loud knock on one of the doors that opened into the corridor.

"Are you decent?" the caretaker asked, pushing the door open before I had a chance to say that I was. "Nourishment for your brain," he said, placing a bamboo tray on the table. He poured me a bowl of clear broth, then urged me to eat the *machaca Sonorense*. "I made it myself," he informed me.

The mixture of scrambled eggs, shredded meat, onions, and hot chilies was delicious.

"When you finish, I'll take you to the movies," he said.

"When I finish eating?" I asked excitedly, stuffing a whole tortilla in my mouth.

"When you finish with your paper," he clarified.

As soon as I was done with the meal, he said that I had to get acquainted with the dog. "Otherwise, you won't be able to go outside. Not even to the outhouse."

I was about to tell him that I had actually met the dog and had gone to the outhouse last night, when with a swift gesture of his chin he motioned me to follow him into the yard. The big black dog lay curled up in the shade of the high fence of plaited cane. The caretaker squatted beside the animal and scratched it behind the ears. Bending even lower, he whispered something in the animal's ear.

Abruptly, the caretaker rose; startled, I stepped backward, falling on my seat. The dog whined, and the caretaker, with one incredible leap, cleared the high fence. I scrambled to my feet and was about to run out of there fast when the dog stretched its forepaws and placed them on my feet. I could feel the pressure of the paws through my shoes. The dog looked up at me and opened its muzzle in a wide, drawn-out yawn. Its tongue and gums were blue-black.

"That's a sign of the finest pedigree."

I was so startled to hear the caretaker behind me that I wheeled around. I lost my balance again and fell over the dog. I didn't dare move at first, then slowly I eased my head to the side. The dog's amber-colored eyes were fixed on me. The dog bared its teeth, not in a growl but in a most friendly, doggish smile.

"Now you're friends," the caretaker pronounced, helping me up. "And it's time for you to start on your paper."

The next three days were dominated entirely by my desire to finish my task. I worked for long stretches but somehow didn't feel the passing of time. It wasn't that I was so engrossed in my work that I lost track of the hours. Rather, time seemed to have transformed itself into a matter of space. That is, I began to count time as interludes, interludes between my sightings of Esperanza.

Every day around midmorning, when I was eating my breakfast—whatever she had left for me in the kitchen—she would suddenly appear. Soundlessly, she seemed to materialize out of the perpetual bluish smoke that hung about the kitchen like a cloud. Invariably, she combed my hair with a coarse wooden comb but never said a word. Neither did I.

I would see her again in the afternoons. As soundlessly as she appeared in the kitchen, she would abruptly materialize in the yard and sit in her custom-made rocking chair under the stone archway. For hours, she would stare into space, as if she could see beyond the limits of human vision. Other than a brief nod or a quick smile, there was no interaction between us at that hour. Yet I knew that I was protected in her silence.

The dog, as if it had been directed by the caretaker, never left my side. It followed me around day and night, even to the

outhouse. I particularly looked forward to our late afternoon out-
ings, when the dog and I would race across the fields toward the
row of trees that divided the plots of land. There we would sit in
the shade, staring into space like Esperanza. It sometimes seemed
to me that I could reach out and touch the distant mountains. I
would listen to the breeze rustling through the branches and wait
until the yellow light of the setting sun turned the leaves into
golden chimes. I waited until the leaves turned blue and finally
black. Then the dog and I would race back to the house, to escape
the faint voice of the wind telling about the loneliness of that
arid land.

On the fourth day I awoke, startled. From beyond the door that
opened to the yard, a voice called out, "Time to get up, lazy bones."
The caretaker's voice was drowsily indifferent.

"Why don't you come in?" I asked. "Where were you all
these days?"

There was no answer.

I sat wrapped in my blanket, waiting for him to appear, too
tense and sleepy to go out and see for myself why he was hiding.
After a while I roused myself and went outside. The yard was deserted. In an effort to chase my sleepiness away, I drew bucket after
bucket of cold water over my head.

My breakfast was different that morning: Esperanza didn't
show up. It was only after I settled down to work that I realized
that the dog had also vanished. Listlessly, I thumbed through my
books. I had very little energy and even less desire to work. I just
sat at my table for hours, gazing at the distant mountains through
my opened door.

The transparent silence of the afternoon was broken now and
then by the faint clucking of hens scratching the ground for seeds
and by the penetrating cry of the cicadas vibrating in the blue,
cloudless light as if it were still noon.

I was about to doze off when I heard some noise in the yard. I
looked up quickly. The caretaker and the dog lay side by side on a
straw mat in the shade of the fence. There was something odd about
the way they lay, sprawled out on the straw mat. They were so still,
they appeared dead.

With a mixture of concern and curiosity, I tiptoed toward them. The caretaker noticed my presence before the dog did. He opened his eyes wide in an exaggerated fashion, then in one swift motion sat up crosslegged and asked, "Did you miss me?"

"I did!" I exclaimed, then laughed nervously. It seemed an odd question for him to ask. "Why didn't you come into my room this morning?" Seeing his blank expression I added, "Where have you been for the past three days?"

Instead of answering, he asked in a harsh tone, "How is your work coming along?"

I was so taken aback by his brusqueness, I didn't know what to say. I didn't know whether I should tell him that my paper was none of his business or whether I should confess that I was stuck.

"Don't upset yourself trying to think up an explanation," he said. "Just tell me the truth. Tell me that you need my expert opinion on your term paper."

Afraid I would burst out laughing, I squatted beside the dog and scratched its head.

"Well?" the caretaker demanded. "Can't you admit that without me you're lost?"

Uncertain about the state of his mind, I decided it was better to humor him than to contradict him. So I said that, indeed, I hadn't written a single line the whole day. I had been waiting for him, knowing that only he could rescue me. I assured him that it wasn't really up to my professors at school but up to him to decide my fate as a graduate student.

The caretaker beamed at me, then asked that I bring him my paper. He wanted to have a look at it.

"It's in English," I said pointedly. "You won't be able to read it."

My impulse to add that even if it were in Spanish, he wouldn't be able to understand it, was checked by the certainty that I wasn't that ill mannered after all.

He insisted I bring him the paper. I did. He spread out the pages all around him, some on the mat, others on the dusty ground, then retrieved from his shirt pocket a pair of metal-rimmed glasses and put them on.

231

"It's important to look like an educated man," he whispered, leaning toward the dog. The animal pricked up one ear, then made a soft growling sound, as if to agree with him. The dog shifted positions, and the caretaker motioned me to sit between him and the animal.

He looked like an owl, erudite and austere, as he pored over the loose sheets on the ground. He made disapproving, clucking sounds with his tongue. He scratched his head. He shuffled and reshuffled the sheets, as if trying to find some order that eluded him.

The muscles in my neck and shoulders ached from sitting in that position. Sighing with impatience, I reclined against the fence and closed my eyes. In spite of my growing irritation, I must have dozed off, for I was suddenly startled by a faint yet insistent buzz. I opened my eyes. Sitting nearby, facing me, sat a tall, gorgeously dressed, beautiful-looking woman. She said something to me, but I couldn't hear what it was. The buzzing in my ears rose.

The woman leaned forward, toward me, and in a loud, clear voice asked, "Aren't you going to say hello to me?"

"Nélida! When did you get here? I was trying to shake off the buzzing in my ears," I explained.

She nodded, then drew up her long, shapely legs under the skirt she was wearing and wrapped her arms around them. "It's good to see you," she said dreamily.

With frowning brows, the caretaker mumbled to himself as he studied the pages before him. "Your scribbles are not only hard to read," he pronounced after a while, "but they don't make much sense."

Nélida stared at me with narrow, critical eyes, as if daring me to contradict him.

I fidgeted, eager to get away, to escape the scrutiny of her unnerving gaze. She leaned forward and grabbed my arm in a firm grip.

The caretaker began to read from the pages with an exasperating slowness. What he read sounded familiar, but whether he actually followed the text I couldn't tell, for I couldn't concentrate. I was too irritated by the capricious manner in which he cut the sentences, the phrases, and sometimes even the words.

"All in all," he stated upon finishing with the last page, "it's a badly written paper." He stacked the loose sheets in a pile, then leaned against the fence. Very deliberately he bent his knees up in the same position Isidoro Baltazar had taught me—the right leg crossed over with the ankle resting on the left thigh—and closed his eyes. He was silent for so long I thought he had fallen asleep and was thus startled when in a slow, measured voice he began to talk about anthropology, history, and philosophy. His thoughts seemed to come into being while he was talking, and words flowed out of him clearly and precisely, with a simplicity that was easy to follow, easy to understand.

I listened to him attentively. Yet at the same time I couldn't help thinking, "How could he possibly know so much about Western intellectual trends? How educated was he? Who was he really?"

"Could you repeat everything again?" I asked the instant he finished speaking. "I'd like to take notes."

"Whatever I said is all in your paper," the caretaker assured me. "It is buried under too many footnotes, quotes, and undeveloped ideas." He leaned closer until his head almost touched mine. "It's not enough to cite works in an effort to supply your paper with the veracity it lacks."

Dumbfounded, I could only stare at him. "Will you help me write my paper?" I asked.

"No, I can't do that," he said with a grave look in his eyes. "That's something you must do on your own."

"But I can't," I protested. "You just pointed out how badly written my paper is. Believe me, that's my best shot."

"It's not!" He contradicted me forcefully, then gazed at me with an air of astonishment that was mingled with a friendly warmth. "I'm sure your professors will accept the paper once it's neatly typed. But I wouldn't. There is nothing original about it."

I was too stunned to be upset.

"You're only paraphrasing what you have read," the caretaker continued. "I demand that you rely more on your own opinions, even if they contradict what is expected of you."

"It's only a term paper," I said defensively. "I know it needs more work, but I also need to please my professors. Whether I agree with

233

the expressed views is beside the point. I need to get accepted into graduate school, and that entails, in part, pleasing my professors."

"If you want to draw strength from the sorcerers' world," he said, "you can no longer work under such premises. Ulterior motives are not acceptable in this magical world of ours. If you want to be a graduate student, then you have to behave like a warrior, not like a woman who has been trained to please. You know, even when you are beastially nasty, you strive to please. Now, whenever you write, since you were not trained to do writing, you can certainly adopt a new mood: the warriors' mood."

"What do you mean by the warriors' mood?" I asked. "Do I have to fight my professors?"

"Not your professors," he said. "You have to fight yourself. Every inch of the way. And you have to do it so artfully and so cleverly that no one will notice your struggle."

I wasn't quite sure what he meant, and I didn't want to know, either. Before he could say anything else, I asked him how he knew so much about anthropology, history, and philosophy.

Smiling, he shook his head. "Didn't you notice how I did it?" he asked, then proceeded to answer his own question. "I picked the thoughts out of thin air. I simply stretched my energy fibers and hooked those thoughts, as one hooks fish with a fishing line, from the immeasurable ocean of thoughts and ideas that is out there." He made a wide gesture with his arms, as though to encompass the very air around him.

"To pick up thoughts, Isidoro Baltazar told me, one must know which are the ones that might be useful," I argued. "So you must have studied history, philosophy, and anthropology."

"Perhaps I did at one time," he said undecidedly, scratching his head in perplexity. "I must have."

"You had to!" I stated sententiously, as if I had made a great discovery.

Sighing loudly, he leaned against the fence and closed his eyes.

"Why do you insist on always being right?" Nélida asked.

Startled to hear her speak, I stared at her open-mouthed. The corners of her lips curled up into a mischievous, secret smile. Then she motioned me to close my mouth. I had been so engrossed in

234

listening to what the caretaker had to say about my paper I had forgotten all about her, even though she had been sitting right in front of me. Or had she? The thought that she might have gone and returned without me noticing it filled me with anxiety.

"Don't let that bother you," Nélida said softly, as if I had voiced my fears out loud. "We are in the habit of coming and going without anyone ever noticing us."

Her tone canceled the chilling effect of her statement. Gazing from one to the other, I wondered whether they would actually vanish, unperceived, before my very eyes. I tried to make sure they wouldn't. Stretching like a cat, I lay flat on the straw mat and inched my foot toward the hem of Nélida's dress, which trailed on the ground; my hand went to the caretaker's jacket. He must have noticed the tug on his sleeve, for he sat up abruptly and stared at me. I closed my eyes but kept watching them through my lashes. They didn't move. Their straight postures betrayed no trace of fatigue, whereas I had to fight to keep my eyes open.

A cool breeze, fragrant with the scent of eucalyptus, sprang up. Streaks of colored clouds trailed across the sky, and the deep, transparent blue grew slowly more diffused. It melted away so languidly, it was impossible to distinguish what was cloud and what was sky, what was day and what was night.

With my foot on the hem of Nélida's dress and clutching onto the caretaker's jacket as if my life depended on it, I fell asleep. It seemed that only moments had passed when I was awakened by a hand touching my face.

"Florinda?" I whispered, knowing instinctively that the woman sitting beside me was someone else. She was murmuring something. I had the feeling she had been murmuring for a long time and I had just awakened to hear what she was saying.

I wanted to sit up. With a gentle but firm touch on my shoulder, the woman prevented me from doing so. A small flame flickered somewhere unsteadily in the darkness. It shed a gentle, wavering pallor upon her face. It made her look ghostlike. She seemed to grow as she moved closer. Her eyes, too, grew larger as they stared down into mine. The arch of her brows, like a curve drawn with a black marker, was concentrated in a frown.

"Nélida!" I sighed with relief.

Smiling faintly, she nodded.

I wanted to ask her about the caretaker and about my term paper, but she pressed her fingers against my lips and continued with her murmurings. The sound grew fainter and fainter. It seemed to come from a great distance, and then it finally faded away altogether.

Nélida rose and motioned me to do the same. I did so and noticed that we were not outside in the yard but in one of the empty bedrooms along the corridor.

"Where is my term paper?" I asked, alarmed at the possibility that the wind might have scattered the pages. The idea that I might have to begin my work from scratch made me feverish.

Nélida made an imperious gesture with her chin, motioning me to follow her. She was much taller than me and looked exactly like Florinda. Had it not been that she was so delicate, I wouldn't have been able to tell them apart. At that moment, she appeared as an unfinished version of Florinda—as Florinda must have been when she was younger. There was something so ethereal about Nélida, so frail, and yet so appealing. I used to joke with Isidoro Baltazar that if I were a man I would go for her. He had retorted—I had hoped in jest—that that was perhaps the reason why Nélida hardly ever talked to me.

We headed toward my room. I heard steps all around me. It couldn't be Nélida, I decided, for she walked so quietly she seemed not to touch the ground. The absurd notion that I was hearing my own steps made me tiptoe as silently as a cat. Yet I still kept hearing the steps. Someone's feet moved like mine did, the same rhythm echoing slightly on the tile floor. I glanced backward several times, but there was, of course, no one behind me. Hoping to dispel my fear, I giggled out loud.

Nélida turned around abruptly. I thought she was going to reprimand me, but she, too, began to laugh. She put her arm around my shoulders. Her touch wasn't particularly warm or tender. I didn't care. I liked her, and her touch was very reassuring to me. Still giggling, and with the sound of footsteps all around us, we entered my room.

A strange brilliance hung about the walls, as if a fog had seeped through the four doors in the room, which at that moment I could not see. The fog had changed the shape of the room, giving it strange contours, almost making it round. Regardless of how much I blinked and squinted, all I could see was the table I had been working on for the past three days. I stepped closer. To my relief, I saw my paper arranged in a neat pile. Next to it were all my pencils; they had been sharpened.

"Nélida!" I cried out excitedly, wheeling around. I could no longer see her. The fog was denser now. It closed around me with every breath I drew. It seeped inside me, filling me with a deep, excited feeling of lightness and lucidity. Guided by some invisible source, I sat at the table and spread out the pages all around me. Right under my watchful eyes the entire structure of my paper emerged, superimposing itself on my original draft like a double exposure on a frame of film.

I lost myself in admiration of the skilled development of the themes. As if they were being maneuvered by some invisible hand that thought and wrote, the paragraphs rearranged themselves, imposing a new order. It was all so gorgeously clear and simple that I laughed out of joy.

"Write it down."

The words echoed softly in the room. Curious, I glanced all around me, but I saw no one. Knowing that whatever I was experiencing was definitely more than a dream, I reached for my notepad and a pencil and began to write with a furious speed. Ideas came to me with an incredible clarity and ease. They pulsated in my head and in my body like sound waves. I simultaneously heard and saw the words. Yet it wasn't my eyes or my ears that perceived what was there before me. Rather, it was some filaments within me that were reaching out and, like some noiseless vacuum cleaner, sucking up the words shining before me like dust particles.

After a while, the order superimposed on my paper began to blur. One by one the lines faded away. Desperately, I tried to hold on to this splendid structure, knowing that it would all vanish without a trace. Only the memory of my awareness of that magnificent lucidity remained. And then that, too, was extinguished, as if a candle had been blown out. A curl of fog, as fine as a thread, lingered in the room. Then it withdrew in little ripples, and an oppressive darkness closed in around me. I was so drained, I knew I was going to faint.

"Lie down!"

I didn't even bother to look up, knowing that I wouldn't be able to see anyone. With great effort, I rose from my chair and staggered to my bed.

16

FOR a moment, I just lay on my bed, vaguely aware of my amazing, astonishing dream, so unlike any other dream. For the first time ever I was conscious of all I had done.

"Nélida?" I whispered as a soft, raspy, murmuring, coming from the other end of the room, intruded on my reveries. I sat up only to lie back quickly as the room began to spin around me. I waited for a few moments, then tried again. I stood and took a few hesitant steps. I collapsed on the floor and hit my head against the wall.

"Shit!" I cried out when the room kept spinning around me. "I'm fainting."

"Don't be so dramatic," Florinda said, then giggled as she saw my bewildered face. She touched first my forehead, then my neck, as if she were afraid I might be running a fever. "You aren't fainting," she pronounced. "You need to replenish your energy."

"Where is Nélida?"

"Aren't you happy to see me?" She took my arm and helped me back to the bed. "You're faint with hunger."

"I'm not." I contradicted her, more out of habit than conviction. Although I didn't feel hungry, I was certain my dizziness was caused by a lack of food. Except for breakfast, I hadn't eaten at all during the day.

"We wondered why you didn't," Florinda said, responding to my thoughts. "We prepared such a delicious stew for you."

"When did you get here?" I asked. "I have been silently calling you for days."

Closing her eyes, Florinda made a humming sound, as if the noise would help her remember. "We have been here for several days, I think," she finally said.

"You think!" I was completely taken aback, my temper getting the better of me. I quickly recovered. "Why didn't you let me know that you were here?" More than hurt, I was puzzled that I had failed to notice their presence. "How could I have been so unaware?" I mumbled, more to myself than to her.

Florinda regarded me with a curious expression in her eyes. She seemed surprised by my bafflement. "If we had let you know that we were here, you wouldn't have been able to concentrate on your work," she remarked sagaciously. "As you well know, instead of writing your paper, you would have been pending on our comings and goings. All your energy would have been spent in trying to find out what we do, wouldn't it?" Her voice was low and raspy, and a strange, excited light made her eyes even more shiny than usual. "It was a deliberate act on our part that you should work without distractions," she assured me.

Then she went on to explain that the caretaker had helped me with my paper only after he was satisfied with what I had done so far. She claimed that in dreaming he found the inherent order of my notes.

"I, too, saw the inherent order of my notes," I said smugly. "I, too, saw it in a dream."

"Of course you did," Florinda readily agreed. "We pulled you into dreaming so you could work on your paper."

"You pulled me into dreaming?" I repeated. There was something startlingly normal about her statement. Yet at the same time it made me feel apprehensive. I had an uncanny sense that I was finally close to understanding what dreaming-awake was, but somehow I couldn't quite grasp it. In an effort to make sense, I told Florinda all that had happened from the moment I saw the caretaker and the dog in the yard.

240

It was difficult to make it sound coherent, for I couldn't decide myself when I had been awake and when I had been dreaming. To my utter bewilderment, I could recall the exact outline of my paper as I had seen it superimposed on my original draft. "My concentration was far too keen for me to have been dreaming," I pointed out.

"That's precisely what dreaming-awake is," Florinda interrupted me. "That's why you remember it so well." Her tone was that of an impatient teacher explaining a simple but fundamental point to a backward child. "I've already told you that dreaming-awake has nothing to do with falling asleep and having a dream."

"I took notes," I said, as if that would invalidate her statement. Seeing her nod, I asked her if I would find whatever I saw in dreaming-awake jotted down in my own handwriting on my pad.

"You will," she assured me. "But before you do, you'll have to eat first." She rose and, holding out her hand, helped me to my feet. To put a semblance of order to my appearance, she tucked my shirt into my jeans and brushed off the pieces of straw sticking to my sweater. She held me at arm's length and regarded me critically. Not satisfied with the results, she began to fuss with my hair, tweaking the unruly strands this way and that.

"You look quite frightful with your hair sticking out all over the place," she pronounced.

"I'm used to taking a hot shower upon awakening," I said, and followed her out into the corridor. Seeing that she was heading toward the kitchen, I told her that I had to go to the outhouse first.

"I'll walk with you." Noticing my displeased face, she added that she only wanted to make sure I didn't get dizzy and fall into the shit hole.

Actually, I was glad to hold on to her arm as we made our way to the yard. I almost fell as we stepped outside, not so much from weakness as from the shock of seeing how late in the day it was.

"What's the matter?" Florinda asked. "Do you feel faint?"

I pointed up at the sky. A faint gleam was all that remained of the sun's light. "I can't possibly have lost a day," I said. My voice had all but vanished even before I finished speaking. I struggled to assimilate the idea that indeed a whole night and the whole day had passed, but my mind would not accept it. Not being able to account for time, measured in the usual manner, unhinged me.

"Sorcerers break time's flux," Florinda answered my thoughts. "Time, in the fashion we measure it, doesn't exist when one dreams the way sorcerers dream. Sorcerers stretch or compress time at will. For sorcerers, time is not a matter of minutes or hours or days but an altogether different matter.

"When dreaming-awake, our perceptual faculties are heightened," she proceeded in a patient, measured tone. "However, when it comes to perceiving time, something altogether different happens. The perception of time does not become heightened but is canceled out completely." She added that time is always a factor of consciousness; that is, to be aware of time is a psychological state that we automatically transform into physical measurements. It is so ingrained in us that we can hear, even when we are not consciously aware of it, a clock ticking inside us, subliminally keeping track of time.

"In dreaming-awake, that capacity is absent," she emphasized. "A thoroughly new, unfamiliar structure, which somehow is not to be understood or interpreted as we normally do with time, takes over."

"Then all I will ever consciously know about dreaming-awake is that time has either been stretched or compressed," I said, trying to come to grips with her elucidation.

"You will understand a great deal more than that," she assured me emphatically. "Once you become adept at entering heightened awareness, as Mariano Aureliano calls it, you'll be aware then of whatever you wish because sorcerers are not involved in measuring time. They are involved in using it, in stretching or compressing it at will."

"You mentioned earlier that you all helped me into dreaming," I said. "Then some of you must know how long that state lasted."

Florinda said that she and her companions were perennially in a state of dreaming-awake, that it was precisely their joint effort that pulled me into dreaming-awake but that they never kept track of it.

"Are you implying that I might be dreaming-awake now?" I asked, knowing the answer before she responded. "If I am, what did I do to reach this state? What steps did I take?"

"The simplest step imaginable," Florinda said. "You didn't let yourself be your usual self. That is the key that opens doors. We have told you many times and in many ways that sorcery is not at all what you think it is. To say that to stop yourself from being your usual self is sorcery's most complex secret sounds like idiocy, but it isn't. It is the key to power, therefore the most difficult thing a sorcerer does. And yet, it isn't something complex or impossible to understand. It doesn't boggle the mind, and for that reason no one can even suspect its importance or take it seriously.

"Judging by the result of your latest dreaming-awake, I can say that you have accumulated enough energy, through preventing yourself from being your usual self."

She patted my shoulder and turned away. "I'll see you in the kitchen," she whispered.

The kitchen door was ajar but no sound came from the inside.

"Florinda?" I whispered.

A soft laughter answered my call, but I couldn't see anyone. As soon as my eyes became accustomed to the penumbra, I saw Florinda and Nélida sitting around the table. Their faces were unnaturally vivid in that tenuous light. Their same hair, their same eyes, their same noses and mouths, gleamed as if lit by an inner light. It was the most eerie thing to see two beings so totally alike.

"You two are so beautiful that you're scary," I said and stepped closer.

The two women gazed at each other, as if to validate my statement, then burst into a most disturbing laughter. I felt a curious prickle running down my spine. Before I had a chance to comment on the odd sound, they stopped. Nélida beckoned me to sit on the empty chair beside her.

I took a deep breath. I had to stay calm, I told myself as I sat down. There was a tenseness and a crispness about Nélida that unnerved me. She served me a plateful of a thick soup from the tureen standing in the middle of the table.

"I want you to eat everything," she said, pushing the butter and a basket with warm tortillas toward me.

I was famished. I attacked my food as if I had not eaten for days. It tasted wonderful. I ate all there was in the tureen and washed down the buttered tortillas with three mugfuls of hot chocolate.

Satiated, I slumped back in my chair. The door to the yard was wide open and a cool breeze rearranged the shadows in the room. Twilight seemed to be lasting forever. The sky was still streaked with heavy layers of color: vermilion, deep blue, violet, and gold. And the air had that transparent quality that brought close the distant hills. As if propelled by some inner force, the night seemed to shoot out of the ground. The shadowed movements of the fruit trees in the wind, rhythmic and graceful, swept the darkness up into the sky.

Esperanza burst then into the room and placed a lit oil lamp on the table. She regarded me with unblinking eyes, as if she had difficulty in focusing. She gave the impression that she was still concerned with some otherworldly mystery, that she wasn't yet quite there. Then slowly her eyes thawed, and she smiled as if she knew now that she had returned from a great distance.

"My paper!" I cried out upon discovering the loose sheets and my notepad under her arm.

Grinning broadly, Esperanza handed me my notes.

Eagerly, I examined the sheets and laughed out loud upon seeing the pages on the pad filled with precise and detailed instructions— written half in Spanish, half in English—on how to proceed with my term paper. The handwriting was unmistakably mine.

"It's all there," I said excitedly. "That's how I saw it in my dream." The thought that I might be able to zoom through graduate school without having to work so hard made me forget all my former anxiety.

"There are no shortcuts to writing good term papers," Esperanza said. "Not even with the aid of sorcery. You should know that without the preliminary reading, the note taking, and the writing and rewriting, you would never have been able to recognize the structure and order of your term paper in dreaming."

I nodded wordlessly. She had spoken with such an incontestable authority that I didn't know what to say.

"What about the caretaker?" I finally managed to ask. "Was he a professor in his youth?"

Nélida and Florinda turned to Esperanza, as if it were up to her to answer.

"I wouldn't know that," Esperanza said evasively. "Didn't he tell you that he's a sorcerer in love with ideas?" She was silent for a moment, then added softly, "When he is not taking care of our magical world, as befits a caretaker, he reads."

"Besides reading books," Nélida elucidated, "he reads a most extraordinary number of scholarly journals. He speaks several languages, so he's quite up to date with the latest of everything. Delia and Clara are his assistants. He taught them to speak English and German."

"Is the library in your house his?" I asked.

"It belongs to all of us," Nélida said. "However, I'm sure he's the only one, beside Vicente, who has read every book on the shelves." Noticing my incredulous expression, she advised me that I shouldn't be fooled by appearances regarding the people in the sorcerers' world. "To reach a degree of knowledge, sorcerers work twice as hard as normal people," she assured me. "Sorcerers have to make sense of the everyday world as well as the magical world. To accomplish that, they have to be highly skilled and sophisticated, mentally as well as physically." She regarded me with narrowed, critical eyes then chuckled softly.

"For three days, you worked on your paper," she explained. "You worked very hard, didn't you?" She waited for my assent then added that, while dreaming-awake, I worked on my term paper even harder than I did while awake.

"Not at all," I hastened to contradict her. "It was all quite simple and effortless." I explained that all I did was see a new version of my paper superimposed on my old draft, and then I copied what I saw.

"To do that took all the strength you had," Nélida maintained. "While dreaming-awake, you channeled all your energy into a single purpose. All your concern and effort went into finishing your paper. Nothing else mattered to you at the moment. You had no other thoughts to interfere with your endeavor."

"Was the caretaker dreaming-awake when he looked at my paper?" I asked. "Did I see what he saw?"

Nélida rose and walked slowly to the door. For a long moment she peered out into the darkness then returned to the table. She whispered something to Esperanza, which I didn't hear, and then sat down again.

Esperanza chuckled softly then said that what the caretaker saw in my paper was different from what I saw and wrote down. "Quite naturally so, for his knowledge is by far more vast than yours."

Esperanza stared at me with her quick, dark eyes that somehow made the rest of her face seem lifeless. "Guided by his suggestions, and according to your own capabilities, you saw what your paper ought to read like. That's what you wrote down."

"While dreaming-awake, we have access to hidden resources, which we never use ordinarily," Nélida said, going on to explain that, the instant I saw my paper, I remembered the clues the caretaker had given me.

Noticing my incredulous expression, she reminded me what the caretaker had said about my paper: "Too many footnotes, too many quotes and sloppily developed ideas." Her eyes radiated sympathy and amusement as she went on to say that since I was dreaming and I am not as stupid as I pretended to be, I immediately saw all kinds of links and connections that I hadn't noticed before within my material. Nélida leaned toward me, a half-smile playing over her lips as she waited for my reaction.

"It's time you know what made you see a better version of your original paper." Esperanza sat up straight and gave me a wink as if to emphasize that she was about to reveal a major secret. "When dreaming-awake, we have access to direct knowledge."

I could see the disappointment in her eyes as she regarded me for a long moment.

"Don't be so dense!" Nélida snapped impatiently. "Dreaming-awake should have made you realize that you have, as all women do, a unique capacity to receive knowledge directly."

Esperanza made a silencing gesture with her hand and said, "Did you know that one of the basic differences between males and females is how they approach knowledge?"

I had no idea what she meant. Slowly and deliberately, she tore off a clean sheet from my notepad and drew two human figures. One head she crowned with a cone and said that it was a man. On the other head, she drew the same cone, but upside down, and said that it was a woman.

"Men build knowledge step by step," she explained, her pencil poised on the figure crowned with a cone. "Men reach up; they climb toward knowledge. Sorcerers say that men cone toward the spirit; they cone up toward knowledge. This coning process limits men on how far they can reach." She retraced the cone on the first figure. "As you can see, men can only reach a certain height. Their path toward knowledge ends up in a narrow point: the tip of the cone."

She looked at me sharply. "Pay attention," she warned me and pointed her pencil to the second figure, the one with the inverted cone on its head. "As you can see, the cone is upside down, open like a funnel. Women are able to open themselves directly to the source, or rather, the source reaches them directly, in the broad base of the cone. Sorcerers say that women's connection to knowledge is expansive. On the other hand, men's connection is quite restricted.

"Men are close to the concrete," she proceeded, "and aim at the abstract. Women are close to the abstract and yet try to indulge themselves with the concrete."

"Why are women, being so open to knowledge or the abstract, considered inferior?" I interrupted her.

Esperanza gazed at me with rapt fascination. She rose swiftly, stretched like a cat until all her joints cracked, then sat down again.

"That women are considered inferior, or, at the very best, that female traits are equated as complementary to the male's, has to do with the manner in which males and females approach knowledge," she explained. "Generally speaking, women are more interested in power over themselves than over others, a power which is clearly what males want."

"Even among sorcerers," Nélida interjected, and the women all laughed.

Esperanza went on to say that she believed that originally women saw no need to exploit their facility to link themselves

247

broadly and directly to the spirit. They saw no necessity to talk about or to intellectualize this natural capacity of theirs, for it was enough for them to put it in action and to know that they had it.

"Men's incapacity to link themselves directly to the spirit was what drove them to talk about the process of reaching knowledge," she stressed. "They haven't stopped talking about it. And it is precisely this insistence on knowing how they strive toward the spirit, this insistence on analyzing the process, that gave them the certainty that being rational is a typically male skill."

Esperanza explained that the conceptualization of reason has been done exclusively by men, and that this has allowed men to belittle women's gifts and accomplishments. And even worse, it has allowed men to exclude feminine traits from the formulation of the ideals of reason.

"By now, of course, women believe what has been defined for them," she emphasized. "Women have been reared to believe that only men can be rational and coherent. By now, men carry with them a load of unearned assets that makes them automatically superior regardless of their preparation or capacity."

"How did women lose their direct link to knowledge?" I asked.

"Women haven't lost their connection," Esperanza corrected me. "Women still have a direct link with the spirit. They have only forgotten how to use it, or rather, they have copied men's condition of not having it at all. For thousands of years, men have struggled to make sure that women forget it. Take the Holy Inquisition, for example. That was a systematic purge to eradicate the belief that women have a direct link to the spirit. All organized religion is nothing but a very successful maneuver to put women in a lower place. Religions invoke a divine law that says that women are inferior."

I stared at her in amazement, wondering to myself how she could possibly be so erudite.

"Men's need to dominate others and women's lack of interest in expressing or formulating what they know and how they know it has been a most nefarious alliance," Esperanza went on. "It has made it possible for women to be coerced, from the moment they're born, into accepting that fulfillment lies in homemaking, in love, in marriage, in having children, and in self-denial. Women have been excluded from the dominant forms of abstract thought and educated into dependence. They have been so thoroughly trained in the belief that men must think for them that women have finally given up thinking."

"Women are quite capable of thinking." I interrupted her.

"Women are capable of formulating what they have learned," Esperanza corrected me. "And what they have learned has been defined by men. Men define the very nature of knowledge, and from it they have excluded that which pertains to the feminine. Or if it is included, it is always in a negative light. And women have accepted this."

"You are years behind the times," I interjected. "Nowadays women can do anything they set their hearts to do. They pretty much have access to all the centers of learning and to almost any job that men can do."

"But this is meaningless as long as they don't have a support system, a support base," Esperanza argued. "What good is it that they have access to what men have when they are still considered inferior beings who have to adopt male attitudes and behaviors in order to succeed? The truly successful ones are the perfect converts. They, too, look down on women.

"According to men, the womb limits women both mentally and physically. This is the reason why women, although they have access to knowledge, have not been allowed to help determine what this knowledge is.

"Take, for instance, philosophers," Esperanza proposed. "The pure thinkers. Some of them are viciously against women. Others are more subtle in that they are willing to admit that women might be as capable as men were it not for the fact that women are not interested in rational pursuits. And if they are, they shouldn't be. For it is more becoming for a woman to be true to her nature: a nurturing, dependent companion of the male."

Esperanza expressed all this with unquestionable authority. Within moments, however, I was assailed by doubts. "If knowledge is but a male construct, then why your insistence that I go to school?" I asked.

249

"Because you are a witch, and as such you need to know what impinges on you and how it impinges on you," she replied. "Before you refuse something, you must understand why you refuse it.

"You see, the problem is that knowledge, in our day, is derived purely from reasoning things out. But women have a different track, never, ever taken into consideration. That track can contribute to knowledge, but it would have to be a contribution that has nothing to do with reasoning things out."

"What would it deal with, then?" I asked.

"That's for you to decide, after you master the tools of reasoning and understanding."

I was very confused.

"What sorcerers propose," she explained, "is that men can't have the exclusive right to reason. They seem to have it now because the ground where they apply reason is a ground where maleness prevails. Let's then apply reason to a ground where femaleness prevails. And that ground is, naturally, the inverted cone I described to you. Women's connection with the spirit itself."

She tilted her head slightly to one side, considering what to say. "That connection has to be faced with a different aspect of reasoning. An aspect never, ever used before: the feminine side of reasoning," she said.

"What is the feminine side of reason, Esperanza?"

"Many things. One of them is definitely dreaming." She regarded me questioningly, but I had nothing to say.

Her deep chuckle caught me by surprise. "I know what you expect from sorcerers. You want rituals, incantations. Odd, mysterious cults. You want to sing. You want to be one with nature. You want to commune with water spirits. You want paganism. Some romantic view of what sorcerers do. Very Germanic.

"To jump into the unknown," she went on, "you need guts and mind. Only with them will you be able to explain to yourself and to others the treasures you might find." She leaned toward me, eager, it seemed, to confide something. She scratched her head and sneezed repeatedly, five times as the caretaker had. "You need to act on your magical side," she said.

"And what is that?"

"The womb." She said this so distantly and calmly, as if she were not interested in my reaction, that I almost missed hearing it. Then suddenly, realizing the absurdity of her remark, I straightened up and looked at the others.

"The womb!" Esperanza repeated. "The womb is the ultimate feminine organ. It is the womb that gives women that extra edge, that extra force to channel their energy."

She explained that men, in their quest for supremacy, have succeeded in reducing woman's mysterious power, her womb, to a strictly biological organ, whose only function is to reproduce, to carry man's seed.

As if obeying a cue, Nélida rose, walked around the table, and came to stand behind me. "Do you know the story of the Annunciation?" she whispered in my ear.

Giggling, I turned to face her. "I don't."

In that same confidential whisper, she proceeded to tell me that in the Judeo-Christian tradition, men are the only ones who hear the voice of God. Women have been excluded from that privilege, with the exception of the Virgin Mary.

Nélida said that an angel whispering to Mary was, of course, natural. What wasn't natural was the fact that all the angel had to say to Mary was that she would bear the son of God. The womb did not receive knowledge but rather the promise of God's seed. A male god, who engendered another male god in turn.

I wanted to think, to reflect on all that I had heard, but my mind was in a confused whirl. "What about male sorcerers?" I asked. "They don't have a womb, yet they are clearly connected to the spirit."

Esperanza regarded me with undisguised pleasure, then looked over her shoulder, as though she were afraid to be overheard, and whispered, "Sorcerers are able to align themselves to intent, to the spirit, because they have given up what specifically defines their masculinity. And they are no longer males."

17

THE manner in which Isidoro Baltazar was pacing about the room was different from the way he usually covered the length of his rectangular studio. Before, I had always been soothed by his pacing. This time, however, his steps rang with a disturbing, oddly menacing sound. The image of a tiger prowling in the bushes—not ready to pounce on a victim but sensing that something was not quite right—came to mind.

I turned away from my paper and was about to ask him what was the matter, when he said, "We are going to Mexico!"

The way he said it made me laugh. The gruffness and seriousness of his voice warranted my joking question, "Are you going to marry me there?"

Glaring at me, he came to an abrupt halt. "This is no joke," he snapped angrily. "This is the real thing." No sooner had he spoken than he smiled and shook his head. "What am I doing?" he said, making a humorous, helpless gesture. "I am getting angry at you, as if I had time for that. What a shame! The nagual Juan Matus warned me that we are crap to the very end."

He hugged me fiercely, as if I had been gone for a long time and had just returned.

"I don't think it's such a good idea for me to go to Mexico," I said.

"Cancel anything pending. There is no more time." He sounded like a military man giving orders. And I was in a festive mood. I couldn't help retorting, "Jawohl, mein Gruppenfuehrer!"

He lost his tightness and laughed.

As we drove through Arizona, a most peculiar feeling suddenly flooded me. It was a bodily sensation, something like a chill, that extended from my womb to my entire body and brought goose bumps all over my skin: the knowledge that something was wrong. There was in that feeling a new element I had not encountered before: absolute certainty, without a tinge of being right or wrong.

"I just had an intuition. Something is wrong!" I said, my voice rising against my will.

Isidoro Baltazar nodded, then said in a matter-of-fact tone, "The sorcerers are leaving."

"When?" My cry was quite involuntary.

"Maybe tomorrow or the next day," he replied. "Or perhaps a month from now, but their departure is imminent."

Sighing in relief, I slumped on my seat and consciously relaxed. "They have been saying that they're leaving since the day I met them, more than three years ago," I murmured, but I didn't really feel right about saying it.

Isidoro Baltazar turned to glance at me, his face a mask of sheer contempt. I could see the effort he was making to erase his dissatisfaction. He smiled, then patted my knee and said softly, "In the sorcerers' world, we can't be that factual. If sorcerers repeat something to you until you're cynically bored with it, it is because they want to prepare you for it." He fixed me momentarily with his hard, unsmiling eyes and added, "Don't confuse their magical ways with your dumbo ways."

I nodded wordlessly. His statement didn't anger me; I was too scared for that. I kept quiet.

The journey didn't take any time at all, or so it seemed to me. We took turns sleeping and driving, and by noon of the following day we were at the witches' house. The instant the car's engine had been shut off, we both jumped out of the car, slammed the doors shut, and ran up to the witches' house.

"What's the idea?" the caretaker said. He was standing by the front door, seemingly bewildered by our abrupt and loud arrival. "Are you two fighting or chasing each other?" He looked at Isidoro Baltazar and then at me. "Gee! Running like this."

"When are you leaving? When are you leaving?" I repeated mechanically, unable to contain my growing anxiety and fear any longer.

Laughing, the caretaker patted my back reassuringly and said, "I'm not going anyplace. You're not going to get rid of me that easily." His words sounded genuine enough, but they didn't relieve my anxiety.

I searched his face, his eyes, to see if I could detect a lie. All I saw was kindness and sincerity. Upon realizing that Isidoro Baltazar was no longer standing beside me, I tensed up again. He had vanished, as noiselessly and swiftly as a shadow.

Sensing my agitation, the caretaker pointed with his chin to the house. I heard Isidoro Baltazar's voice, rising as if he were protesting, and then I heard his laughter.

"Is everybody here?" I asked, trying to move past the caretaker.

"They are inside," he said, blocking my way with his outstretched arms. "They can't see you at the moment." Seeing that I was about to protest, he added, "They were not expecting you. They want me to talk to you before they do." He took my hand and led me away from the door. "Let's go to the back and pick up some leaves," he proposed. "We'll burn them and leave the ashes for the water fairies. Perhaps they'll turn them into gold."

We didn't talk at all as we gathered pile after pile of leaves, but the physical activity, the sound of the rake scratching the ground, soothed me.

It seemed we had been gathering and burning leaves for hours when suddenly I knew that there was someone else in the yard. I turned my head quickly and saw Florinda. Dressed in white pants and jacket, sitting on the bench under the zapote tree, she was like an apparition. Her face was shaded by a wide-brimmed straw hat, and in her hand she held a lace fan. She seemed not quite human and so remote that I just stood motionless, absolutely amazed.

Wondering whether she was going to acknowledge me, I took a few hesitant steps toward her. Upon noticing that she didn't in any way register my presence, I waited, undecided. It wasn't that I was trying to protect myself against being refused or being slighted by her. Rather, some undetermined yet unconsciously understood rule kept me from demanding that she pay attention to me.

However, when the caretaker joined Florinda on the bench, I reached for the rake propped against a tree and inched my way toward them. Grinning absentmindedly, the caretaker looked up at me, but his attention was on what Florinda was saying. They spoke in a language I didn't understand. Yet I listened to them, entranced. Whether it was the language or her affection for the old man, I didn't know, but her raspy voice was unusually soft and strange and hauntingly tender.

Abruptly, she rose from the bench. As if she were propelled by some hidden spring, she zigzagged across the clearing like a hummingbird, pausing for an instant beside each tree, touching a leaf here and a blossom there.

I raised my hand to call her attention, but I was distracted by a bright blue butterfly weaving blue shadows in the air. It flew toward me and alighted on my hand. The wide, quivering wings fanned out and their shadow fell darkly over my fingers. It rubbed its head with its legs, and after opening and closing its wings several times, it took off again, leaving on my middle finger a ring in the shape of a triangular butterfly.

Certain that it was but an optical illusion, I shook my hand repeatedly. "It's a trick, isn't it?" I asked the caretaker in a shaky voice. "It's an optical illusion?"

The caretaker shook his head, and his face crinkled into a most radiant smile. "It's a lovely ring," he said, holding my hand in his. "It's a magnificent gift."

"A gift," I repeated. I had the briefest flash of insight, but it disappeared, leaving me lost and bewildered. "Who put the ring on my finger?" I asked, staring at the jewel. The antennae and the thin, elongated body dividing the triangle were fashioned in white gold filigree and were studded with tiny diamonds.

"Didn't you notice the ring before?" the caretaker asked.

"Before?" I repeated, baffled. "Before what?"

"You've been wearing that ring since Florinda gave it to you," he replied.

"But when?" I asked, then held my hand over my mouth to stifle my shock. "I can't remember Florinda giving me the ring," I mumbled more to myself than to him. "And why haven't I noticed the ring before?"

The caretaker shrugged, at a loss to explain my oversight, then suggested that perhaps I hadn't noticed the ring because it fit so perfectly on my finger. He seemed about to say something else but stopped himself and instead suggested that we pick up some more leaves.

"I can't," I said. "I have to talk to Florinda."

"You do?" he mused, in the manner of one hearing a ridiculous and probably unsound idea, but he didn't persuade me to the contrary. "She's gone for her walk," he explained, pointing with his chin toward the path that led to the hills.

"I'll catch up with her," I stated. I could see her white-clad figure weaving in and out of the high chaparral in the distance.

"She goes far," the caretaker warned me.

"That's no problem," I assured him.

I ran after Florinda, then slowed down before I caught up with her.

She had the most beautiful walk; she moved with a vigorous, athletic motion, effortlessly, her back erect.

Sensing my presence, she came to an abrupt halt, then turned and held out her hands in a gesture of greeting. "How are you, darling?" she said, gazing at me. Her raspy voice was light and clear and very soft.

In my eagerness to learn about the ring, I didn't even greet her properly. Stumbling over my words, I asked her if she had put the ring on my finger. "Is it mine now?" I said.

"Yes," she said. "It's yours by right." There was something in her tone, a sense of certainty that both thrilled and terrified me. Yet it didn't even occur to me to refuse the no doubt expensive gift.

"Does the ring have magical powers?" I asked, holding up my hand against the light so that each stone sparkled with a dazzling radiance.

"No," she laughed. "It doesn't have powers of any sort. It is a special ring, though. Not because of its value or because it belonged to me, but because the person who made this ring was an extraordinary nagual."

"Was he a jeweler?" I inquired. "Was he the same person who built the odd-looking figures in the caretaker's room?"

"The same one," she replied. "He wasn't a jeweler, though. He wasn't a sculptor either. The mere thought that he might be considered an artist made him laugh. Yet anyone who saw his work couldn't help but see that only an artist could have executed the extraordinary things he did."

Florinda moved a few steps away from me and let her eyes roam across the hills, as if she were searching for memories in the distance. Then she turned once more toward me and in a barely audible whisper said that whatever this nagual made, whether it was a ring, a brick wall, tiles for the floor, the mysterious inventions, or simply a cardboard box, it invariably turned out to be an exquisite piece, not only in terms of its superb craftsmanship, but because it was imbued with something ineffable.

"If such an extraordinary individual made this ring, then it has to have some kind of power," I insisted.

"The ring in itself has no power, regardless of who made it," Florinda assured me. "The power was in the making. The nagual who made this ring was aligned so thoroughly with what sorcerers call intent that he was able to produce this lovely jewel without him being a jeweler. The ring was an act of pure intent."

Reluctant to sound stupid, I didn't dare admit that I had no inkling what she meant by intent. So I asked her what had prompted her to make me such a marvelous gift. "I don't think I deserve it," I added.

"You will use the ring to align yourself with intent," she said. A wicked grin spread across her face as she added, "But, of course, you already know about aligning yourself with intent."

"I know nothing of the sort," I mumbled defensively, then confessed that I didn't really know what intent was.

"You might not know what the word means," she said offhandedly, "but something in you intuits how to tap that force." She brought her head close to mine and whispered that I had always used intent to move from dream to reality or to bring my dream—whatever it might have been—to reality. She glanced at me expectantly, waiting no doubt for me to draw the obvious conclusions. Seeing my uncomprehending expression, she added, "Both the inventions in the caretaker's room and the ring were made in dreams."

"I still don't get it," I complained.

"The inventions frighten you," she said equably. "And the ring delights you. Since both are dreams, it can easily be the reverse . . ."

"You frighten me, Florinda. What do you mean?"

"This, dear, is a world of dreams. We are teaching you how to bring them about all by yourself." Her dark, shiny eyes held mine for a moment, and then she added, "At the moment, all the sorcerers of the nagual Mariano Aureliano's party help you enter into this world and are helping you to stay in it now."

"Is it a different world? Or is it that I am different myself?"

"You are the same but in a different world." She was silent for a moment, then conceded that I had more energy than before. "Energy that comes from your savings and from the loan all of us made you."

Her banking metaphor was very clear to me. What I still didn't grasp was what she meant by a different world.

"Look around you!" she exclaimed, holding her arms out wide. "This is not the world of everyday life." She was silent for a long time, then in a voice that was but a low, gentle murmur, added, "Can butterflies turn into rings in the world of daily affairs? In a world that has been safely and rigorously structured by the roles assigned to all of us?"

I had no answer. I looked around me, at the trees, at the bushes, at the distant mountains. Whatever she meant by a different world still eluded me. The difference had to be a purely subjective one, was the thought that finally occurred to me.

"It isn't!" Florinda insisted, reading my thoughts. "This is a sorcerer's dream. You got into it because you have the energy."

She regarded me quite hopelessly, and said, "There is really no way to teach dreaming to women. All that can be done is to prop them up, so as to make them realize the enormous potential they carry in their organic disposition.

"Since dreaming, for a woman, is a matter of having energy at her disposal, the important thing is to convince her of the need to modify her deep socialization in order to acquire that energy. The act of making use of this energy is automatic; women dream sorcerers' dreams the instant they have the energy."

She confided that a serious consideration about sorcerers' dreams, stemming from her own shortcomings, was the difficulty of imbuing women with the courage to break new ground. Most women—and she said she was one of them—prefer their safe shackles to the terror of the new.

"Dreaming is only for courageous women," she whispered in my ear. Then she burst into loud laughter and added, "Or for those women who have no other choice, because their circumstances are unbearable—a category to which most women belong, without even knowing it."

The sound of her raspy laughter had an odd effect on me. I felt as if I had suddenly awakened from a deep sleep and remembered something quite forgotten while I had slept. "Isidoro Baltazar told me about your imminent departure. When are you leaving?"

"I'm not going anywhere yet." Her voice was firm, but it rang with a devastating sadness. "Your dreaming teacher and I are staying behind. The rest are leaving."

I didn't quite understand what she meant, and to hide my confusion I made a joking comment. "My dreaming teacher, Zuleica, hasn't said a single word to me in three years. In fact, she has never even talked to me. You and Esperanza are the only ones who have really guided me and taught me."

Florinda's gales of laughter reverberated around us, a joyous sound that brought me intense relief, and yet I felt puzzled.

"Explain something to me, Florinda," I began. "When did you give me this ring? How come I went from picking leaves with the caretaker to having this ring?"

Florinda's face was full of enjoyment as she explained that it could easily be said that picking leaves is one of the doors into a sorcerers' dream, provided one has enough energy to cross that threshold. She took my hand in hers and added, "I gave you the ring while you were crossing; therefore, your mind didn't record the act. Suddenly, when you were already in the dream, you discovered the ring on your finger."

I looked at her curiously. There was something in her elucidation I couldn't grasp, something so vague, so indistinct.

"Let's return to the house," she suggested, "and recross that threshold. Perhaps you'll be aware of it this time."

Leisurely, we retraced our steps, approaching the house from the back. I walked a few steps ahead of Florinda so I could be perfectly aware of everything. I peered at the trees, the tiles, the walls, eager to detect the change or anything that might give me a clue to the transition.

I didn't notice anything, except that the caretaker was no longer there. I turned around to tell Florinda that I most definitely had missed the transition, but she was not behind me. She was nowhere in sight. She was gone and had left me all alone there.

I walked into the house. It was, as had happened to me before, deserted. This feeling of aloneness no longer frightened me, no longer gave me the sensation I had been abandoned. Automatically, I went to the kitchen and ate the chicken tamales that had been left in a basket. Then I went to my hammock and tried to put my thoughts in order.

I woke up and found myself lying on a cot, in a small, dark room. I looked desperately about me, searching for some inkling of what was going on. I sat bolt upright as I saw big, moving shadows lurking by the door. Eager to find out whether the door was open and the shadows were inside, I reached under the cot for the chamber pot—which somehow I knew to be there—and threw it at the shadows. The pot landed outside with an excessively loud clatter.

The shadows vanished. Wondering whether I had simply imagined them, I went outside. Undecided, I stared at the tall mesquite fence encircling the clearing. And then I knew, in a flash, where I was: I was standing in back of the small house.

All this went through my mind as I searched for the chamber pot, which had rolled all the way to the fence. As I bent to pick it up, I saw a coyote squeeze through the mesquite fence. Automatically, I threw the pot at the animal, but it hit a rock instead. Indifferent to the loud bang and to my presence, the coyote crossed the clearing. It turned its head audaciously several times to look at me. Its fur shimmered like silver. Its bushy tail swept over the various rocks like a magic wand. Each rock it touched came to life. The rocks hopped about with shiny eyes and moved their lips, asking peculiar questions in voices too faint to be heard.

I screamed; the rocks moved appallingly fast toward me.

I immediately knew that I was dreaming. "This is one of my usual nightmares," I mumbled to myself. "With monsters and fear and everything else." Convinced that once I had recognized and voiced the problem, I had neutralized its effects on me, I was about to give in and settle down to live a nightmare terror when I heard a voice say, "Test the track of dreams."

I wheeled around. Esperanza was standing under the ramada tending to a fire on a raised platform made of cane heavily coated with mud. She looked strange and remote in the gleaming, moving light of the fire, as if she were separated from me by a distance that had nothing to do with space.

"Don't be frightened," she ordered. Then she lowered her voice to a murmur and said, "We all share one another's dreams, but now you are not dreaming." Doubt must have been written all over my face. "Believe me, you are not dreaming," she assured me.

I stepped a bit closer. Not only did her voice sound unfamiliar, but she herself was different. From where I was standing she was Esperanza; nonetheless, she looked like Zuleica. I moved very close to her. She was Zuleica! Young and strong and very beautiful. She couldn't have been more than forty years old. Her oval face was framed by curly, black hair that was turning grey. Hers was a

261

smooth, pale face, highlighted by liquid, dark eyes set wide apart. Her gaze was indrawn, enigmatic, and very pure. Her short, thin upper lip hinted at severeness, while the full, almost voluptuous lower lip gave an indication of gentleness and also passion.

Fascinated by the change in her, I simply stared at her, enthralled. I definitely must be dreaming, I thought.

Her clear laughter made me realize that she had read my thoughts. She took my hand in hers and said softly, "You're not dreaming, my dear. This is the real me. I am your dreaming teacher. I am Zuleica. Esperanza is my other self. Sorcerers call it the dreaming body."

My heart thumped so violently it made my chest ache. I almost choked with anxiety and excitement. I tried to pull my hand away, but she was holding me with a firm grip that I couldn't break. I pressed my eyes tightly shut. More than anything I wanted her to be gone when I opened them again. She was there, of course, her lips parted in a radiant smile. I closed my eyes again, then jumped up and down and stomped on the ground as if I had gone berserk. With my free hand, I slapped my face repeatedly, until it burned with pain. All to no avail; I couldn't wake up. Every time I opened my eyes, she was there.

"I think you've got enough," she laughed, and I commanded her to hit me.

She readily obliged, striking two sharp blows on my upper arms with a long, hard walking stick.

"It's no use, dear." She spoke slowly, as if she were very tired. She took a deep breath and let go of my hand. Then she spoke again. "You're not dreaming. And I am Zuleica. But when I dream, I am Esperanza and something else, too. But I am not going to go into that now."

I wanted to say something, anything, but I couldn't speak. My tongue was paralyzed and all I managed to produce was a whimpering, doglike sound. I tried to relax with breathing I had learned in a yoga class.

She chuckled, seemingly taken with my antics. It was a reassuring sound that had a soothing effect on me; it radiated so much warmth, such deep confidence, that my body relaxed instantaneously.

262

"You're a stalker," she proceeded. "And you belong, by all rights, to Florinda." Her tone brooked no argument, no contradiction. "You're also a somnambulist and a great natural dreamer, and by virtue of your ability, you also belong to me."

One side of me wanted to laugh out loud and tell her that she was raving mad. But another side was in complete agreement with her claim.

"By which name do you want me to call you?" I asked hesitantly.

"By which name?" she repeated, gazing at me as if it should have been self-evident. "I'm Zuleica. What do you think this is? A game? We don't play games here."

Taken aback by her vehemence, I could only mumble, "No, I don't think this is a game."

"When I dream, I am Esperanza," she continued, her voice sharp with intensity. Her face was stern but radiant, open without pity, all at the same time. "When I don't dream, I am Zuleica. But whether I am Zuleica or Esperanza or anything else, it shouldn't matter to you. I am still your dreaming teacher."

All I could do was nod idiotically. Even if I had had something to say, I wouldn't have been able to do so. A cold, clammy sweat of fear ran down my sides. My bowels were loose and my bladder about to burst. I wanted to go to the bathroom and relieve myself and puke.

I finally couldn't hold it any longer. It was a matter of disgracing myself right there or running to the outhouse. I had enough energy to opt for the latter.

Zuleica's laughter was the laughter of a young girl; it followed me all the way to the outhouse.

When I returned to the clearing, she urged me to sit beside her on the nearby bench. I automatically obeyed her and sat down heavily on the edge, nervously putting my hands over my closed knees.

There was an undeniable gleam of hardness but also of kindness in her eyes. It came to me in a flash, as if I had known it before, that her ruthlessness was, more than anything else, an inner discipline. Her relentless self-control had stamped her whole being with a most appealing elusiveness and secretiveness, not the secretiveness

263

of covert and furtive behavior, but the secretiveness of the mysterious, the unknown. That was the reason I followed her around, whenever I saw her, like a puppy dog.

"You've had two transitions today," Zuleica explained. "One from being normally awake to dreaming-awake and the other from dreaming-awake to being normally awake. The first was smooth and unnoticeable; the second was nightmarish. That's the normal state of affairs. All of us experience those transitions just like that."

I forced a smile. "But I still don't know what I did," I said. "I am not aware of any steps. Things just happen to me, and I find myself in a dream, without knowing how I got there."

There was a glint in her eyes. "What is ordinarily done," she said, "is to start dreaming by sleeping in a hammock or in some kind of a strapping contraption hanging from a roof beam or a tree. Suspended in that fashion, we don't have any contact with the ground. The ground grounds us, remember that. In that suspended position, a beginning dreamer can learn how energy shifts from being awake to dreaming and from dreaming a dream to dreaming-awake.

"All this, as Florinda already told you, is a matter of energy. The moment you have it, off you go.

"Your problem now is going to be whether you'll be able to save enough energy yourself since the sorcerers won't be able to lend it to you anymore." Zuleica raised her brows in an exaggerated manner and added, "We'll see. I'll try to remind you, the next time we share one another's dreams." Seeing the dismay on my face, she laughed with childlike abandon.

"How do we share one another's dreams?" I asked, gazing into her astonishing eyes. They were dark and shiny, with beams of light radiating from the pupils.

Instead of answering, Zuleica dropped a few more sticks into the fire. Embers burst and spilled, and the light grew brighter. For an instant she stood still, her eyes fixed on the flames as if she were gathering in the light. She turned sharply and glanced briefly at me, then squatted and wrapped her strong, muscular arms around her shins. Looking into the darkness, listening to the crackling fire, she rocked from side to side.

"How do we share one another's dreams?" I asked again.

Zuleica stopped rocking. She shook her head, then looked up, startled, as if suddenly awakened.

"That's something impossible for me to explain now," she stated. "Dreaming is incomprehensible. One has to feel it, not discuss it. As in the everyday world, before one explains something and analyzes it, one has to experience it." She spoke slowly and deliberately. She admitted that it was important to explain as one went along. "Yet, explanations sometimes are premature. This is one of those times.

"One day it will all make sense to you," Zuleica promised, seeing the disappointment in my face.

With a quick, light motion, she rose to her feet and went to stare at the flames, as if her eyes needed to feed on the light. Her shadow, thrown by the fire, grew enormous against the wall and the ceiling of the ramada. Without so much as a nod, she turned with a sweep of her long skirt and disappeared inside the house.

Unable to move, I stood rooted to the spot. I could barely breathe as the clatter of her sandals grew fainter and fainter. "Don't leave me here!" I yelled in a panic-stricken voice. "There are things I need to know."

Zuleica materialized by the door instantly. "What do you need to know?" she asked in a detached, almost distracted tone.

"I'm sorry," I gabbled, glancing into her shiny eyes. I examined her, almost hypnotized. "I didn't mean to shout," I added apologetically. "I thought you had gone into one of the rooms." I looked at her beseechingly, hoping she would explain something to me.

She didn't. All she did was ask me again what it was I wanted to know.

"Would you talk to me when I see you again?" I blurted out the first thing that came into my head, afraid she would leave if I didn't keep on talking.

"When I see you again, we won't be in the same world as before," she said. "Who knows what we'll do there?"

"But a while ago," I insisted, "you, yourself, told me you are my dreaming teacher. Don't leave me in darkness. Explain things to me. The torment I experience is more than I can bear. I am split."

"You are," she admitted casually. "You certainly are split." She looked at me, her eyes brimming with kindness. "But that's only because you don't let go of your old ways. You're a good dreamer. Somnambulist brains have formidable potential. That is . . . if you would cultivate your character."

I hardly heard what she said. I tried to put my thoughts in order, but I couldn't. A succession of images of events I didn't quite remember went through my mind with incredible speed. My will exercised no control upon their order or their nature. Those images were transformed into sensations that, however precise, refused to be defined, refused to be formulated into words, even into thoughts.

Obviously aware of my incapacity, Zuleica's face lit up in an expansive grin. "We have all helped the nagual Mariano Aureliano to push you into the second attention all along," she said slowly and softly. "In there, we find fluency and continuity as we do in the world of everyday life. In both states, the practical is dominant. We act efficiently in both states. What we can't do in the second attention, however, is to break what we experience into pieces so we can handle it, so we can feel secure, so we can understand it."

While she talked, I was thinking to myself, 'She's wasting her time telling me all this. Doesn't she know that I am too stupid to understand her explanations?' But she continued to speak, smiling broadly, obviously knowing that for me to admit that I was not too bright meant that I had changed somehow; otherwise, I would never admit such a notion, even to myself.

"In the second attention," she continued, "or as I prefer to call it, when dreaming-awake, one has to believe that the dream is as real as the everyday world. In other words, one has to acquiesce. For sorcerers, all worldly or otherworldly pursuits are ruled by irreproachable acts, and in back of all irreproachable acts lies acquiescence. And acquiescence is not acceptance. Acquiescence involves a dynamic element; it involves action." Her voice was very soft, and there was a feverish gleam in her eyes as she finished. "The moment

266

one begins dreaming-awake, a world of enticing, unexplored possibilities opens up. A world where the ultimate audacity becomes a reality. Where the unexpected is expected. That's the time when man's definitive adventure begins. The world becomes limitless with possibilities and wonder."

Zuleica was silent for a long time; she seemed to be debating what else to say. "With the help of the nagual Mariano Aureliano, you once even saw the glow of the surem," she began, and her soft voice, turning wistful, became softer still. "Magical creatures that exist only in Indian legends, the surem are beings that sorcerers can see only while dreaming-awake at the deepest level. They are beings from another world; they glow like phosphorescent human beings."

She wished me good night, turned, and disappeared inside the house. For a second I stood numbed, then I dashed after her. Before I reached the threshold I heard Florinda behind me say, "Don't follow her!"

Florinda's presence was so unexpected that I had to lean against the wall and wait for my heartbeat to return to normal. "Come and keep me company," Florinda said. She was sitting on the bench, feeding the fire. The elusive light in her eyes, the ghostly whiteness of her hair, was more like a memory than a vision. I stretched out on the bench beside her, and, as if it were the most natural thing to do, I placed my head in her lap.

"Never follow Zuleica, or any one of us, for that matter, unless you're asked to do so," Florinda said, combing her fingers through my hair. "As you know now, Zuleica isn't what she appears to be. She's always more, much more than that. Never try to figure her out, because when you think you have covered all the possibilities, she'll flatten you out by being more than you can imagine in your wildest fantasies."

"I know," I sighed contentedly. I could feel the tension draining from my face. I could feel it leaving my body. "Zuleica is a surem from the Bacatete Mountains," I said with absolute conviction. "I've known about these creatures all along." Seeing the astonishment in Florinda's face, I went on daringly, "Zuleica wasn't born like an ordinary human being. She was established. She's sorcery itself."

"No," Florinda contradicted me emphatically. "Zuleica was born. Esperanza wasn't." She smiled down into my face and added, "This should be a worthy riddle for you."

"I think I understand," I murmured, "but I am too insensitive and can't formulate what I understand."

"You're doing fine," she chuckled softly. "Being as insensitive as you normally are, you must wait until you are really, really awake, 100 percent in order to understand. Now you are only 50 percent awake. The trick is to remain in heightened awareness. In heightened awareness, nothing is impossible to comprehend for us." Feeling that I was about to interrupt her, she covered my lips with her hand and added, "Don't think about it now. Always remember that you're compulsive, even in heightened awareness, and your thinking is not thorough."

I heard someone moving in the shadows behind the bushes. "Who is there?" I asked, sitting up. I looked all around me but couldn't see anyone.

Women's laughter echoed across the yard.

"You can't see them," Florinda said sleepily.

"And why are they hiding from me?" I asked.

Florinda smiled. "They are not hiding from you," she explained. "It's just that you can't see them without the nagual Mariano Aurliano's help."

I didn't know what to say to that. On one level, it made perfect sense, yet I found myself shaking my head. "Can you help me see them?"

Florinda nodded. "But your eyes are tired; they are tired from seeing too much. You need to sleep."

Purposefully, I kept my eyes wide open, afraid to miss whoever was going to come out of the bushes the moment my attention slackened. I stared at the leaves and the shadows, no longer knowing which was which, until I fell into a deep, dreamless sleep.

18

THE caretaker was dozing on his favorite bench in the shade of the zapote tree. That's all he had been doing for the past two days. He no longer swept the patios or raked the leaves outside but instead sat for hours on that bench, dozing or staring into the distance, as if he had a secret understanding with something that only he could see.

Everything had changed in the house. Did I do wrong to come to see them? I asked myself incessantly. I felt, as usual, guilty and defensive. And all I did was to sleep uninterrupted for hours on end. When awake, however, I was disturbingly aware that nothing was the same. Aimlessly, I wandered about the house. But it was to no avail. Something seemed to have fled from the house.

The caretaker's long and loud sigh intruded on my thoughts. Unable to contain my anxiety any longer, I pushed my book aside, rose to my feet, and covered the short distance between us. "Won't you rake and burn some leaves today?" I asked.

He looked up, startled, but did not answer. He was wearing sunglasses. I couldn't see the expression in his eyes through the dark lenses. I didn't know whether to stay or to leave or to wait for his reply. Afraid he might doze off again, I asked in a loud, impatient tone, "Is there a reason why you aren't raking and burning leaves any longer?"

He parried my question with one of his own, "Have you seen or heard a leaf fall for the past two days?" His eyes seemed to drill through me as he lifted his glasses.

"No," I said. It was the seriousness of his tone and demeanor, rather than his statement, which I found ridiculous, that compelled me to answer.

He beckoned to me to sit beside him on the bench. Leaning close to me, he whispered in my ear, "These trees know exactly when to let go of their leaves." He glanced all around him, as if he were afraid we might be overheard, then added in that same confidential whisper, "And now the trees know that there's no need for their leaves to fall."

"Leaves wilt and fall, regardless of anything," I pronounced pompously. "It's a law of nature."

"These trees are utterly capricious," he maintained stubbornly. "They have a mind of their own. They don't follow the laws of nature."

"What has prompted the trees not to drop any leaves?" I asked, trying to keep an earnest expression.

"That's a good question," he mused, rubbing his chin thoughtfully. "I'm afraid I don't know the answer yet. The trees haven't told me." He smiled at me inanely and added, "I've already told you, these trees are temperamental."

Before I had a chance to retort, he asked, out of the blue, "Did you make yourself your lunch?"

His abrupt change of subject took me by surprise. "I did," I admitted, then hesitated for a moment. An almost defiant mood took hold of me. "I don't care all that much about food. I'm quite used to eating the same food day in and day out. If it weren't for the fact that I get pimples, I would live on chocolates and nuts."

Throwing all caution to the winds, I began to complain. I told the caretaker that I wished the women would talk to me. "I would appreciate if they'd let me know what is going on. Anxiety is taking its toll on me." After I had said all I wanted to say, I felt much better, much relieved. "Is it true that they are leaving forever?" I asked.

"They have already left forever," the caretaker said. Seeing my uncomprehending expression, he added, "But you knew that, didn't you? You're just making conversation with me, aren't you?"

Before I had a chance to recover from my shock, he asked me in a genuinely puzzled tone, "Why should this be shocking to you?" He paused for a moment, as if to give me time to think, then answered the question himself. "Ah, I've got it! You are furious because they took Isidoro Baltazar with them." He patted me repeatedly on my back, as though to emphasize each word. His gaze told me that he didn't care if I gave in to either anger or tears.

To know that I had no audience gave me an instantaneous sense of equanimity.

"I didn't know that," I murmured. "I swear, I didn't know it." I stared at him in mute despair. I felt all the blood drain from my face. My knees ached. My chest was so tight I couldn't breathe. Knowing that I was about to faint, I held on to the bench with both hands.

I heard the caretaker's voice like a distant sound. "No one knows if he'll ever be back. Not even I know that." Leaning toward me, he added, "My personal opinion is that he has gone with them temporarily, but he'll come back; if not right away, some day. That's my opinion."

I searched his eyes, wondering whether he was mocking me. His cheerful face radiated sheer goodwill and honesty. And his eyes were as guileless as a child's.

"However, when he returns, he won't be Isidoro Baltazar anymore," the caretaker warned me. "The Isidoro Baltazar you knew, I think is already gone. And do you know what's the saddest part?" He paused, then answered his own question. "You took him so for granted that you didn't even thank him for all his care, his help, his affection for you.

"Our great tragedy is to be buffoons, oblivious to anything else, except our buffoonery."

I was too devastated to say a word.

Abruptly, the caretaker rose to his feet. Without another word, as if he were too embarrassed to stay with me, he walked toward the path that led to the other house.

"You can't just leave me here by myself," I shouted after him.

He turned, waved at me, and then began to laugh. It was a loud, joyful sound that raised echoes across the chaparral. He waved once again, then vanished, as if the bushes had swallowed him.

Incapable of following him, I waited for him to return or to appear suddenly in front of me and scare me half to death. I was almost bracing myself for a fright I intuited in my body more than I anticipated in my mind.

As it had happened before, I didn't see or hear Esperanza approach, but I sensed her presence. I turned around and there she was, sitting on the bench under the zapote tree. I became elated just watching her.

"I thought I was never going to see you again," I sighed. "I had nearly resigned myself to it. I thought you were gone."

"Goodness gracious!" she chided me in mock consternation.

"Are you really Zuleica?" I blurted out.

"Not a chance," she retorted. "I am Esperanza. What are you doing? Driving yourself nuts with questions no one can answer?"

Never in my life have I been so close to a total breakdown as at that moment. I felt that my mind was not going to take in all that pressure. I was going to be ripped apart by my anguish and turmoil.

"Brace yourself, girl," Esperanza said harshly. "The worst is yet to come. But we can't spare you. To stop the pressure now, because you're about to go bonkers, is unthinkable to sorcerers. It's your challenge to be tested today. You either live or you die. And I don't mean this metaphorically."

"I'll never see Isidoro Baltazar?" I asked, hardly able to speak through my tears.

"I can't lie to you to spare your feelings. No, he'll never be back. Isidoro Baltazar was only a moment of sorcery. A dream that passed after being dreamed. Isidoro Baltazar, as the dream, is gone already."

A small, almost wistful smile curved her lips. "What I don't know yet," she continued, "is if the man, the new nagual, is gone forever as well. You understand, of course, that even if he returns, he won't be Isidoro Baltazar. He'll be someone else you have to meet all over again."

"Would he be unknown to me?" I asked, not quite sure whether I wanted to know.

"I don't know, my child," she said with the weariness of uncertainty. "I simply don't know. I am a dream myself. And so is the new nagual. Dreams like us are impermanent, for it is our impermanence that allows us to exist. Nothing holds us, except the dream."

Blinded by my tears, I could barely see her.

"To ease your pain, sink deeper into yourself," she said softly. "Sit up with your knees raised and grab your ankles with crossed arms, right ankle with the left hand. Put your head on your knees and let the sadness go.

"Let the earth soothe your pain. Let the earth's healing force come to you."

I sat on the ground in exactly the manner she prescribed. Within moments my sadness vanished. A deep bodily sensation of well-being replaced my anguish. I lost sight of myself, in any context except the context of the moment at hand. Without my subjective memory I had no pain.

Esperanza patted the place beside her on the bench. As soon as I was seated, she took my hand in hers and rubbed it for an instant, as if she were massaging it, then said that it was quite a fleshy hand for being so bony. She turned the palm up and studied it intently. She didn't say a word, but gently curled my hand into a fist.

We sat in silence for a long time. It was late afternoon; nothing could be heard but the rhythmic sound of leaves moved by the breeze.

As I stared at her, a most uncanny certainty possessed me: I knew that Esperanza and I had already talked at length about my coming to the witches' house and the sorcerers' departure.

"What is it with me, Esperanza?" I asked. "Am I dreaming?"

"Well," she began slowly. There was a gleam in her eyes as she proposed I test the dream. "Sit on the ground and test it."

I did. All I felt was the coldness of the rock I had sat on. No feeling was sent back to me. "I'm not dreaming," I asserted. "Then why do I feel that we've already talked?" I searched her face to see if I could find a clue to my dilemma stamped on her features. "This is the first time I've seen you since my arrival, but I feel we've been together every day," I mumbled, more to myself than to be heard. "It's been seven days now."

"It's been much longer. But you must resolve this puzzle yourself, with minimal help," Esperanza said.

I nodded in agreement. There was so much I wanted to ask, but I knew and accepted that it would be useless to talk. I knew without knowing how I knew it that we had already covered all my questions. I was saturated with answers.

Esperanza regarded me thoughtfully, as if she doubted my realization. Then, very slowly, enunciating her words carefully, she said, "I want you to know that the awareness you have gotten here, no matter how deep and permanent it may seem to you, is only temporary. You'll get back to your nonsense soon enough. That's our women's fate, to be especially difficult."

"I think you are wrong," I protested. "You don't know me at all."

"It's precisely because I know you that I'm saying this." She paused for a moment, and when she spoke again her voice was harsh and serious. "Women are very cagey. Remember, being reared to be a servant makes you extremely shifty and clever." Her explosive, resonant laughter erased any desire I might have had to protest.

"The best thing you can do is not to say anything," she declared. Taking my hand, she pulled me up and suggested that we go to the small house for a long, much-needed talk.

We didn't go inside the house but sat down on a bench by the front door. Silently, we just sat there for nearly an hour. Then Esperanza turned toward me; she didn't seem to see me. In fact, I wondered if she had forgotten that I had come with her and was sitting beside her. Without acknowledging my presence, she stood up and moved a few steps away from me and gazed at the other house, nestled among a clump of trees. It was quite a while before she said, "I'm going far."

I couldn't tell whether it was hope, excitement, or apprehension that gave me a strangely sickening sensation in the pit of my stomach. I knew that she wasn't referring to distance in terms of miles but in terms of other worlds.

"I don't care how far we're going," I said. It was a bravado I was far from feeling. I desperately wished to know, but didn't dare ask, what would be at the end of our journey.

Esperanza smiled and opened her arms wide as if to embrace the setting sun. The sky in the west was a fiery red; the distant mountains, a shadowy purple. A light breeze swept through the trees; the leaves shimmered and rustled.

A silent hour went by, and then all was still. The spell of twilight immobilized everything around us. Every sound and movement ceased; the contours of bushes, trees, and hills were so precisely defined, they appeared to have been etched against the sky.

I moved closer to Esperanza as the shadows crawled up on us and blackened the sky. The sight of the other silent house, with its lights twinkling like glowworms in the dark, aroused some deeply buried emotion within me. It wasn't connected to any particular feeling of the moment but to a vaguely sad, nostalgic memory buried in childhood.

I must have been totally engrossed in my reveries; suddenly I found myself walking alongside Esperanza. My tiredness, my former anxiety, had all vanished. Filled with an overwhelming sense of vigor, I walked in a kind of ecstasy, a silent happiness, my feet drawn forward but not by my volition alone.

The path we were walking on ended abruptly. The ground rose and trees stretched high above us. Huge boulders were scattered here and there. From somewhere in the distance came the sound of running water, like a soft, comforting chant. Sighing with sudden fatigue, I leaned against one of the boulders and wished that this was the end of our journey.

"We haven't reached our destination yet!" Esperanza shouted. She was already halfway up some rocks and she moved with the agility of a goat. She didn't wait for me. She didn't even look back to see if I was following her. My short rest had robbed me of my last strength. Gasping for breath, I slipped repeatedly on the stones as I scrambled after her.

Halfway up, the trail continued around a huge boulder. The dry and brittle vegetation gave way to luscious growth, dark in the early evening light. The air, too, was no longer the same; it was humid and, for me, easier to breathe. Esperanza moved unerringly along a narrow path; it was full of shadows, full of silences and rustlings. She knew each of the night's mysterious sounds. She identified each of its pulsating croaks, cries, calls, and hisses.

The path came to an end in front of some steps cut into the rock. The steps led to a concealed mound of stones.

"Pick one," she ordered, "and put it in your pocket."

Worn as smooth as pebbles in a brook, the stones all looked the same at first. Upon closer examination, however, I discovered that they were all different. Some were so smooth and shiny they appeared to have been polished in a tumbler.

It took me quite some time until I found one I liked. It was heavy, yet it fit easily in my palm. Its light brown, bulky mass was wedge-shaped and crisscrossed by almost translucent milky veins.

Startled by a noise, I almost dropped the stone. "Someone is following us," I whispered.

"Nobody is following us!" Esperanza exclaimed, with a look halfway between amusement and incredulity. Seeing me draw back behind a tree, she giggled softly and said that it was probably a toad jumping through the underbrush.

I wanted to tell her that toads don't jump in the darkness, but I wasn't sure it was true. It surprised me that I hadn't just said it with the most absolute certainty, as was my habit. "Something is wrong with me, Esperanza," I said in an alarmed tone of voice. "I'm not myself."

"There is nothing wrong with you, dear," she assured me absentmindedly. "In fact, you are more yourself than ever."

"I feel strange . . ." My voice trailed off. I had begun to see a pattern in what had been happening to me since the first time I arrived at the witches' house.

"It's very hard to teach something so unsubstantial as dreaming," Esperanza said. "Especially to women. We are extremely coy and clever. After all, we've been slaves all our lives; we know how to precisely manipulate things when we don't want anything to upset what we have worked so hard to obtain: our status quo."

"Do you mean that men don't?"

"They certainly do, but they are more overt. Women fight underhandedly. Their preferred fighting technique is the slave's maneuver: to turn the mind off. They hear without paying attention, and they look without seeing." She added that to instruct women was an accomplishment worthy of praise.

"We like the openness of your fighting," she went on. "There is high hope for you. What we fear the most is the agreeable woman who doesn't mind the new and does everything you ask her to do and then turns around and denounces you as soon as she gets tired or bored with the newness."

"I think I am beginning to understand," I mused uncertainly.

"Of course you have begun to understand!" Her assertion was so comically triumphant, I had to laugh. "You have even begun to understand what intent is."

"You mean I am beginning to be a sorceress?" I asked. My whole body shook as I tried to suppress a fit of giggles.

"Since you arrived here, you've been dreaming-awake on and off," Esperanza stated. "That's why you fall asleep so much." There was no mockery, not even a trace of condescension in her smiling face.

We walked in silence for a while, and then she said that the difference between a sorcerer and an ordinary person was that the former could enter into a state of dreaming-awake at will. She tapped my arm repeatedly, as if to emphasize her point, and in a confidential tone added, "And you are dreaming-awake because, in order to help you hone your energy, we have created a bubble around you since the first night you arrived."

She went on to say that from the moment they first met me, they had nicknamed me *Fosforito*, little match. "You burn too fast and uselessly." She gestured for me to remain quiet and added that I didn't know how to focus my energy. "It's deployed to protect and uphold the idea of yourself." Again she motioned me to be silent, and said that what we think is our personal self is, in actuality, only an idea. She claimed that the bulk of our energy is consumed in defending that idea.

Esperanza's eyebrows lifted a little, an elated grin spreading across her face. "To reach a point of detachment, where the self is

277

just an idea that can be changed at will, is a true act of sorcery and the most difficult of all," she explained. "When the idea of the self retreats, sorcerers have the energy to align themselves with intent and be more than what we believe is normal.

"Women, because they have a womb, can focus their attention with great facility on something outside their dreams while dreaming," she explained. "That's precisely what you have been doing all along, unbeknownst to yourself. That object becomes a bridge that connects you to intent."

"And what object do I use?"

There was a flicker of impatience in her eyes. Then she said that it was usually a window or a light or even the bed. "You're so good at it, that's second nature with you," she assured me. "That's why you have nightmares. I told you all this when you were in a deep state of dreaming-awake, and you understood that as long as you refuse to focus your attention on any object, prior to sleeping, you don't have bad dreams.

"You are cured, aren't you?" she asked.

My initial reaction, of course, was to contradict her. However, upon a moment's thought, I couldn't but agree with her. After my meeting with them in Sonora, I had been fairly free from nightmares.

"You'll never be really free from them as long as you persist in being yourself," she pronounced. "What you should do, of course, is to exploit your dreaming talents deliberately and intelligently. That's why you're here. And the first lesson is that a woman must, through her womb, focus her attention on an object. Not an object from the dream itself, but an independent one, one from the world prior to the dream.

"Yet, it isn't the object that matters," she hastened to point out. "What's important is the deliberate act of focusing on it, at will, prior to the dream and while continuing the dream." She warned me that although it sounded simple enough, it was a formidable task that might take me years to accomplish. "What normally happens is that one awakens the instant one focuses one's attention on the outside object," she said.

"What does it mean to use the womb?" I interjected. "And how is it done?"

"You are a woman," Esperanza said softly. "You know how to feel with your womb."

I wanted to contradict her, to explain that I didn't know any such thing. Before I could do so, however, she went on to explain that, in a woman, feelings originate in the womb.

"In men," she claimed, "feelings originate in the brain." She poked me in the stomach and added, "Think about it. A woman is heartless except with her brood because her feelings are coming from her womb.

"In order to focus your attention with your womb, get an object and put it on your belly or rub it on your genitalia." She laughed uproariously at my look of dismay, then, in between fits of laughter, chided me. "I wasn't that bad. I could have said that you need to smear the object with your juices, but I didn't.

"Once you establish a deep familiarity with the object," she continued, her tone serious again, "it'll always be there to serve you as a bridge."

We walked in silence for a stretch; she was seemingly deep in thought; I was itching to say something yet knew that I didn't have anything to say. When she finally spoke, her voice was stern, demanding. "There is no more time for you to waste," she said. "It's very natural that in our stupidity we screw things up. Sorcerers know this better than anyone else. But they also know that there are no second chances. You must learn control and discipline because you have no more leeway for mistakes.

"You screwed up, you know. You didn't even know that Isidoro Baltazar had left."

The ethereal dike that was holding the avalanche of feelings broke down. My memory was restored and sadness overtook me again. It became so intense that I didn't even notice I had sat and was sinking into the ground as if it were made out of sponge. Finally, the ground swallowed me. It was not a suffocating, claustrophobic experience because the sensation of sitting on the surface coexisted simultaneously with the awareness of being swallowed by the earth, a dual sensation that made me yell, "I'm dreaming now!" That loudly spoken announcement triggered something within me; a new landslide of different memories flooded in on top of me. I knew what was wrong with me: I had screwed up and had no energy to dream. Every night since my arrival, I had dreamt the same dream, which I had forgotten about until that very moment. I dreamt that all the women sorcerers came to my room and drilled me in the sorcerers' rationales. They told me, on and on, that dreaming is the secondary function of the womb—the primary being reproduction and whatever is related to it. They told me that dreaming is a natural function in women, a pure corollary of energy. Given enough energy, the body of a woman by itself will awake the womb's secondary functions, and the woman will dream inconceivable dreams.

That needed energy, however, is like aid to an underdeveloped country: it never arrives. Something in the overall order of our social structures prevents that energy from being free so women can dream.

Were that energy free, the women sorcerers told me, it would simply overthrow the "civilized" order of things. But women's great tragedy is that their social conscience completely dominates their individual conscience. Women fear being different and don't want to stray too far from the comforts of the known. The social pressures put upon them not to deviate are simply too overpowering, and rather than change, they acquiesce to what has been ordained: women exist to be at the service of man. Thus they can never dream sorcery dreams, although they have the organic disposition for it.

Womanhood has destroyed women's chances. Whether it be tinted with a religious or a scientific slant, it still brands women with the same seal: their main function is to reproduce, and whether they have achieved a degree of political, social, or economic equality is ultimately immaterial.

The women told me all this every night. The more I remembered and understood their words, the greater was my sorrow. My grief was no longer for me alone but for all of us, a race of schizoid beings trapped in a social order that has shackled us to our own incapacities. If we ever break free, it is only momentarily, a short-lived clarity, before we plunge, willingly or forced, back into the darkness.

"Stop this sentimental garbage," I heard a voice say. It was a man's voice. I looked up and saw the caretaker bending over, peering at me.

"How did you get here?" I asked. I was perplexed and a little flustered. "You've been following us?" More than a question, it was an accusation.

"Yes, I've been following you in particular," he leered at me.

I searched his face. I didn't believe him. I knew he was poking fun at me, yet I was neither annoyed nor frightened by the intense glint in his eyes.

"Where is Esperanza?" I asked. She was nowhere in sight. "Where did she . . . ?" I stammered nervously, unable to get the words out.

"She's around," he said, smiling. "Don't worry. I'm also your teacher. You are in good hands."

Hesitantly, I put my hand in his. Effortlessly, he pulled me up to a flat boulder overlooking a large, oval-shaped pool of water. It was fed by a murmuring stream, trickling from somewhere in the darkness.

"And now, take off your clothes," he said. "It's time for your cosmic bath!"

"My what?" Certain that he was joking, I began to laugh.

But he was serious. He tapped me repeatedly on the arm, just like Esperanza did, and urged me to take off my clothes. Before I knew what he was doing, he had already untied the laces on my sneakers. "We don't have all that much time," he admonished, then pressed me to get on with it. The look he gave me was cold, clinical, impersonal. I might have been the toad Esperanza had claimed was jumping around.

The sheer idea of getting into that dark, cold water, infested, no doubt, with all sorts of slimy creatures, was appalling to me. Eager to put an end to that preposterous situation, I sidled down the boulder and stuck my toes into the water. "I don't feel a thing!" I cried out, shrinking back in horror. "What's going on? This is not water!"

"Don't be childish," the caretaker scolded me. "Of course it's water. You just don't feel it, that's all."

281

I opened my mouth to let out an imprecation but controlled myself in time. My horror had vanished. "Why don't I feel the water?" I asked, trying hard to gain time, although I knew that stalling for time was a useless affair, for I had no doubt that I was going to end up in the water whether I felt the water or not. However, I had no intention of giving in gracefully.

"Is this waterless water some kind of a purification liquid?" I asked.

After a long silence, charged with menacing possibilities, he said that I might call it a purification liquid. "However, I should warn you that there isn't a ritual capable of purifying anyone," he emphasized. "Purification has to come from within. It's a private and lonely struggle."

"Then why do you want me to get into this water, which is slimy even if I don't feel it?" I said with all the force I could invoke.

His lips twitched as if he were about to laugh, but seemingly reluctant to give in, his face grew grave again, and he said, "I'm going to dive into that pool with you." And without any further hesitation he completely undressed.

He stood in front of me, barely five feet away, stark naked. In that strange light that was neither day nor night, I could see with utter clarity every inch of his body. He didn't make bashful attempts to cover his nakedness. Quite the opposite; he seemed to be more than proud of his maleness and paraded it in front of me with defiant insolence.

"Hurry up and take off your clothes," he urged me. "We don't have much time."

"I'm not going to do that. It's insane!" I protested.

"You are going to do that. It's a decision you'll make all by yourself." He spoke without vehemence, without anger, yet with quiet determination. "Tonight, in this strange world, you will know that there is only one way to behave: the sorcerers' way." He stared at me with a curious mixture of compassion and amusement.

With a grin that was meant to reassure me but didn't, the caretaker said that jumping into the pool would jolt me. It would shift something within me. "This shift will serve you, at a later time, to understand what we are and what we do."

A fleeting smile lit up his face as he hastened to point out that jumping into the water would not give me the energy to dream-awake on my own. He warned me that it would certainly take a long time to save and hone my energy and that I might never succeed. "There are no guarantees in the sorcerers' world," he said. Then he conceded that jumping into the pool might shift my attention away from my everyday concerns: the concerns expected of a woman of my age, of my time.

"Is this a sacred pool?" I asked.

His brows shot up in obvious surprise. "It's a sorcerers' pool," he explained, gazing at me steadily. He must have seen that my decision had been made, for he unfastened the watch around my wrist. "The pool is neither holy nor evil." He shrugged his thin shoulders and fastened my watch around his own wrist. "Now look at your watch," he ordered me. "It's been yours for many years. Feel it on my wrist." He chuckled as he started to say something and decided against it. "Well, go on, take off your clothes."

"I think I'll just wade in with my clothes on," I mumbled. Although I wasn't prudish, I somehow resisted the idea of standing naked in front of him.

He pointed out that I would need dry clothes when I got out of the water. "I don't want you to catch pneumonia." A wicked smile dawned in his eyes. "This is real water even though you don't feel it," he said.

Reluctantly, I took off my jeans and shirt.

"Your panties too," he said.

I walked around the grassy edge of the pool, wondering whether I should just dive in and get it over with or whether I should get wet little by little, cupping water in my hands, letting it trickle down my legs, my arms, my stomach, and, last, over my heart, as I remembered old women doing in Venezuela before wading into the sea.

"Here I go!" I cried out, but instead of jumping in I turned to look at the caretaker.

His immobility frightened me. He seemed to have turned into stone, so still and erect did he sit on the boulder. Only his eyes seemed to have life; they shone in a curiously compelling way, without any source of light to account for it. It astounded more than saddened me to see tears trickling down his cheeks. Without know-ing why, I, too, began to weep, silently. His tears made their way down, I thought, into my watch on his wrist. I felt the eerie weight of his conviction, and suddenly my fear and my indecision were gone, and I dove into the pool.

The water was not slimy but transparent like silk, and green. I wasn't cold. As the caretaker had claimed, I didn't feel the water. In fact, I didn't feel anything; it was as if I were a disembodied aware-ness swimming in the center of a pool of water that did feel liquid but not wet. I noticed that light emanated from the depths of the water. I jumped up like a fish to gather impetus, then dove in search of the light.

I came up for air. "How deep is this pool?"

"As deep as the center of the earth." Esperanza's voice was clear and loud; it carried such certainty that, just to be myself, I wanted to contradict her. But there was something uneasy in the air that stopped me, some unnatural stillness, some tension, that was suddenly broken by a crisp, rustling sound all around us. A sort of warning whisper, a rushing, ominous warning that something was odd.

Standing on the exact same spot where the caretaker had stood was Esperanza; she was stark naked.

"Where is the caretaker?" I shouted in a panic-stricken voice.

"I am the caretaker," she said.

Convinced that those two were playing some horrendous trick on me, I propelled myself, with one great sidestroke, toward the overhanging boulder Esperanza was standing on. "What's going on?" I demanded to know in a voice that was but a whisper, for I could hardly breathe.

Gesturing for me to remain still, she moved toward me with that boneless, uncoiling movement so characteristic of her. She craned her neck to look at me, then stepped closer and showed me my watch strapped around her wrist.

"I am the caretaker," she repeated.

I nodded automatically. But then, right there in front of me, instead of Esperanza, was the caretaker, naked as he had been be-fore, pointing at my watch on his wrist. I didn't look at the watch; all my attention was focused on his sexual organs. I reached out to touch him, to see if perhaps he was a hermaphrodite. He wasn't. With my hand still probing, I felt, more than saw, his body fold into itself, and I was touching a woman's vagina. I parted the lips to make sure the penis was not hidden somewhere in there.

"Esperanza . . ." My voice faded as something clamped around my neck. I was conscious of the water parting as something pulled me into the depths of the pool. I felt cold. It wasn't a physical coldness but rather the awareness of the absence of warmth, of light, of sound; the absence of any human feeling in that world where that pool existed.

I awoke to the faint sound of snoring; Zuleica was sleeping beside me on a straw mat laid on the ground. She looked as beautiful as ever, young and strong, yet vulnerable—unlike the other women sorcerers—in spite of the harmony and power she exuded.

I watched her for a moment then sat up as all the events of the night came flooding into my mind. I wanted to shake her awake and demand that she tell me what had happened, when I noticed that we were not by the pool up in the hills but in the exact same spot where we had been sitting earlier, by the front door of the real witches' house.

Wondering whether it had all been a dream, I gently shook her by the shoulder.

"Ah, you finally woke up," she murmured sleepily.

"What happened?" I asked. "You have to tell me everything."

"Everything?" she repeated, yawning noisily.

"Everything that happened at the pool," I snapped impatiently.

Again she yawned, and then she giggled. Studying my watch, which was on her wrist, she said that something in me had shifted more than she had anticipated. "The sorcerers' world has a natural barrier that dissuades timid souls," she explained. "Sorcerers need tremendous strength to handle it. You see, it's populated by monsters, flying dragons, and demonic beings, which, of course, are nothing but impersonal energy. We, driven by our fears, make that impersonal energy into hellish creatures."

285

"But what about Esperanza and the caretaker?" I interrupted her. "I dreamt that both were really you."

"They are," she said, as if it were the most natural thing in the world. "I've just told you. You shifted deeper than I anticipated and entered into what dreamers call *dreaming in worlds other than this world.*

"You and I were dreaming in a different world. That's why you didn't feel the water. That's the world where the nagual Elías found all his inventions. In that world, I can be either a man or a woman. And just like the nagual Elías brought his inventions to this world, I bring either Esperanza or the caretaker. Or rather, my impersonal energy does that."

I couldn't put my thoughts or feelings into words. An incredible urge to run away screaming took hold of me, but I couldn't put it into action. My motor control was no longer a volitional matter with me. Trying to rise and scream, I collapsed on the ground.

Zuleica wasn't in the least concerned or moved by my condition. She went on talking as if she hadn't seen my knees give, as if I weren't lying sprawled on the ground like a rag doll. "You're a good dreamer. After all, you've been dreaming with monsters all your life. Now it's time you acquired the energy to dream like sorcerers do, to dream about impersonal energy."

I wanted to interrupt her, to tell her that there was nothing impersonal about my dream of Esperanza and the caretaker, that, in fact, it was worse than the monsters of my nightmares, but I couldn't speak.

"Tonight, your watch brought you back from the deepest dream you have ever had," Zuleica continued, indifferent to the weird sounds emerging from my throat. "And you even have a rock to prove it."

She came to where I lay open-mouthed, staring at her. She felt in my pocket. She was right. There it was, the rock I had picked from the pile of stones.

19

A loud, shattering noise woke me. I sat up in my hammock, peering into the darkness, and saw that the wooden panels covering the windows were down. A cold, sucking wind swirled up around me. Leaves rustled across the patio outside my room; the rustling grew, then abruptly faded to a gentle swishing sound. A dim brightness seeped into the room; like mist, it clung to the bare walls.

"Nagual!" I cried out. For a moment, as if I were conjuring him up, Isidoro Baltazar stood at the foot of my hammock. He looked real, yet there was something undefined about him, like an image seen in water. I cleared my throat to speak but only a faint croak escaped my lips as the image dissolved in the mist. Then the mist moved, restless and abrupt like the wind outside.

Too tense to sleep, I sat wrapped in my blanket, pondering whether I had done the right thing to come to the witches' house looking for the nagual Isidoro Baltazar. I didn't know anywhere else to go. I had patiently waited for three months, then my anxiety had become so acute that it finally prompted me to act. One morning—seven days ago—I had driven nonstop to the witches' house. And there had been no question in my mind then about whether I had proceeded correctly—not even after I had to climb over the wall at the back of the house and let myself in through an unlocked window. However, after seven days of waiting, my certainty had begun to falter.

I jumped out of my hammock onto the tiled floor, landing hard on the heels of my bare feet. Shaking myself that way had always helped me dispel my uncertainties. It didn't work this time, and I lay down again in my hammock.

If there is one thing I should have learned in the three years I had spent in the sorcerers' world, it is that sorcerers' decisions are final and my decision had been to live and die in the sorcerers' world. Now it was time for me to prove it.

An unearthly sounding laughter startled me out of my reveries. Eerily it reverberated throughout the house, then all was silent again. I waited tensely, but there was no other sound except that of dry leaves being pushed by the wind on the patio. They sounded like a faint, raspy whisper.

Listening to that sound not only lulled me to sleep but pulled me into the same dream I had been dreaming for the past seven nights.

I am standing in the Sonoran desert. It is noon. The sun, a silvery disk so brilliant as to be almost invisible, has come to a halt in the middle of the sky. There is not a single sound, not a movement around. The tall saguaros, with their prickly arms reaching toward that immobile sun, stand like sentries guarding the silence and the stillness.

The wind, as if it has followed me through the dream, begins to blow with tremendous force. It whistles between the branches of the mesquite trees and shakes them with systematic fury. Red dust devils well up in powdery swirls all around me. A flock of crows scatter like dots through the air then fall to the ground a bit farther away, softly, like bits of black veil.

As abruptly as it has begun, the wind dies down. I head toward the hills in the distance. It seems I walk for hours before I see a huge, dark shadow on the ground. I look up. A gigantic bird hangs in the air with outstretched wings, motionless, as though it were nailed to the sky. It is only when I gaze again at its dark shadow on the ground that I know that the bird is moving. Slowly, imperceptibly, its shadow glides ahead of me.

Driven by some inexplicable urge, I try to catch up with
the shadow. Regardless of how fast I run, the shadow moves
farther and farther away from me. Dizzy with exhaustion, I
stumble over my own feet and fall flat on the ground.

As I rise to dust off my clothes, I discover the bird perched
on a nearby boulder. Its head is slightly turned toward me, as
though beckoning me. Cautiously, I approach it. It is enor-
mous and tawny, with feathers that glisten like burnished cop-
per. Its amber-colored eyes are hard and implacable and as
final as death itself.

I step back as the bird opens its wide wings and takes off.
It flies high up until it is only a dot in the sky. Yet its shadow
on the ground is a straight dark line that stretches into infinity
and holds together the desert and the sky.

Confident that if I summon the wind I will catch up with
the bird, I invoke an incantation. But there is no force, no
power in my chant. My voice breaks into a thousand whispers
that are quickly absorbed by the silence. The desert regains its
eerie calm. It begins to crumble at the edges, then slowly fades
all around me . . .

Gradually, I became conscious of my body lying in the hammock. I discerned, through a shifting haze, the book-lined walls of
the room. Then I was fully awake, and the realization hit me, as it
had hit me every time during the past week, that this had not been
an ordinary dream, and that I knew what it meant.

The nagual Mariano Aureliano had once told me that sorcerers,
when they talk among themselves, speak of sorcery as a bird; they
call it the bird of freedom. They say that the bird of freedom only
flies in a straight line and never comes around twice. They also say
that it is the nagual who lures the bird of freedom. It is he who
entices the bird to shed its shadow on the warrior's path. Without
that shadow, there is no direction.

The meaning of my dream was that I had lost the bird of freedom. I had lost the nagual and, without him, all hope and purpose.

And what weighed the most on my heart was that the bird of freedom flew away so fast it didn't give me time to thank them properly, didn't give me time to express my endless admiration.

I had assured the sorcerers all along that I never took their world or their persons for granted, but I did, in particular Isidoro Baltazar's. He surely was going to be with me forever, I thought. Suddenly, they were gone, all of them, like puffs of air, like shooting stars. And they took Isidoro Baltazar with them.

I had sat for weeks on end in my room, asking myself the same question: How can it be possible that they vanished like that? A meaningless, superfluous question, considering what I had experienced and witnessed in their world. All it revealed was my true nature: meek and doubting. For the sorcerers had told me for years that their ultimate purpose was to burn, to disappear, swallowed by the force of awareness. The old nagual and his party of sorcerers were ready, but I didn't know it. They had been preparing themselves nearly all their lives for the ultimate audacity: to dream-awake that they sneak past death—as we ordinarily know death to be—and cross over into the unknown, enhancing, without breaking, the unity of their total energy.

My regret was most intense upon recalling how my usual doubting self would emerge when I least expected it. It was not that I didn't believe their stupendous, otherworldly, yet so practical aim and purpose. Rather, I would explain them away, integrate them, make them fit into the everyday world of common sense—not quite, perhaps, but certainly coexisting with what was normal and familiar to me.

The sorcerers certainly tried to prepare me to witness their definitive journey; that they would one day vanish was something I was almost aware of. But nothing could have prepared me for the anguish and despair that followed. I sunk into a well of sadness from which I knew I would never come out. That part was for me alone to deal with.

Afraid I would only give in to more despair if I stayed a moment longer in my hammock, I got up and made breakfast. Or rather, I warmed up last night's leftovers: tortillas, rice, and beans—my standard meal of the last seven days, except that for lunch I would add a can of Norwegian sardines. I had found them at a grocery store in the nearest town. I had bought all the cans they had. The beans were also canned.

I washed the dishes and mopped the floor. Then, with broom in hand, I went from room to room looking for some new dirt, a spider web in some forgotten corner. From the day I had arrived, I had done nothing else but scrub floors, wash windows and walls, sweep patios and corridors. Cleaning tasks had always distracted me from my problems, had always given me solace. Not this time. Regardless of how eagerly I went about my chores, I couldn't still the anguish, the aching void within me.

A quick rustling of leaves interrupted my cleaning chores. I went outside to look. There was a strong wind blowing through the trees. Its force startled me. I was ready to close the windows when the wind abruptly died out. A profound melancholy settled over the yard, over the bushes and trees, over the flower and vegetable patches. Even the bright purple bougainvillea hanging over the wall added to the sadness.

I walked over to the Spanish colonial–motif fountain, built in the middle of the yard, and knelt on the wide stone ledge. Absent-mindedly, I picked out the leaves and the blossoms that had fallen in the water. Then, bending over, I searched for my image on the smooth surface. Next to my face appeared the very beautiful, stark, and angular face of Florinda.

Dumbfounded, I watched her reflection, mesmerized by her large, dark, luminous eyes, which contrasted dazzlingly with her braided white hair. Slowly, she smiled. I smiled back.

"I didn't hear you come," I whispered, afraid that her image might vanish, afraid that she might be only a dream.

She let her hand rest on my shoulder, then sat beside me on the stone ledge. "I'm going to be with you only for a moment," she said. "I'll come back later, though."

I turned around and poured out all the anguish and despair that had accumulated in me.

Florinda stared at me. Her face reflected an immeasurable sadness. There were sudden tears in her eyes, tears that were gone as fast as they had come.

"Where is Isidoro Baltazar?" I asked her.

I averted my face and gave free rein to my pent-up tears. It wasn't self-pity or even sorrow that made me weep but a deep sense of failure, of guilt and loss; it was drowning me. Florinda had certainly warned me in the past about such feelings.

"Tears are meaningless for sorcerers," she said in her deep, husky voice. "When you joined the sorcerers' world you were made to understand that the designs of fate, no matter what they are, are merely challenges that a sorcerer must face without resentment or self-pity." She paused for a moment, then in her familiar, relentless manner she repeated what she had said to me on previous occasions: "Isidoro Baltazar is no longer a man but a nagual. He may have accompanied the old nagual, in which case he'll never return. But then, he may not have."

"But why did he . . ." My voice died away before I had asked the question.

"I really don't know at this time," Florinda said, raising her hand to forestall my protest. "It is your challenge to rise above this. And as you know, challenges are not discussed or resented. Challenges are actively met. Sorcerers either succeed in meeting their challenges or they fail at it. And it doesn't really matter which, as long as they are in command."

"How do you expect me to be in command when the sadness is killing me? Isidoro Baltazar is gone forever," I said resentfully, irked by the prosaicness of her feelings and attitudes.

"Why don't you heed my suggestion and behave impeccably regardless of your feelings," she retorted sternly. Her temper was as quick as her brilliant smile.

"How can I possibly do that? I know that if the nagual is gone the game is over."

"You don't need the nagual to be an impeccable sorceress," she remarked. "Your impeccability should lead you to him even if he's no longer in the world. To live impeccably within your circumstances is your challenge. Whether you see Isidoro Baltazar tomorrow or in a year or at the end of your life should make no difference to you."

Florinda turned her back to me. She was silent for a long time. When she faced me again, her face was calm and oddly bland, like a mask, as though she were making a great effort to control her emotions. There was something so sad about her eyes it made me forget my own anguish.

"Let me tell you a story, young woman," she said in an unusually harsh voice, as if her tone was meant to cancel the pain in her eyes. "I didn't go with the nagual Mariano Aureliano and his party. And neither did Zuleica. Do you know why?"

Numb with anticipation and fear, I stared at her, open-mouthed. "No, Florinda. I don't," I finally managed to say.

"We are here because we don't belong to that party of sorcerers," she said, her voice now low and soft. "We do, but then we don't really. Our feelings are with another nagual, the nagual Julián, our teacher. The nagual Mariano Aureliano is our cohort, and the nagual Isidoro Baltazar, our pupil.

"Like yourself, we've been left behind. You, because you were not ready to go with them; we, because we need more energy to take a greater jump and join perhaps another band of warriors, a much older band. The nagual Julián's."

I could feel Florinda's aloneness and solitude like a fine mist settling all around me. I barely dared to breathe lest she stop talking.

At great length she told me about her teacher, the nagual Julián, famous by all accounts. Her descriptions of him were compressed yet so evocative I could see him before my very eyes: the most dashing being that ever lived. Funny, sharp-witted, and fast-thinking; an incorrigible prankster. A storyteller, a magician who handled perception as a master baker handles dough, kneading it into any shape or form without ever losing sight of it. To be with the nagual Julián, Florinda assured me, was something unforgettable. She confessed that she loved him beyond words, beyond feelings. And so did Zuleica.

Florinda was silent for a long time, her gaze fixed on the distant mountains, as if drawing strength from those sharp-edged peaks. When she spoke again her voice was a barely audible whisper. "The

293

world of sorcerers is a world of solitariness, yet in it, love is forever. Like my love for the nagual Julián. We move in the world of sorcerers all by ourselves, accounting only for our acts, our feelings, our impeccability." She nodded, as if to underline her words. "I've no longer any feelings. Whatever I had went away with the nagual Julián. All I have left is my sense of will, of duty, of purpose.

"Perhaps you and I are in the same boat." She said this so smoothly that it passed before I realized what she had said.

I stared at her, and as always, I was dazzled by her splendid beauty and youthfulness, which the years had left bewitchingly intact.

"Not me, Florinda," I finally said. "You had the nagual Isidoro Baltazar and me and all the other disciples I've heard about. I have nothing. I don't even have my old world." There was no self-pity in me, only a devastating knowledge that my life, as I had known it until now, had ended. "The nagual Isidoro Baltazar is mine, by right of my power. I'll wait, dutifully, a bit longer, but if he's not here in this world anymore, neither am I. I know what to do!" My voice trailed off as I realized that Florinda was no longer listening to me. She was absorbed in watching a small crow making its way toward us along the fountain ledge.

"That's Dionysus," I said, reaching into my pocket for his pieces of tortilla. I had none with me. I looked up at the marvelously clear sky. I had been so engrossed in my sadness, I hadn't noticed that it was already past noon, the time this little crow usually came for its food.

"That fellow is quite upset." Florinda laughed at the bird's outraged caws and then, looking me in the eye, said, "You and the crow are quite alike. You get easily upset, and you're both quite loud about it."

I could barely contain myself from blurting out that the same could be said about her. Florinda chuckled, as though she knew the effort I was making not to weep.

The crow had perched on my empty hand and stared at me sidelong with its shiny, pebblelike eyes. The bird opened its wings but didn't fly away; its black feathers sparkled blue in the sun.

I calmly told Florinda that the pressures of the sorcerers' world were unbearable.

"Nonsense!" she chided, as if she were talking to a spoiled child. "Look, we scared Dionysus away." Enraptured, she watched the crow circle over our heads, then she fixed her attention back on me.

I averted my face. I didn't know why, for there was nothing unkind in the gaze of those shiny, dark eyes. They were calm and utterly indifferent as she said, "If you can't catch up with Isidoro Baltazar, then I and the rest of the sorcerers who taught you would have failed to impress you. We would have failed to challenge you. It's not a final loss for us, but it certainly will be a final loss for you." Seeing that I was about to weep again, she challenged me, "Where is your impeccable purpose? What happened to all the things you've learned with us?"

"What if I never catch up with Isidoro Baltazar?" I asked tearfully.

"Can you go on living in the sorcerers' world if you don't make an effort to find out?" she asked sharply.

"This is a time when I need kindness," I mumbled, closing my eyes to prevent my tears from spilling. "I need my mother. If I could only go to her."

I was surprised at my own words, yet I really meant them. Unable to hold back my tears any longer I began to weep.

Florinda laughed. She wasn't mocking me; there was a note of kindness, of sympathy in her laughter. "You're so far away from your mother," she said softly, with a pensive, distant look in her eyes, "that you'll never find her again." Her voice was but a soft whisper as she went on to say that the sorcerers' life builds impassable barriers around us. Sorcerers, she reminded me, don't find solace in the sympathy of others or in self-pity.

"You think that all my torment is caused by self-pity, don't you, Florinda?"

"No. Not just self-pity but morbidity, too." She put her arms around my shoulders and hugged me as if I were a small child. "Most women are damn morbid, you know," she murmured. "You and I are among them."

I didn't agree with her, yet I had no desire to contradict her. I was far too happy with her arms around me. In spite of my somber mood, I had to smile. Florinda, like all the other women in the sorcerers' world, lacked the facility to express maternal feelings. And although I liked to kiss and hug the people I loved, I couldn't bear to be in someone's arms for more than an instant. Florinda's embrace was not as warm and soothing as my mother's, but it was all I could hope to get.

Then she went into the house.

I came suddenly awake. For a moment I simply lay there—on the ground at the foot of the fountain—trying to remember something Florinda had said before I fell asleep in the leaf-spotted sunlight. I had obviously slept for hours. Although the sky was still bright, the evening shadows had already stolen into the yard.

I was about to look for Florinda in the house when an unearthly sounding laughter echoed across the yard; it was the same laughter I had heard during the night.

I waited and listened. The silence around me was unsettling. Nothing chirped; nothing hummed; nothing moved. Yet, still as it was, I could sense noiseless footsteps, silent as shadows, behind me.

I wheeled around. At the far edge of the yard, almost concealed by the blooming bougainvillea, I saw somebody sitting on a wooden bench. Her back was turned to me, but I immediately recognized her.

"Zuleica?" I whispered uncertainly, afraid that the sound of my voice might scare her away.

"How happy I am to see you again," she said, beckoning me to sit beside her.

Her deep, clear voice, vibrant with the briskness of the desert air, didn't seem to come from her body but from far away. I wanted to embrace her, but I knew better. Zuleica never liked to be touched, so I just sat beside her and told her that I, too, was happy to see her again. But to my utter surprise, she clasped my hand in hers, a small, delicate hand. Her pale, copperish-pink, beautiful face was oddly blank. All the life was concentrated in her incredible eyes: neither black nor brown but strangely in between and oddly clear. She fixed them on me in a prolonged stare.

"When did you get here?" I asked.

"Just this moment," she replied, her lips curling into an angelic smile.

"How did you get here? Did Florinda come with you?"

"Oh, you know," she said vaguely, "women sorcerers come and go unnoticed. Nobody pays attention to a woman, especially if she's old. Now, a beautiful young woman, on the other hand, attracts everybody's attention. That's why women sorcerers should always be disguised if they are handsome. If they are averagely homely, they have nothing to worry about."

Zuleica's sudden light tap on my shoulder jolted me. She clasped my hand again, as though to dispel my doubts, then gazed at me calmly and keenly and said, "To be in the sorcerers' world one has to dream superbly." She looked away. An almost full moon hung over the distant mountains. "Most people don't have the wits nor the size of spirit to dream. They cannot help but see the world as ordinary and repetitious. And do you know why?" she asked, fixing me with her keen gaze. "Because if you don't fight to avoid it, the world is indeed ordinary and repetitious. Most people are so involved with themselves that they have become idiotic. Idiots have no desire to fight to avoid ordinariness and repetitiousness."

Zuleica rose from the bench and put on her sandals. She tied her shawl around her waist so her long skirt wouldn't drag, and walked to the middle of the patio. And I knew what she was going to do before she even started. She was going to spin. She was going to perform a dance in order to gather cosmic energy. Women sorcerers believe that by moving their bodies they can get the strength necessary to dream.

With a barely perceptible gesture of her chin, she motioned me to follow her and imitate her movements. She glided on the dark brown Mexican tiles and brown bricks that had been laid out in an ancient Toltec pattern by Isidoro Baltazar himself, a sorceric design binding generations of sorcerers and dreamers throughout the ages in webs of secrets and feats of power—a design into which he had put himself, around and inside it, with all his strength, all his intent, willing myth and dream into reality.

Zuleica moved with the certainty and agility of a young dancer. Her movements were simple, yet they required so much speed, balance, and concentration that they left me exhausted. With uncanny agility and swiftness, she spun around, away from me. For an instant she vacillated amidst the shadows of the trees, as though to make sure I was following her. Then she headed toward the recessed, arched doorway built into the wall encircling the grounds behind the house. She paused momentarily by the two citrus trees growing outside the walls, the ones that stood like two sentries on either side of the path leading to the small house across the chaparral.

Afraid of losing sight of her, I dashed along the narrow, dark trail. Then, curious and eager, I followed her inside the house, all the way to the back room. Instead of turning on the light, she reached for an oil lamp hanging from one of the rafters. She lit it; the lamp cast a flickering glow all around us but left the corners of the room in shadows. Kneeling in front of the only piece of furniture in the room, a wooden chest sitting under the window, she pulled out a mat and a blanket.

"Lie down, on your stomach," she said softly, spreading the mat on the tiled floor.

I heaved a deep sigh and gave in to a pleasant sense of helplessness as I lay, face down, on the mat. A feeling of peace and well-being spread through my body. I felt her hands on my back; she wasn't massaging me but tapping my back lightly.

Although I had often been in the small house, I still didn't know how many rooms it had or how it was furnished. Florinda had once told me that that house was the center of their adventure. It was there, she said, where the old nagual and his sorcerers wove their magic web. Like a spider's web, invisible and resilient, it held them when they plunged into the unknown, into the darkness and the light, as sorcerers do routinely.

She had also said that the house was a symbol. The sorcerers of her group didn't have to be in the house or even in its vicinity when they plunged into the unknown through dreaming. Everywhere they went, they carried the feeling, the mood of the house in their hearts. And that feeling and mood, whatever they were for each of them, gave them the strength to face the everyday world with wonder and delight.

Zuleica's sharp tap on my shoulder startled me. "Turn on your back," she commanded.

I did so.

Her face, as she bent down, was radiant with energy and purpose. "Myths are dreams of extraordinary dreamers," she said. "You need a great deal of courage and concentration in order to maintain them. And above all, you need a great deal of imagination. You are living a myth, a myth that has been handed down to you for safekeeping."

She spoke in a tone that was almost reverent. "You cannot be the recipient of this myth unless you are irreproachable. If you are not, the myth will simply move away from you."

I opened my mouth to speak, to say that I understood all that, but I saw the hardness in her eyes. She was not there to have a dialogue with me.

The repetitive sound of branches brushing against the wall outside died out and turned into a throb in the air, a pulsating sound that I felt rather than heard. I was on the verge of falling asleep when Zuleica said that I should follow the commands of the repetitive dream I had had.

"How did you know I've been having that dream?" I asked, alarmed, trying to sit up.

"Don't you remember that we share one another's dreams?" she whispered, pushing me back onto the mat. "I'm the one who brings you dreams."

"It was just a dream, Zuleica." My voice trembled because I was seized by a desperate desire to weep. I knew it wasn't just a dream, but I wanted her to lie to me. Shaking her head, she looked at me. "No. It wasn't just a dream," she said quietly. "It was a sorcerers' dream, a vision."

"What should I do?"

"Didn't the dream tell you what to do?" she asked in a challenging tone. "Didn't Florinda?" She watched me with an inscrutable expression on her face. Then she smiled, a shy, childlike smile. "You have to understand that you cannot run after Isidoro Baltazar. He's no longer in the world. There is nothing you can give him or do for him anymore. You cannot be attached to the nagual as a person, but only as a mythical being." Her voice was soft yet commanding as she repeated that I was living a myth. "The sorcerers' world is a mythical world separated from the everyday one by a mysterious barrier made out of dreams and commitments.

"Only if the nagual is supported and upheld by his fellow dreamers can he lead them into other viable worlds from which he can entice the bird of freedom." Her words faded in the shadows of the room as she added that the support Isidoro Baltazar needed was dreaming energy, not worldly feelings and actions.

After a long silence, she spoke again. "You have witnessed how the old nagual, as well as Isidoro Baltazar, by their mere presence, affect whoever is around them, be it their fellow sorcerers or just bystanders, making them aware that the world is a mystery where nothing can be taken for granted under any circumstances."

I nodded in agreement.

For a long time I had been at a loss to understand how naguals could, by their mere presence, make such a difference. After careful observation, comparing opinions with others, and endless introspection, I concluded that their influence stemmed from their renunciation of worldly concerns. In our daily world, we also have examples of men and women who have left worldly concerns behind. We call them mystics, saints, religious people. But naguals are neither mystics nor saints and are certainly not religious men. Naguals are worldly men without a shred of worldly concerns.

At a subliminal level, this contradiction has the most tremendous effect on whoever is around them. The minds of those who are around a nagual can't grasp what is affecting them, yet they feel the impact in their bodies as a strange anxiety, an urge to break loose, or as a sense of inadequacy, as if something transcendental is taking place somewhere else, and they can't get to it.

But the naguals' built-in capacity to affect others doesn't only depend on their lack of worldly concerns or on the force of their personalities but rather on the force of their unreproachful behavior. Naguals are unreproachful in their actions and feelings, regardless of the ambushes—worldly or otherworldly—placed on their interminable path. It isn't that naguals follow a prescribed pattern of rules and regulations in order to have unreproachful behavior, for there are none. But rather, they use their imaginations for adopting or adapting to whatever it takes to make their actions fluid.

For their deeds, naguals, unlike average men, don't seek approval, respect, praise, or any kind of acknowledgment from anyone, including their fellow sorcerers. All they seek is their own sense of flawlessness, of innocence, of integrity.

It is this that makes a nagual's company addictive. One becomes dependent on his freedom as one would to a drug. To a nagual, the world is always brand new. In his company, one begins to look at the world as if it had never happened before.

"That's because naguals have broken the mirror of self-reflection," Zuleica said, as if she had followed my train of thoughts. "Naguals are able to see themselves in the mirror of fog, which reflects only the unknown. It is a mirror that no longer reflects our normal humanity, expressed in repetition, but reveals the face of infinity.

"Sorcerers believe that when the face of self-reflection and the face of infinity merge, a nagual is totally ready to break the boundaries of reality and disappear as though he wasn't made of solid matter. Isidoro Baltazar had been ready for a long time."

"He can't leave me behind!" I cried out. "That would be too unfair."

"It's downright foolish to think in terms of fairness and unfairness," Zuleica said. "In the sorcerers' world, there is only power. Didn't every one of us teach you that?"

"There are many things I learned," I conceded gloomily. After a few moments, I mumbled under my breath, "But they are not worth anything at the moment."

"They are worth the most now," she contradicted me. "If you have learned one thing, it's that at the bleakest moments warriors rally their power to carry on. A warrior doesn't succumb to despair."

"Nothing of what I've learned and experienced can alleviate my sadness and despair," I said softly. "I've even tried the spiritual chants I learned from my nanny. Florinda laughed at me. She thinks I am an idiot."

"Florinda is right," Zuleica pronounced. "Our magical world has nothing to do with chants and incantations, with rituals and

301

bizarre behavior. Our magical world, which is a dream, is willed into being by the concentrated desire of those who participate in it. It is held intact at every moment by the sorcerers' tenacious wills. The same way the everyday world is held together by everybody's tenacious will."

She stopped abruptly. She seemed to have caught herself in the middle of a thought that she didn't wish to express. Then she smiled. Making a humorous, helpless gesture, she added, "To dream our dream, you have to be dead."

"Does that mean I have to drop dead right here and now?" I asked in a voice that was getting hoarse. "You know that I am ready for that, at a drop of a hat."

Zuleica's face lit up, and she laughed as though I had told the best of jokes. Seeing that I was as serious as I could be, she hastened to clarify, "No, no. To die means to cancel all your holdings, to drop everything you have, everything you are."

"That's nothing new," I said. "I did that the moment I joined your world."

"Obviously you didn't. Otherwise you wouldn't be in such a mess. If you had died the way sorcery demands, you would feel no anguish now."

"What would I feel, then?"

"Duty! Purpose!"

"My anguish has nothing to do with my sense of purpose," I shouted. "It's apart, independent. I am alive and feel sadness and love. How can I avoid that?"

"You're not supposed to avoid it," Zuleica clarified, "but to overcome it. If warriors have nothing, they feel nothing."

"What kind of an empty world is that?" I asked defiantly.

"Empty is the world of indulging, because indulging cuts off everything else except indulging." She gazed at me eagerly, as if expecting me to agree with her statement. "So it's a lopsided world. Boring, repetitious. For sorcerers, the antidote of indulging is dying. And they don't just think about it, they do it."

A cold shiver went up my back. I swallowed and remained silent, looking at the splendid sight of the moon shining through the window. "I really don't understand what you're saying, Zuleica."

302

"You understand me perfectly well," she maintained. "Your dream began when you met me. Now it's time for another dream. But this time, dream dead. Your error was to dream alive."

"What does that mean?" I asked restlessly. "Don't torment me with riddles. You, yourself, told me that only male sorcerers drive themselves nuts with riddles. You're doing the same to me now."

Zuleica's laughter echoed from wall to wall. It rustled like dry leaves pushed by the wind. "To dream alive means to have hope. It means that you hold on to your dream for dear life. To dream dead means that you dream without hope. You dream without holding on to your dream."

Not trusting myself to speak, all I could do was to nod.

Florinda had told me that freedom is a total absence of concern about oneself, a lack of concern achieved when the imprisoned bulk of energy within ourselves is untied. She had said that this energy is released only when we can arrest the exalted conception we have of ourselves, of our importance, an importance we feel must not be violated or mocked.

Zuleica's voice was clear but seemed to come from a great distance as she added, "The price of freedom is very high. Freedom can only be attained by dreaming without hope, by being willing to lose all, even the dream.

"For some of us, to dream without hope, to struggle with no goal in mind, is the only way to keep up with the bird of freedom."